METHOD
IN
MINISTRY

METHOD IN MINISTRY

Theological Reflection and Christian Ministry

James D. Whitehead

AND

Evelyn Eaton Whitehead

The Seabury Press

Library of Congress Catalog Card Number: 80-13704
ISBN: 0-86683-459-1 (previously ISBN: 0-8164-2363-6)

Printed in the United States of America
5   4   3   2   1

Winston Press, Inc.
430 Oak Grove
Minneapolis, Minnesota 55403

This book is dedicated to
John J. Egan
and
Jerome A. O'Leary,

mentors in ministry

Acknowledgments

W e are grateful to the Lilly Endowment, whose gracious funding made possible both the research and preparation of this book. We are especially thankful to Fred Hofheinz of the Lilly Endowment for his support throughout the project.

The method and model discussed in this book were developed by a four-person team and tested in a series of workshops with experienced ministers. We thank Gordon Myers and Eugene Ulrich for the wisdom and imagination they contributed to the design and execution of these workshops. The ministers who participated with us contributed significantly at every stage. We salute these colleagues-become-friends: Judith Anne Beattie, Gregory Green, Thomas Jones, John Phalen, Joy O'Grady, Jane Pitz, Mary Anne Roemer, Frank Quinlivan, Michael Rosswurm, and Richard Stieglitz.

We acknowledge the other theological locus in which this method was developed and tested—Moreau Seminary and the M.Div. Program in the Theology Department of the University of Notre Dame. We are deeply grateful to two colleagues whose collaboration and friendship continue to shape our theology and our ministry: Mary Virginia Ulrich and Peggy Roach.

Two of the chapters included here have appeared previously in somewhat different form. We thank the Campaign for Human Development in Washington, D.C., for permission to include here material that Peter Henriot prepared for them; we thank the editors of *Review for Religious* for permission to include in Chapter Ten material which appeared initially in their journal.

J.D.W.
E.E.W.

CONTENTS

x   *Contents*

PART IV
Reflection in Ministry—The Method in Action   113

PART V
Implications for Ministerial Education   165

METHOD
IN
MINISTRY

Introduction
THE CONTEMPORARY NEED
FOR METHOD

Theological reflection in ministry is the process of bringing to bear in the practical decisions of ministry the resources of Christian faith. In this book we propose both a model and a method for doing theological reflection in ministry. In the model we indicate three sources of information that are relevant to decision making in contemporary ministry: the Christian Tradition, personal experience, and cultural information. Faithful and effective pastoral activity depends on the ability of Christians—and, in a special way, Christian ministers—to recognize and use the religiously significant insights available in these three sources. In the method we suggest a three-step process—attending, assertion, and decision—through which this information is clarified, coordinated, and allowed to shape pastoral action.

Theological reflection in ministry is not new. It is our conviction that effective ministry is and has been the result of an ongoing dynamic of reflection and action. What we attempt to do here is to examine that process, to name its elements, and to suggest ways in which it can be strengthened in the life of Christian ministry today.

While theological reflection in ministry is not new, its contemporary context is complex. Influenced by the explosion of information and the expansion of historical consciousness that mark this century, ministers are more keenly aware of the limits of their own knowledge. Recent research in Scripture has elaborated not only the richness of this central source of Christian revelation, but its complexity and variation. The forms of worship, the understanding of sexuality, the relation of the Church to political life—in these and other areas profound cultural changes have called into question earlier certitudes that were once the foundation of confident pastoral action.

This exciting but often bewildering complexity in contemporary Christian life heightens the need for a method of reflection: a systematic way to approach the various sources of religious information, one that leads not just to theoretical insight, but to pastoral decision. Christian ministry today requires a method of reflection that is at once theological and practical. As theological, it must attend confidently and competently to the resources of Scripture and the historical Tradition. As practical, it must be more than theoretically sound; it must be able to assist a wide range of ministers in their efforts to reflect and act in complex pastoral contexts. The method must be sufficiently clear and concrete that it can actually be used by persons and groups in ministry. And it must be focused on action; its process cannot end in religious insight but must move on to pastoral action. It is the need for such a method that is addressed in this book.

A Model and a Method

A *model* of theological reflection provides an image of the elements that are involved. The model we discuss points to sources of information that are important in pastoral decision making: Christian Tradition, personal experience, and cultural information. In this understanding, theological reflection in ministry is the process by which a community of faith correlates the religious information from these sources in pursuit of insight that will illumine and shape pastoral activity.

The *method* describes the dynamic or movement of the reflection. It outlines the stages through which the correlation proceeds. The initial stage (attending) involves seeking out the diverse information residing, often in a partly-hidden fashion, in the religious Tradition, the culture, and personal experience. An intermediate stage (assertion) instigates a dialogue among these sources of information in order to clarify, challenge, and purify the insights and limits of each. The final stage (decision) moves the reflection from insight toward practical and corporate pastoral action.

Situating the Method in Theological Context

The contribution of this method to the recent history of theological reflection can best be elucidated by recalling the reciprocal relationship of ministry and theology. Theology intends an understanding of faith that is ultimately practical. Its insights are meant to shape ministry. Ministry, on the other hand, is both shaped by theology and critiques the adequacy of theological formulations to the life of the Church. Reflections on faith occur along this continuum, differing as they are more influenced by the

A CONTINUUM OF THEOLOGICAL REFLECTION

M I N I S T R Y → T H E O L O G Y

scope	_immediate_ and _concrete_ (this pastoral question)	_intermediate_ (this pastoral question in its Christian and cultural context)	_broad_ (a theological question in its philosophical and historical context)
length of reflection	_brief_ (one or two sessions)	_intermediate_ (several weeks or months)	_indeterminate_ (complexity of reflection and commitment to insight rather than action; therefore, reflection is viewed as ongoing)
conversation partners	personal and ministerial experience	theology and social sciences as well as experience	philosophy and history
example: Christian community	This community's effort to live its Christian ideals; skills for community building and resolution of problems	This community's experience in explicit relation to the Christian Tradition and the American culture	Christian community as interpreted by scriptural images and historical understandings of Church; ecclesiology

Figure 1

immediacy of a pastoral concern or by the historical, scriptural, or philo-sophical complexity of a religious question. At the extremes of the min-istry-theology continuum are styles of behavior familiar to every profes-sional minister: theological reflection so abstract that its religious import is all but indiscernible and, at the other extreme, ministerial activity in which reflection enjoys almost no role.

Moving in from these extremes we encounter important models of theo-logical reflection being developed. On the theology side of the continuum, the work of Tillich, Lonergan, Ogden, Tracy, and others has contributed significantly to our understanding of the nature of theological reflection.[1] Important as these contributions are, they remain too complex for all but the most astute minister. This is partly due to the scope of the inquiry, its length, and the conversation partners of such theological reflections. A theological reflection in systematic or fundamental theology on the faith statement, "Jesus is the Christ,"[2] will focus more on the historical inter-pretations of this phrase than on contemporary experiences of Jesus as the Lord. With such historical and exegetical scope this inquiry will require a relatively extended period of reflection. Finally, the conversation partners for such a reflection are history, philosophy, and hermeneutics—sources familiar to the professional theologian, but less so to the professional min-ister. Thus the scope, length of inquiry, and the conversation partners of this reflection suggest that this model will not likely be available to the minister. This is not to denigrate such models of reflection, but only to suggest the need for their being complemented by other models of theo-logical reflection.

On the ministry side of the continuum, two recently elaborated models of reflection suggest themselves. The first model of reflection, influenced by the methods of Clinical Pastoral Education (CPE), focuses on a specific pastoral concern through the report of a "critical incident." In a small group setting, a minister explores his or her own emotional and cognitive response and then, with the group, examines theological implications of the incident and considers possibilities for pastoral response. A second model of theological reflection, the case study method,[3] begins with the preparation of a "case," a pastoral question in its concrete historical set-ting. The case is presented to a group and its religious and pastoral impli-cations are explored. The strength of these two models of reflection is their immediacy and concreteness; the scope of inquiry is narrowed to an im-mediate concern. An added strength of the first method is its attention to the minister's relationship (emotional and cognitive) to the concern.

Weaknesses sometimes experienced in both methods are a paucity of explicit attention given to the Christian Tradition in regard to this pastoral concern and a difficulty of moving from such concrete incidents to broader theological understanding. Each of these methods has contributed significantly to the development of theological reflection in ministry. Both differ from the academic model of theological reflection discussed previously in immediacy of scope, in the length of the reflection (usually being completed in one or two sessions), and in the conversation partners (giving little attention to either historical or philosophical considerations).

The process of theological reflection elaborated in this book situates itself midway on the ministry-theology continuum. It focuses on a pastoral concern in both its immediate dimension (What is *my* experience of it? What has been its impact on *this* community?) and its broader religious import (How has the Christian Tradition responded to this kind of concern?). Thus, the scope of this method is broader than a straightforward reflection on an immediate concern, but more experientially rooted than a reflection in the method of Lonergan or Tracy. These characteristics suggest the kind of minister for whom this model was devised: the minister who is neither exclusively an activist nor a professional theologian; the minister who needs and wants time for reflection in ministry; the minister who wants to be more critically aware of the influence of the Christian Tradition, culture, and personal experience on pastoral decision making.

Pastoral Reflection: A Corporate Task

A contemporary shift in ecclesiology, our understanding of the nature and structure of the Church, has significantly influenced the shape of theological reflection in ministry. Previously, we have been familiar with a Church in which an individual authority (whether Catholic pope, Episcopal bishop, or Methodist pastor) reflected on and made decisions for the believing community. The emphasis today moves toward understanding the community of faith as the locus of theological and pastoral reflection. Pastoral insight and decision are not just *received* in the community but are *generated* there as well. Theological reflection becomes a responsibility of the community itself, a corporate task. This shift is evidenced in the recent growth of ministry teams and in the increased involvement of the laity at all levels of Christian life and ministry. This shift requires new pastoral skills—group reflection, conflict resolution, and decision making—for the community and for its ministers.

The method which we discuss here is intended to assist the corporate task of theological reflection. Its development itself has been a corporate endeavor. The model and method were formulated initially over the course of a two-year research project undertaken with the support of the Lilly Endowment. The research group consisted of a theologian, a biblical scholar, a social scientist, and a ministry educator. At the core of the project was a year-long conversation, structured in eight workshop sessions, which engaged ten Roman Catholic women and men experienced in ministry in dialogue with the research group. Together, the participants explored a series of questions: the nature of Christian vocation and ministry, the contemporary experience of Christian community, the shape of adult religious growth, Christian understandings of sexuality and marriage, the mission of the Church in the world. The intent of the dialogue was twofold: to discover how effective ministers do, in fact, reflect on these questions as they arise in their ministry and to describe and further elaborate the process through which persons in ministry reach decisions for pastoral action.

These sessions produced a preliminary statement of the shape of theological reflection in ministry. Further clarification was achieved in dialogue with colleagues in education for ministry at the Biennial Convocation of the Association for Theological Field Education held in Berkeley, California, in January 1977; the Institute for Theological Reflection at Notre Dame in June 1978; and the Bairnwick School of Theology of the University of the South in September 1979. In addition, the model and method were presented for discussion and critique to ecumenical groups of ministers in St. Louis, Chicago, Denver, Michigan, New York, and California. Finally, in the essays which make up this book, our collaboration is expanded to include contributions of three colleagues in ministry and education for ministry who share our interest in the articulation of a practical method for theological reflection in ministry.

It is our hope that this method of reflection, tested and refined in a variety of settings, will be useful both to Christian ministers and to ministry education. The value of such a practical method will be confirmed, not by its sophistication, but by its effectiveness as a tool of reflective Christians in their efforts of ministry and service.

Notes

1. See Paul Tillich's presentation of method in theology in Volume One of his *Systematic Theology* (Chicago: University of Chicago Press, 1951). See also Bernard Lonergan, *Method in Theology* (New York: Herder and Herder, 1972);

Shubert Ogden, "What Is Theology?" in *Journal of Religion* 52 (January 1972); and David Tracy, *Blessed Rage for Order* (New York: Seabury, 1975). The methods of these theologians will be examined in more detail in the following chapter. See also Gordon Kaufman's *An Essay on Theological Method* (Missoula, MT: Scholars Press, 1975) and Bernard Meland's *Fallible Forms and Symbols* (Philadelphia: Fortress Press, 1976).

2. David Tracy describes such a reflection in his *Blessed Rage for Order*, p. 49f.

3. See the range of articles on the case study method in *Theological Education* 10 (Spring 1974). See also Oliver Williams and John Houck, *Full Value: Cases in Christian Business Ethics* (San Francisco: Harper and Row, 1978).

PART I

Theological Reflection in Ministry

In a complex and changing world we are challenged to discern the contin-uing presence and action of God and to respond, faithfully and effectively, to this presence. For the adult Christian and especially for the minister this necessitates a method of reflection.

In Part One we outline a model of reflection in ministry which invites the reflective Christian to attend to three sources of religiously relevant in-formation: the Christian Tradition, our own life experience, and the in-sights (and biases) of our culture. The dynamic at work in this model is a three-stage movement of attending, assertion, and decision. First listening to the Word, we are then called to witness to it. This witnessing occurs in a pluralistic setting; we challenge and support each other's witness to faith as we move from religious insight toward religious action.

The goal of this model and method of reflection is the development of reflective Christian communities and ministers whose faith finds effective expression in today's world.

·1·

REFLECTION IN MINISTRY—
A MODEL AND A METHOD

In every age the community of faith must discover the shape of its ministry. We must discern how we are to be faithful to the gospel and effective in our mission: to celebrate God's saving presence and to contribute, by word and action and sacrament, to the fullness of this presence—the coming of the Kingdom. Theological reflection is an essential tool in this discernment of contemporary ministry. In this chapter we outline a model and method of theological reflection in ministry. The *model* points to three sources of religiously significant information to be brought to bear on pastoral decisions. The *method* indicates how this information can influence pastoral action. Both the model and the method are presented as working tools. Their goal is not simply to help ministers understand more clearly, but to help them to act more effectively—that is, in ways that are faithful to the good news of salvation made known to us in Jesus Christ—and to help them become competent in proclaiming this good news in our own time.

An Overview of Model and Method

Method has been defined as "a normative pattern of recurrent and related operations yielding cumulative and progressive results."[1] In theology today this pattern of operations is understood by many as an ongoing correlation of the Christian Tradition and human experience. Paul Tillich's formulation of this correlation was simply (and, from the vantage point of the 1980s, simplisticly) in terms of "existential questions and theological answers in mutual interdependence."[2] This relationship is altered by Shubert Ogden to read "the correlation of the Christian witness of faith and human existence."[3] David Tracy further shifts the vocabulary of the correlation to that of "common human experience" and "the Christian fact."[4]

If it is agreed that theological reflection involves a correlation of these two facets, broadly understood as Tradition and experience, ambiguity and disagreement abound concerning the meaning, content, and theological weight of each. The delineation of a method of theological reflection thus chiefly consists in a definition of each part of the correlation and of the dynamic that moves the reflection toward its conclusion. For a model of reflection in ministry it will also be imperative to describe a method which is *performable* (that is, a method that can not only be appreciated, but practically used by a range of ministers) and which issues in pastoral decisions and ministerial strategies.

In the pursuit of such a performable model we have described a manner of reflection which seeks to correlate three sources of religiously relevant information. Tradition is the first and obvious source for a theological reflection. By this term we understand both the Sacred Scripture and the history of the Christian Church, with its multiple interpretations of Scripture and of itself. Tradition here embraces Ogden's "Christian witness of faith" and Tracy's "Christian fact." The aspects of this pole most relevant to reflection in ministry will be discussed in detail after we first outline the other poles of the reflection and the dynamic which moves the process.

That which is to be correlated with Christian Tradition is at once clear and endlessly complicated. We have distinguished Tracy's "common human experience" and Ogden's "human existence" into two separable poles of reflection. For the first of these we have retained the name "experience." By this admittedly amorphous term we signify the personal experience of the minister and the collective experience of the community in which the reflection is taking place.

The pole of experience in this model, then, bears an importantly different meaning than Tracy's "common human experience." While Tracy's "experience" refers to the common and general experience of a culture (not yet recognized as religiously relevant), experience in this model refers to the specific experience of *this* minister and *this* community concerning *this* pastoral concern. Such concrete and immediate experience is, of course, a distillate of religious, cultural, and personal influence. It is neither simply "religious experience" nor "cultural experience." The initial challenge at this pole of the reflection is carefully to apprehend what this experience is. In a model that is ministerial in orientation this pole of the reflection and methods of inquiry proper to it take on great importance.

The third pole of the reflection, that of cultural information, is separable from the more immediate experience of the minister and the reflecting community. By "cultural information," we mean that sort of understanding, conviction, or bias in the culture which contributes explicitly or implicitly to any theological reflection in ministry. We have distinguished cultural information as a distinct source of theological reflection since the inclusion of it within the already overburdened pole of (personal) experience results in a category too cumbersome for a practical method of reflection. In the following pages we shall discuss how this pole of cultural information functions not only as a secular or demonic force to be overcome, but also at times as a force which assertively confirms Christian insight or challenges the limitations of past formulations of Christian self-understanding.

If these are the three poles of the correlation that describes theological reflection in ministry, the dynamic which moves this correlation toward insight and decision is a dual movement of attending and assertion. In Christianity, hearing the Word is followed by witnessing to it. In a movement that parallels this hearing/witnessing dynamic[5] this model of reflection attends to the three sources of religiously relevant information and then places these different "hearings" in an assertive relationship. These operations of listening and assertion demand a complex set of skills. The minister must possess not only textual and hermeneutical abilities—the theological skills of attending—but also the interpersonal and ministerial skills of attending. Assertion skills of a similar breadth are required if a ministerial reflection is to sustain the tension of differing interpretations not only among those participating in the reflection, but also in Scripture and Tradition. Out of such assertively maintained tensions, theological insight and pastoral decisions begin to emerge. The final stage of this method, pastoral decision, is intimately related to and flows from a critical execution of the prior stages of attending and assertion. We will return to these theological and ministerial skills in greater detail in the subsequent discussion on the dynamic of this model of reflection.

The Model

Theological reflection in ministry involves three sources of religiously relevant information—Christian Tradition, the experience of the community of faith, and the resources of the culture.

Tradition

This pole of theological reflection represents that information we draw both from Scripture and from Church history concerning a specific pastoral concern. At the outset it must be recalled that in a ministerial reflection the goal is not simply a clarification of our historical understanding of

---

THEOLOGICAL REFLECTION IN MINISTRY

Tradition   *Cultural Information*

pluriform in   data from the culture
Scripture      (e.g., social sciences)
and history   that influence the
                                                         issue

Personal Experience

what the individual believer and
the community bring to the reflection

Figure 2

a religious question. The goal is a pastoral decision, a ministerial response to a contemporary situation. Tradition, as we are using the term in this model of reflection, includes both the revelation found in the Old and New Testaments and those ecclesial decisions of the past two millennia which incline the minister toward certain pastoral responses rather than toward others.

When we confront this massive and complex source of religious information called Tradition, we are immediately faced with questions about the nature and locus of revelation. Current studies in the theology of revelation,[6] as well as in the development of dogma and the influence of historical consciousness on our understanding of the Christian Tradition, are delivering Catholic theology from earlier ahistorical understandings of a *depositum fidei* and a stress on *tradita* (the content of tradition) to the neglect of *traditio* (the process of traditioning). The pursuit of the ramifications of these changes for a method of theological reflection is a most important task, but one that we will not undertake here. Instead, we will understand the theological information available in the different historical stages of the Christian Tradition as grounded in the Christian conviction of the continuing, formative presence of the Spirit in the Church. Differing theological weight will certainly be assigned to these different stages of the Tradition. Thus, scriptural judgments about a pastoral concern will outweigh practices of the medieval Church in this regard; decisions of Chalcedon will outweigh religious practices and beliefs which arose in opposition to these decisions. The important point in the present context is a recognition of the multiple and varied presence of God in our

Christian Tradition and of the need for ministers to be aware of the different responses of the Tradition to this enduring presence.

The Tradition as Pluriform

The characteristic of the Tradition that has special relevance for this method of reflection in ministry is its *pluriformity*. Christian Tradition has been pluriform from its inception. The Church at Antioch formulated a Christology slightly different from that of Corinth;[7] the eschatology of the Fourth Gospel differs from that of the synoptics. This level of pluriformity, so familiar to the professional theologian, remains a scandal for many believers and a source of confusion for many ministers. The method of reflection we discuss here assumes an understanding of Christian pluralism not only as scandal and sign of disunity (which it has been), but also as a sign of richness. The variety of expressions of belief within our Tradition points to the ineffably diverse ways God is with us. This model of theological reflection, as an educational tool, attempts to develop a greater awareness of and an increased comfort with this pluriformity.

The second level of pluriformity in the Christian Tradition is longitudinal—pluriformity resulting from historical change. The Tradition, diverse at its inception, is most notably pluriform over time.[8] Historically, the Tradition has developed as the Christian Church interacted (with varying effectiveness and faithfulness) with different cultural contexts and challenges. Such historical pluriformity means that the Tradition is rich with different and differing responses to a single pastoral concern. With the recognition of this pluriformity the minister may more clearly discern the role of Tradition in a theological reflection today.

The minister does not look to the Christian Tradition to provide a simple, proof-text answer to a contemporary pastoral question, but to provide parameters for a solution—examples of how Christians, in faith, have addressed similar problems. Different responses within Scripture, the Church Fathers, medieval theology, and in twentieth-century Christianity guide the minister to a genuinely Christian resolution of the question.

To approach this historical pluriformity from another viewpoint, it is useful to recall that, for an unreflective believer or minister, Tradition might well mean "how we have always done it." "Always" in such instances will likely go back only as far as the past generation. The method of reflection we discuss here can function as an educational tool in a community to introduce the faithful to the diversity of belief and expression which, in fact, constitutes the larger Christian Tradition.

The third level of pluriformity in the Christian Tradition refers to its divine and human elements. The Church and the two millennia of its history are not only a sacred event (the doing of God), but simultaneously a human event. It is a frail construction of human choices, subject to God's guiding will, but likewise to those multiple, clouded motives that mark the construction of our own lives. This pluriformity, still a scandal for those who envision the Church as an unmixed God-event, suggests one of the dynamics involved in a reflection on the Tradition. This dynamic is one of preserving and overcoming: preserving the gracefulness of the theological and pastoral choices of our Tradition while overcoming some of the limitations of their formulations.[9]

The minister attends to the diverse (and sometimes conflicting) information concerning a specific pastoral concern that arises from the Tradition. This plural information from the Tradition itself is set in interaction with cultural information and personal experience on this question. In such an assertive relationship, necessarily tense but potentially invigorating theological insight and pastoral strategies can begin to emerge.

Befriending the Tradition

If such is the meaning of Tradition in this method of reflection in ministry, an important practical question remains concerning the minister's relation to this pole of the reflection. The riches of the Christian Tradition, as a source of pastoral reflection for ministry, are, ironically, not available to many ministers. It has been our experience that many in ministry feel alienated from the Tradition. This is not an emotional alienation or rejection of what the Tradition may hold. It is, rather, an intellectual alienation, a pervasive sense of *distance.* Most in ministry display great respect for the heritage of their religious past, yet their most consistent experience of it is an intimidating one. When faced with a specific pastoral question, ministers often judge the Tradition to be irrelevant, unhelpfully ambiguous, or simply unapproachable. They feel they lack both the tools and the time to learn from it. Their formal preparation for ministry has given them an appreciation of the complexity and sacredness of the Tradition, but not the skills of access to it that are appropriate to their own profession.

Thus, a challenge for theological reflection in ministry is to develop methods of access to the Tradition that are appropriate not to the Scripture scholar or systematic theologian, but to those working directly within the community of faith. The intent for both minister and faithful appears to be not mastery of the Tradition, but befriending—an increase in intimacy with the Tradition. The image of "befriending" suggests that a more-than-intellectual grasp is required for ministry. The minister's familiarity with the Tradition must include both critical awareness of and comfort with the diverse testimony of the Tradition on a specific pastoral concern.

The Sense of the Faithful

The Tradition to which the minister must be alert exists not only in Scripture and Church history. Theological reflection requires (and leads to) a more explicit awareness of the lively presence of the Tradition *within* the minister and the believing community today. This Tradition-in-experience phenomenon recalls an important, if atrophied, category in the Christian theological tradition—that of the *sensus fidelium*.[10] This category, which refers to the sense of faith residing in the Christian community, can be interpreted as the Tradition alive in the contemporary experience of the minister and the community. We will expand this discussion of the *sensus fidelium* in our consideration of experience as a source for theological reflection in ministry.

Experience

The pole of experience in the model of theological reflection in ministry is at once simple and complex. It is simple when we understand this pole to refer to the minister's and the community's awareness of a specific pastoral concern. Thus, if the question concerns the morality of some political behavior, the minister recognizes that her or his attitude and feelings about politics, as well as the attitudes of the community, will and should influence the reflection. It is important that these feelings and attitudes come to critical awareness in order that their influence in the reflection can be acknowledged, evaluated, and used to full advantage.

The pole of experience represents that source of information—religious, Christian, and cultural—as it is available within the individual minister and within that specific community where the reflection occurs. The present tripolar model of reflection begins at this pole. Initiating reflection at the pole of experience reverses the theological proclivity to begin its reflections "at the beginning" (Scripture and early Church history) and work forward. Such reflections have a way of not reaching the present, of not coming to terms with the contemporary experience of faith. To avoid or postpone serious reflection on personal and communal experience in favor of a reflection of the Tradition and cultural information does not evade the influence of this experience. It avoids only an awareness of its influence.

The challenge of this practical method is to assist the minister and the community to come to a reflective grasp of their own experience (convictions, feelings, ideas, biases) about a specific pastoral concern. Such apprehension depends on skills of awareness and listening. In the workshops in which this model of theological reflection was developed, a variety of experiential learning strategies were used to invite participants to explore their experience and conviction concerning specific ministerial questions. Exercises of the imagination, journal keeping, and structured small group sessions were among the methods employed to approach deeper levels of the minister's experience. The intention of this stage of the method is that self-knowledge which has always been a central part of Christian spirituality and ministerial asceticism. As believers come to greater consciousness and clarity about their personal feeling and convictions on a particular pastoral question this experience can be placed in an assertive conversation with understandings of this same question found in Christian Tradition and the culture.

Attention to experience as a source of theological reflection is a relatively recent development in Catholic thought.[11] Historically, Catholic theology has been very suspicious of "experience." It has seemed too susceptible to subjectivism, excess of feeling, and sectarian enthusiasm.[12] The events of the past two decades, including the work of John Courtney Murray on freedom of conscience and the reforms in liturgical practice, have altered this Catholic bias against the theological relevance of experience. American Catholics have taken a new interest in their own experiences and in the relation of these experiences to the expression of Catholic faith. Widespread rejection of the Vatican's teaching on birth control (which contradicts, for many Catholic couples, their *experience* of the responsible use of contraceptives) and a more active participation in the celebration of the Eucharist are but two indicators of this renewed interest. This interest argues for a more assertive role of personal experience in ministerial reflection. Thus, it becomes imperative to develop among ministers those skills that enable them to attend critically to this most immediate and potentially volatile source of religiously significant information.

Again: The Sense of the Faithful

Our discussion of experience as a distinct source in theological reflection must recognize that for the Christian minister there is significant overlap between experience and Tradition. When ministers explore their own awareness of an issue of pastoral concern they may expect to come in contact not merely with experience that is the product of their culture or with their own idiosyncrasies, but with awareness that has been already "Christianized"—that is in dialogue with the Tradition by which it has been formed. We return here to the notion of the sense of the faithful.

There has been a tendency in Catholic theology, as Mackey has shown,[13] to interpret this sense of the faithful in a thoroughly passive fashion. In this understanding the faith of the community is simply the result of the formative influence of the teaching Church, the Magisterium. In their discussion of the Church (*Lumen Gentium,* #12), however, the Council Fathers of Vatican II recognized the sense of the faithful as a powerful, unerring expression of Christian faith.[14] Even this document, however, by stressing inerrancy and universal agreement, neglects two central features of the *sensus fidelium:* the sense of faith as an *active* expression of belief,[15] and its factual pluriformity. As an active source of faith, the *sensus fidelium* must be attended to and included as an element in any theological reflection. As pluriform, the sense of the faithful finds diverse expressions in the many communities which comprise the Christian Church. Both of these features argue that a practical theological reflection must develop methods which give access to this important source of religious information.

In the context of this tripolar model of theological reflection the *sensus fidelium* represents the overlap of Tradition and experience, reminding us that these poles converge in the Christian community and its ministers. That is, the experiential pole in ministry is not divorced from the Christian Tradition since the pole of experience refers to the accumulated experience of the minister and the community as shaped by the culture and also as formed by the Christian Tradition. The challenge is to develop means of critical access to this sense of the faithful—specific, practical means which rescue this category of *sensus fidelium* from its current rhetorical status and bring its religious informaton into the processes of pastoral decision making.

Cultural Information

This pole of the method of theological reflection in ministry refers to that information—confirming, ambiguous, and demonic—which arises from the culture. It includes understandings—of the human person, of community, of success and failure—which have influenced and continue to influence Christian efforts of self-understanding. Tillich defined one of the sources of systematic theology as "the material presented by the history of religions and culture."[16] Recent discussion of theological method has been impressed by the importance of language in shaping Christian thought.[17] Such language, however, is but one central instance of the influence of culture. In the method under consideration here we have distinguished cultural information from experience as a source of theological reflection. There is certainly considerable overlap of the poles of experience and cultural information, as we noted between Tradition and experience. But it is useful to distinguish the information present in the minister's own experiences and that information which arises more explicitly in the symbols, mores, and sciences of a culture. Instances of such cultural information will clarify the contribution of this pole to theological reflection in ministry.

In our model, cultural information includes both historical and contemporary aspects of a culture, aspects which influence Christian self-understanding. Thus, past philosophical understandings of man as rational animal can be seen as influencing the shape of Christian spirituality. Heidegger's philosophical thought has influenced Karl Rahner and, through him, the shape of current Catholic theology.

A second category within cultural information, after that of philosophy, would be political interpretations of human community. Thus, we can note the monarchical structure of medieval Europe and its contribution to Christian ecclesiologies or Marxism's orientation to the future and the influence of this orientation, through such intermediaries as Ernst Bloch, on the theological rethinking of Christian eschatology.

A third category, closely related to the two above, is the contribution of the social sciences to our understanding of the person and society. In the workshops in which this model of reflection was developed, information from the social sciences played a central part. The possible contributions of psychological theories of adult maturation to a contemporary Christian spirituality were probed and sociological perspectives on community were examined for insight into the nature and forms of Christian life together.

A fourth category of cultural information for Christian reflection is that of other religious traditions. The data of this category is ambiguously included in "cultural" information since its content is specifically religious. This increasingly influential source of data for theological reflection can be assigned to this pole of the reflection because its information originates outside both the Christian Tradition and the Christian's usual experience. These religious traditions function as some of the diverse ways that God speaks to us from the broader culture which lies beyond our own limited experience and the historically specific tradition of Christianity.

Cultural information in all four of these categories is understood in both a positive and negative cast. Neither simply demonic nor unambiguously enlightened, culture produces interpretations which the Christian Tradition rejects, but also provides interpretations which challenge Christian reflection to reconsider and correct limitations within its own self-understanding. Sexuality provides a good example of this ambiguity. Christians struggle against the influence of pornography in American society, but benefit from the culture's contribution, through physiological and psychological research, to a clearer understanding of mature sexuality. The pole of cultural information thus represents not a realm of unredeemed nature, but a mixed environment, partly antithetical to and partly complementary to Christian life.

An important challenge regarding such information and the challenge which marks this method as ministerial in orientation is to make this information available in usable form to reflective ministers. The minister cannot be asked to become either a philosopher or social scientist. We must continue to explore ways to put such cultural information at the disposal of the reflecting minister, both critically and practically.

The Method

How does this model of theological reflection work for the minister confronted by a situation that requires a pastoral response? A family in crisis calls and asks for help. A local community organization seeks the parish's support for a petition encouraging low-income housing in the area. A newspaper article draws attention to the isolation and loneliness that exists among older widows and widowers in the city. The parish women's group proposes one of its members to be formally recognized as a "Minister of Worship." The model of theological reflection in ministry suggests resources that can help persons in ministry to respond faithfully and effectively to the concerns that challenge the community of faith. The method describes a process by which these resources can become part of pastoral decision making and thus influence pastoral action. The process can be understood as three overlapping stages: attending, assertion, and decision for action.

Attending

The initial posture for theological reflection is that of the listener; attending is the first activity of the method. Faced with a particular concern or pastoral issue, the reflective community seeks out the information that is

---

**Three-stage method
of Theological Reflection in Ministry**

I. ATTENDING
Seek out the information on a particular pastoral concern that is available in personal experience, Christian Tradition, and cultural sources.

II. ASSERTION
Engage the information from these three sources in a process of mutual clarification and challenge in order to expand and deepen religious insight.

III. DECISION
Move from insight through decision to concrete pastoral action.

Figure 3

available in experience, in the Tradition, and in the culture's understandings. A range of listening skills is required here. Benefiting from recent biblical scholarship, ministers today must have the skills required to attend critically to the texts and contexts of the writings of the Bible. They must also be able to approach Scripture as a religious resource that can influence their personal lives and inform their practical ministerial decisions.

Other listening skills pertinent to the other sources of religiously relevant information described in the model are required. To attend to experience as a source in theological reflection will require skills of intrapersonal and interpersonal attending. Skills of intrapersonal attending alert me to the movements of my own mind and heart; they contribute to my growing awareness of my own motives, biases, convictions and values. Such self-awareness is an essential part of a minister's spiritual growth. It is also critical to any process of reflection and decision making. Interpersonal attending skills enhance the minister's ability to discern the experience of the community. We are reminded here that the role of the minister is not only to direct and govern the community of faith, but to learn from it. The community is not merely the passive recipient of religious truth. It is an active source of theological information. As one part of the *sensus fidelium* the community has a contribution to make to the ongoing theological reflection of the Church, a contribution that is possible only as ministers and theologians learn to listen more skillfully and expectantly to this source. Listening skills are also required if reflection is to benefit from cultural information. While the minister cannot be expected to learn the skills of a professional social scientist, some critical ability to learn from the culture is imperative.

A necessary ingredient in effective listening to each of these sources is the ability to suspend premature judgment. The conviction here is not that evaluation and judgment are secondary, but that they are subsequent. A person rigidly convinced of a single interpretation—whether of a text or of another person—is not able to hear something new or unexpected and thus is unable to engage in the critical attending required for theological reflection. To suspend judgment[18] is, of course, a threatening venture.[18] It leaves me vulnerable to new information that may challenge the way I see things and perhaps require that I change. Yet the effectiveness of this first stage of theological reflection depends on my ability to explore the information available in the three sources. A tendency to quick evaluation will cut short this exploration and lessen the chance of new insight that may lead to creative pastoral response.

Assertion

It is our conviction that all three sources of information described in the model contribute to theological reflection in ministry. The contribution of each is not made in isolation, but in an assertive relationship of challenge and confirmation. There are two assumptions that ground this conviction: that God is revealed in all three sources and that the religious information available in each is partial. While the limitation of personal experience and cultural information as religious resources may be more immediately evident, there are limitations to be recognized in the Tradition as well—limitations that arise from the human interpretations and cultural contexts that have shaped the Tradition. Culturally rooted biases within the Church today *for* hierarchical models of leadership and *against* equal access of women to positions of ministerial leadership are two examples of such limitations. Our faithful efforts to both preserve and overcome the Tradition are facilitated by placing the Tradition's insights on a pastoral concern in tension with the community's experience and with cultural information. It is in this dialogue of mutual interpretation that new insight is generated and the shape of pastoral response begins to emerge.

This second stage in the method can be clarified by defining assertion and then exemplifying its use in a theological reflection. Assertion is a style of behavior which acknowledges the value of my own needs and convictions in a manner that respects the needs and convictions of others.[19] Assertive behavior functions between the extremes of not being able to share a conviction (nonassertiveness) and forcing a conviction on others (aggressiveness). A theological reflection is aborted when either nonassertiveness or aggressiveness dominates the process. This can happen in a variety of ways. A minister or member of the community may be so impressed by his or her experience about a specific concern that he or she becomes deaf to the Christian Tradition's judgments about it. Here, experience is an aggressor and frustrates the reflection. Likewise, a person may be so overwhelmed by an interpretation in the Tradition of a ministerial question that he or she is closed to any cultural information or even to personal experience and its testimony. Here, the Tradition (really, one interpretation of one aspect of the Tradition) is an aggressor in the reflection. Thirdly, a person may be so impressed by the culture's understanding of a question that the Christian Tradition appears utterly irrelevant and is ignored. Again the reflection is aborted due to the failure to establish a genuinely assertive relationship among the three sources of information. Assertiveness, at both a theological and an interpersonal level, is required of the minister at this stage of the reflection. An ability to face diversity and to tolerate ambiguity is essential. With these, the minister is able to sustain different and possibly conflicting testimony about a single issue. This model of reflection argues that only with the mature development of this stage of mutual assertion can the reflective process move toward the final stage of pastoral decision.

Decision

The assertive interaction of Tradition, experience, and culture generates insight. The challenge of the third stage of the method is to translate this insight into action. The effectiveness of this stage depends on the quality of the information and reflection at earlier stages. The choices made at this point arise out of the insights developed in the assertion stage. The decisions of this stage must be expressive of and in continuity with these insights.

At this point in the reflective process a crucial difference between theological decisions and ministerial decisions becomes more apparent. The minister reflects in order to act. In the face of insufficient information or conflicting facts a reflection accountable only to the criteria of academic theology can decide not to decide. Instead, the theologian can, appropriately, reinitiate the process of reflection in the hope of coming to greater clarity sometime in the future. A ministerial reflection most generally focuses on a question that demands practical resolution now. In many situations the minister or the community must act even in the face of insufficient information. This particular characteristic of decisions in ministry and in other areas of practical life—that they must be made even in the face of ambiguity—has been little studied. Negatively, we know that ministerial reflection which takes as its criteria those standards of clarity and comprehensiveness appropriate in academic theological reflection will necessarily fall short of practical usefulness.

The decision stage of pastoral reflection requires its own set of skills. Skills of problem analysis and conflict resolution are required as the minister and the community attempt to bring to bear in the concrete questions of life the force of their theological reflection. Many pastoral decisions fail because they are arrived at apart from the communities in which they will be implemented. Thus, the ability to develop group consensus and to move an emerging consensus from insight to a plan for community action becomes a skill of pastoral reflection. This move from insight to action can be assisted by the use of strategies of effective decision making. Central to these are the ability to generate alternatives, to choose among these partial solutions, and to keep these choices accountable to the larger vision.

Conclusion

The ideal of Christian ministry is the formation of a reflective community which is alive to the presence of God. The model that we suggest here can be a tool to expand this awareness, inviting believers to develop skills which will enable them to discern religiously significant information in three important sources. Such a community is attentive to the normative statements of the Tradition (which, within the Catholic community, include the teachings of the Magisterium) and is sensitive to its cultural milieu and to its own experience of faith. Aware that, as a single community, it is not the sole arbiter of faith, the community is yet confident as it asserts itself and its convictions within the Church. These convictions will be expressed in pastoral decisions that are at once practical and open to revision as the community continues to attend to convictions that arise in other communities of believers.

In a Church that is truly Catholic, that is, plural, different communities will come to differing conclusions in many concrete pastoral situations. Some of these differences may arise from ignorance or error or even "bad will." More often, however, these differences will be appropriate and expectable variations that reflect the rich diversity within the Christian experience of God's Word and God's will.

Notes

1. Bernard Lonergan, *Method in Theology* (New York: Herder and Herder, 1972), p. 4.

2. Paul Tillich, *Systematic Theology* (Chicago: University of Chicago Press, 1951), 1:60.

3. See his "What is Theology?" in *Journal of Religion* 52 (January 1972):23.

4. In his *Blessed Rage for Order* (New York: Seabury, 1975), Tracy defines theology as "philosophical reflection upon the meanings present in common human experience and language, and upon the meanings present in the Christian fact" (p. 43). In the final footnote of the previous chapter, he admits that "the word 'tradition' covers the same ground as the expression 'the christian fact' " (p. 42).

5. Lonergan (*Method in Theology*, p. 133) distinguishes these operations as assimilating Tradition, then passing it on; and as encountering the past and then confronting the future. His first three phases of theology (research, interpretation, and history) are preeminently stages of attending. Phases four to seven (dialectics, foundations, doctrine, and systematics) are exercises in assertion. His final phase of theology, communications, "is concerned with theology in its external relations" (p. 132). The model of ministerial reflection outlined in this book elaborates this movement of theology into explicit contact with the culture and practical expression (ministry).

6. See Avery Dulles' excellent "The Meaning of Revelation" in Joseph Papin, ed., *The Dynamics of Christian Thought* (Villanova, PA: Villanova University Press, 1970), pp. 52–80; and Thomas O'Meara's "Toward a Subjective Theology of Revelaton," in *Theological Studies* 36 (September 1975):410–27.

7. See Helmut Koester's "*Gnomai Diaphorai:* The Origins and Nature of Diversification in the History of Early Christianity" in *Harvard Theological Review* 58 (1965):279–318. On the broader question of the Church's struggle to come to terms with diversity and change, see Jaroslav Pelikan's "Theology and Change" in *Crosscurrents* (Fall 1969):277–84. Raymond Brown describes the different and differing communities out of which was generated the Fourth Gospel in his excellent *The Community of the Beloved Disciple* (New York: Paulist Press, 1979).

8. See Robert Wilken's *The Myth of Christian Beginnings* (New York: Doubleday, 1972). On the crisis-inducing efforts of the Catholic Church to deal with this historical pluriformity, see Raymond Brown's chapter, "The curent crisis in theology as it affects the teaching of Catholic doctrine," in his *Crises Facing the Church* (New York: Paulist, 1975).

9. Karl Rahner employs this method in examining the christological formulations of Chalcedon in "Current Problems in Christology," *Theological Investigations* (Baltimore: Helicon, 1961), 1:149–54.

10. This sense of the faithful refers to the believing community's intuitions and instincts of belief and recalls the notion in early Christianity of "vox populi vox Dei." Thomas More and Cardinal Newman each recognized the importance of this notion and its relationship to a theology of the laity. See our discussion of experience which follows for references to a study of Thomas More on the *sensus fidelium* and to Vatican II's understanding of this category.

11. See, for example, Anne Carr, "Theology and Experience in the Thought of Karl Rahner" in *Journal of Religion* 53 (July 1973):359–76.

12. John Coleman has noted three striking exceptions to this attitude in his "Vision and Praxis in American Theology: Orestes Brownson, John A. Ryan and John Courtney Murray" in *Theological Studies* 37 (November 1976):3–40.

13. J. P. Mackey, *The Modern Theology of Tradition* (New York: Herder and Herder, 1963), p. 97f.

14. "Thanks to a supernatural sense of the faith which characterizes the People as a whole, it manifests this unerring quality when, 'from the bishops down to the last member of the laity,' it shows universal agreement in matters of faith and morals." Walter M. Abbott, ed., *The Documents of Vatican II* (New York: America Press, 1966), p. 29.

15. Mackey quotes Scheeben (*Katholische Dogmatik*) on this active contribution of the *sensus fidelium:* "The profession of faith by the body of believers is not of value *only* by reason of the influence of the Magisterium, which begets it, but possesses its own intrinsic, relatively autonomous value as a result of the direct working of the Holy Spirit on the faithful" (p. 121).

For a discussion of the *sensus fidelium* as a source of theological authority (which comes to surprisingly conservative conclusions), see James Hitchcock's "Thomas More and the Sensus Fidelium," in *Theological Studies* 36 (March 1975):145–54.

16. Tillich, *Systematic Theology*, 1:38.

17. Gordon Kaufman discusses the role of language in his *An Essay on Theological Method* (Missoula, MT: Scholars Press, 1975), p. 5f. Also see David Tracy's *Blessed Rage for Order*, in which one member of the correlation of theological reflection is "common human experience and language."

18. Such suspension of judgment does not mean the abandonment of beliefs; it simply means that I am not so taken with my interpretation of a gospel passage, for example, or of human sexuality that I cannot hear another person's interpretation. The ability to listen well suggests not an absence of personal conviction, but a comfort with these convictions, knowing they can coexist alongside others.

19. For a definition and brief discussion of assertiveness, see Lawrence Percell et al., "The Effects of Assertive Training on Self-Concept and Anxiety" in *Archives of General Psychiatry* 31 (October 1974):502–4.

PART II

The Model of Reflection in Ministry

Each of the three sources of religiously relevant information to which the reflective Christian must attend is complex and plural.

The Christian Tradition comprises not only the Old and New Testaments, but the two millennia of interpretations and decisions that have shaped Christian history. The minister's approach to this rich and dense heritage is not one of mastery, but of befriending.

The community's own lived experience, another source of information, is both shaped and challenged by this religious heritage and by its cultural milieu. Of central importance in a critical appreciation of this source of information is the question of access: How are we, carefully, to clarify our own insights and biases as these are a part of our reflection and decision?

Cultural information, a third source of information, is likewise ambiguous. Literature, philosophy, and the social sciences can contribute positively to our religious understanding of life; other aspects of our cultural life—racism, materialism, pornography—can influence our awareness in a destructive fashion.

In Part Two we explore the complexity of each of these sources in terms of their contribution to theological reflection in ministry.

·2·

THE TRADITION
AS A RESOURCE
IN THEOLOGICAL REFLECTION—
SCRIPTURE AND THE MINISTER

Eugene C. Ulrich and
William G. Thompson

The previous chapter presented a model for theological reflection in ministry. The model is tripolar, specifying three sources of religiously relevant information and suggesting a dynamic which moves from a sympathetic listening to the information from these sources, through a constructively assertive dialogue generating insight, to a decision translating the theological insight into pastoral action.

The purpose of this chapter is to focus on the Tradition pole of the model, especially the biblical resources within our Tradition. First, we will reflect on Sacred Scripture itself. Then we will explore the function of the Bible in theological reflection, describing a way of approaching Scripture in ministry that listens to the Tradition, uses cultural information, and respects personal experience. Our aim is to elaborate an approach that is theologically rooted, designed for use by those in ministry rather than for the academic community, and genuinely available to persons in ministry.

The particular context in which the Bible is read determines how it is to be approached, what questions may be asked appropriately, and what methods are to be employed in answering these. Contemporary contexts for studying the Bible are many and varied. In humanities programs, for example, the Bible is studied alongside the *Iliad* and the plays of Shakespeare, as a classic of Western culture. In the history of religions, the Bible is approached as a religious text like other religious texts, such as the

Koran and the Bhagavad Gita. Comparison reveals both the common and distinctive characteristics of these writings and of the religions that consider them sacred. Viewing the Bible as a Western classic or as one religious text alongside others does not demand religious commitment to Judaeo-Christianity and to a particular community of believers.

In church-related situations an explicit commitment to a community of believers determines the perspective from which to approach the Bible. Christian theologians in every age have claimed that the biblical writings constitute a norm for Christian theology. In education for Christian ministry a central question is how the Church is to use the Bible in its practice of prayer, in its preaching, in its liturgical life, and in its theology. In this chapter we approach the Bible from this viewpoint of faith. We ask how Scripture functions in the method of theological reflection described in the previous chapter, and how the Bible can become practically available to the minister engaged in such reflection.

Many persons in ministry today, as we noted in Chapter One, have come to the honest but disconcerting realization that their day-to-day pastoral ministry is quite divorced from Scripture and Tradition. With high esteem and reverence for their religious roots, they nevertheless feel distant from these sources, without personal access to them. They see the need and the value of incorporating Scripture and Tradition into what they do as ministers. But they are less clear about how this can be done.

Seminary or divinity school is likely to have implanted in ministers an awareness of the immense complexity of biblical scholarship and Christian history. It may also have awakened an appreciation of the importance of these areas of the Christian heritage, instilling a genuine love for them and a desire to use them in ministry. But, so often, ministers have not learned the skills that could provide access to the Tradition at the level appropriate to their profession. Generally, ministers are educated not by ministers, but by scholars whose tools of inquiry and criteria of effectiveness pertain more to academic theology than to theological reflection in ministry.

Once energetically involved in pastoral work, ministers can begin to lose touch with the attitudes and convictions that permeated their seminary education. How can persons whose hours and weeks are filled with the demands and responsibilities of ministry keep abreast of the developments in biblical scholarship? How can they make this information relevant to the people they serve? For many in ministry Scripture continues as a profound resource for personal piety. But its relevance as a resource in one's ministry becomes clouded. What *should* be the function of the Bible in relation to one's ministry? Is there a realistic way to bring Scripture to bear on actual pastoral concerns? How can its power be released in the daily tasks of ministry? We turn to these questions now, first examining *what* the Christian Scriptures are and, then, *how* these central resources of the Tradition can be used in reflection in ministry.

For centuries the vision of reality in Western society was shaped by the worldview presented in the Bible. In this intellectual milieu the biblical narratives were taken both seriously and literally. Over the last six centuries in the West the biblical construct of the world has gradually lost its power. Fewer people refer happenings to the biblical narratives for clarification, explanation, or interpretation. Even fewer refer happenings to the Bible for assessment. The biblical world construct has been replaced by the evolutionary, the Marxist, the Freudian, and other approaches to reality.

In the nineteenth and twentieth centuries the rise of historical consciousness gave birth to the historical-critical approach, a method that has helped us recognize that the biblical texts were produced in cultural and religious situations very different from the present. Recognizing this distance and the difference in worldview has been, and continues to be, experienced as alienating in both a negative and a positive sense. Negatively, the historical approach to the Bible makes it no longer possible to take biblical narratives literally. It also forces the question: Can we continue to take them seriously? Positively, in using the historical-critical method we try to distance ourselves from the Bible, to push it away from us, so that it might be viewed on its own terms, rather than on ours. For only then does it become an object of critical examination.

The critical study of the Bible, then, is a historical discipline. Its first and most crucial task is to provide an empathetic description and understanding of the biblical writings, each on its own terms. It uses categories appropriate to the culture in which these writings emerged. It interprets what they meant in their historical setting without borrowing categories from later times. It provides, in Krister Stendahl's terms, "a frontal nonpragmatic, nonapologetic attempt to describe OT or NT faith and practice from within its own presuppositions, and with due attention to its own organizing principles, regardless of its possible ramifications for those who live by the Bible as the Word of God."[1]

In the historical-critical investigation of the Bible, philological, literary, historical, and structural methodologies are used to make the past come alive. By attending to the historical setting and the "literal sense" (i.e., the meaning intended by the author), we gain a "feel" for the biblical text in its own environment. Such historical reconstruction requires disciplined imagination and calls upon the social sciences (sociology, economics, anthropology, psychology, politics, history of religions), as well as the historical sciences in the more traditional sense.

What does all this have to do with persons in ministry and with a method for their theological reflection? Some would argue from the historical-critical investigation of the Bible that, since the biblical worldview is no longer our own, and since it has been demonstrated how distant the environment of the biblical writings is from our own, the Bible can at most have a negative role in Christian ministers' reflection. As they seek to listen to individual and collective experience, to make assertions, and to move toward pastoral decisions, ministers should use the Bible as a negative norm—checking whether those assertions and decisions are consistent with, or at least do not contradict, biblical statements.

Another group, and we include ourselves here, would claim more for the Bible. Fully aware of the distance that separates the biblical world from our own, we affirm that the biblical writings can, indeed should, inform, influence, and inspire ministers as they make decisions in ministry. We do not mean that, because the Bible is the Word of God, it must speak the same literal message to every age. But we also do not consider the biblical writings so culturally conditioned that they cannot speak at all to our present situation.

Christian Scripture may at times appear distant and alien to the contemporary believer. Set in very different times and cultural contexts, the stories and teachings of the Bible have also attained an authority as revelation which can further distance them from our own frail but immediate experience of life. It is most useful to recall that the Scriptures represent revelation not as magically descended from heaven, but as gradually discerned and recorded within human experience. Moses, Isaiah, Matthew, and Paul experienced God's presence in their own lives and in their communities. These special experiences were shared with others, retold, and finally written down. Christians believe that the writers of the Scriptures were inspired; this inspiration was, in part, their enlightened recognition of some of their experiences as extraordinary, as revealing the presence and power of God.

In the next section we will examine in greater detail how these sacred writings were gradually recorded and edited. Here we emphasize that the Scriptures and, more broadly, the Christian Tradition, *began* in experience. The Scriptures are a record of special experiences, experiences which originally revealed the Lord to Moses, Isaiah, Matthew, and Paul, and continue to do so today. Among the many experiences of the Israelites and the first Christians, only a portion were recorded and became, in time, "canonized"—gathered into the canon of sacred texts which Christians named the Old and New Testaments.

When we recognize Scripture and Tradition as rooted in experience, as recalling specific human experiences, we do not reduce the Scriptures to *mere* experience or suggest they are *only* a human record. We can continue to believe in the divine inspiration of these texts and to affirm that these accounts are the core of revelation for Christians, and yet recognize the events recorded in Scripture as not so distant from our own lives. They are both rooted in experience—human experience recognized in faith as shaped by God's presence. This recollection—of our Scriptural tradition as grounded in experience—stresses the congruence between the poles of Tradition and experience in our model of theological reflection.

If the Christian Scriptures are, in fact, recordings of and reflections on special, revelatory experiences, it will also be useful to recall the historical processes through which these recordings were collected and passed on from believing community to believing community.

The Composition of the Scriptures

In the following examples, that of the Fourth Gospel and the story of the Exodus, we will elaborate the plural stages and participants in the historical development of these two parts of Scripture. The text of John's Gospel, for example, was not composed in the same way a modern author composes a book. The text whose final written form lies before us today is the last of a series of multiple editions which developed through at least three distinct stages.

First, at the historical stage, Jesus' life included many sayings and actions. Second, at the preaching stage, Jesus' disciples later proclaimed his sayings and deeds in the light of their post-resurrection faith. Third, at the writing stage, the evangelists wrote down in continuous narrative the traditional teachings about Jesus which had developed in oral and written units and collections. At each stage the material was adapted: Jesus adapted "himself to the mentality of his listeners"; the disciples "took into account the needs and circumstances of their listeners"; and the evangelists "adapted what they narrated to the situation of their readers and to the purpose they themselves had in mind."[2]

In the composition of the Gospel of John, then, from sometime after Jesus' death and resurrection to about 100 A.D., a dynamic interaction took place which involved the traditions about Jesus received from the past, the present reflection and experience of John and his disciples, and the lived experience of the communities to which they belonged.[3] Through this interaction, both oral and written, the text was shaped and reshaped through multiple editions until it reached the form in which we now possess it.

COMPOSITION OF SCRIPTURE

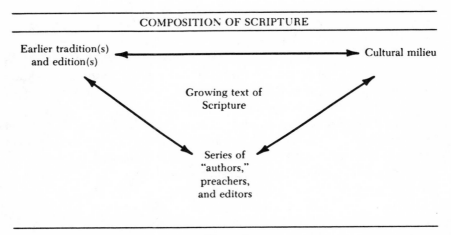

Figure 4

Thus, the culmination of God's self-revelation took the concrete form of Jesus' historical life, interpreted and transmitted through the disciples' and evangelists' formulations, all of which was adapted to the historical and theological categories of those to whom the revelation was addressed. The point to stress is that this is a *process* and that the process of the development of Scripture is dialectical—*Scripture, which began as experience, was produced through a process of tradition(s) being formulated about that experience and being reformulated by interpreters in dialogue with the experience of their communities and with the larger culture.* The diagram in Figure Three, schematizing the composition of Scripture, is thus not only congruent with, but fundamentally gives rise to, the schema suggested in Chapter One as a model for theological reflection.

A similar dynamic of composition can be seen in the centrally important and plural accounts of the Exodus. The Exodus is the primary foundational event for the religion of Israel, and it is the biblical prototype of saving redemption through Christ.[4] An event in the experience of our cultural ancestors, it was a historical event,[5] the nucleus of which was some sort of historical escape from the Egyptian kingdom by a band of slaves.

The details in the classical text of Exodus we read today are not "eyewitness descriptions of what really happened." It would be strange for slaves fleeing through the desert to find time to compose a written account of their escape. Not written down by Moses or any of the participants, neither was it, understandably, preserved in Egyptian records. Rather, there was a long series of steps between that historical event and the multilayered text in our present Bible.

It will prove illuminating in getting to know the inner workings of our Tradition to analyze the composition and development of this central text. It will help us understand even more deeply the interrelations among Scripture, Tradition, and experience, and it will have the added advantage of displaying how pluralism in contemporary religious interpretation is grounded in the pluralism of Scripture itself.

We must begin with the differentiation of epistemological levels along the ladder from the experience or "raw event" of the escape to final written text. In addition to the *event* itself, there was the variegated *perception* by the participants of what had happened, the on-the-spot *understanding* of what had happened, a process of *conceptualization* and *categorization,* involving subjective *interpretation.* To be sure, there must have been an assortment of initial *articulations* of the individuals' conceptions and interpretations of what had happened. Obviously, the Egyptians interpreted and articulated the event differently from the escapees, and the escapees presumably differed among themselves in their own interpretations and articulations—from "lucky break" to "our God saved us."[6]

Historical critics would be wary of saying that any of these stages thus far, other than the nucleus of the raw event itself and the final testimony that "God saved us," can be confidently isolated in the text of Exodus. But later, some of the articulations were considered more appropriate and were retold as the *"classic retelling(s)"* of the story. The classic retelling(s) were taken and, with whatever adaptations deemed necessary, incorporated into the larger tapestry of *national narrative traditions,* the oral epic and the written Yahwist and Elohist accounts.[7] In *ritual celebrations* commemorating that saving act by their God, anonymous individuals would celebrate the event in *lyric poetry:*

> *Sing to the* LORD, *for he is gloriously triumphant;*
> *horse and chariot he has cast into the sea* (Exod. 15:21).

This poetic fragment is considered to be perhaps the oldest element of the present Exodus narrative. But it is clear that the lyric enthusiasm has adopted an Israelite interpretation of the event and shifted from indirect to direct causality. That is, whereas natural forces caused the overthrow of the pursuing Egyptians (see the prose accounts below), the poem looks behind the forces of nature to the God who used those forces as means.

In a *separate hymn,* the "Song of Moses" (Exod. 15:1–18) from the period of the Judges (twelfth to eleventh centuries B.C.), different imagery is used:

A blast from your nostrils and the waters piled high. . . .

One breath of yours you blew, and the sea closed over them; they sank like lead in the terrible waters.

. . . you stretched your right hand out, the earth swallowed them! (Exod. 15:8, 10, 12)

In the tenth-century B.C. *Yahwist's narrative,* "Yahweh drove back the sea with a strong easterly wind all night," making "dry land of the sea," and "threw the army into confusion" (Exod. 14:21, 24).

In contrast to the Yahwist's pillar of cloud (14:19b), the ninth-century *Elohist* tells of an "angel of Yahweh, who marched at the front of the army of Israel" (14:19a). Finally, the sixth-century *Priestly Writer* (whose imagery predominates in Hollywood tastes) has Moses lift his rod and divide the sea, the waters being "walls of water to right and to left of them" (14:16, 22).

Thus, there are at least five different voices from across the centuries retelling the escape in differing sets of imagery.[8] Attempts at harmonizing the conflicting details prove to be misguided hyperliteralism. The different "authors" are not intending to describe factual details of what we would call "what really happened." Only two descriptions date within even two centuries of the event, and they are lyrically intent upon pointing out not natural details, but only that it was God who purposefully caused whatever it was that happened.[9]

Thus, the exodus *began in human experience* but was not limited to raw, unreflective experience. It was human experience recognized in faith as shaped by God's presence and purpose. That is, it was *interpreted and formulated in traditional religious categories,* and it was told and retold, shaped and reshaped, in light of the developing needs and *worldviews* of the believing *communities*. A cross-section of the compositional development of the Exodus narrative at the time of the Priestly Writer, its last major contributor, can be seen in Figure Five.

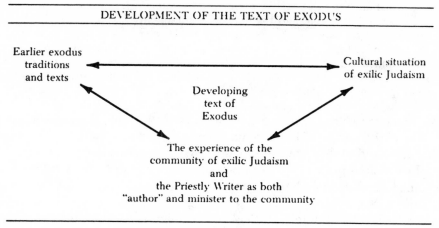

DEVELOPMENT OF THE TEXT OF EXODUS

Earlier exodus traditions and texts ⟷ Cultural situation of exilic Judaism

Developing text of Exodus

The experience of the community of exilic Judaism and the Priestly Writer as both "author" and minister to the community

Figure 5

We have emphasized in this chapter the Sacred Scripture as grounded in human experience and as plural in its accounts of God's actions among us. The enormous advance in biblical scholarship has taught us, as theologians and ministers, to attend more thoroughly to the plural cultural and historical contexts in which Christian revelation has occurred and been recorded. We have also learned not simply to search out individual biblical passages as proofs of our own theological convictions. Scripture does not serve the contemporary community of faith by providing specific solutions to contemporary questions. In the face of this realization, ministers must learn new modes of faithful and effective access to this central source of revelation and Christian wisdom.

The Use of Scripture in Reflection in Ministry

With this understanding of Scripture, how is the minister to approach it? How does the Bible function, theoretically and practically, in a reflection in ministry? One way to describe how we see the Bible functioning in theological reflection is to say it provides ministers with "paradigms" that can inform, influence, and inspire them as they approach pastoral issues. James M. Gustafson has provided a most useful description of biblical paradigms:

> Paradigms are basic models of a vision of life, and of the practice of
> life, from which flow certain consistent attitudes, outlooks (or "on-
> looks"), rules or norms of behavior, and specific actions. . . . Rather the
> paradigm *in*-forms and *in*-fluences the life of the community and its
> members as they become what they are under their own circum-
> stances. By *in*-form I wish to suggest more than giving data or infor-
> mation; I wish to suggest a formation of life. By *in*-fluence I wish to
> suggest a flowing into the life of the community and its members. A
> paradigm allows for the community and its members to make it their
> own, to bring it into the texture and fabric of life that exists, condi-
> tioned as that is by its historical circumstances, by the sorts of limita-
> tions and extensions of particular capacities and powers that exist in
> persons and communities.[10]

Once produced in their historical contexts, the biblical texts assumed a
life of their own and began to function as "paradigms," as they were read
and reread in different life situations. When, for example, the Gospel of
John won its place in the Christian canon of Scripture, it began to be read
and interpreted in relation to Mark, Matthew, and Luke, as well as to the
other Old and New Testament writings. New contexts generated new,
more-than-literal interpretations. When John was read in the context of
the christological debates that led to the councils of Nicaea (325 A.D.) and
Chalcedon (451 A.D.), understandings were generated that were totally
unavailable to the evangelist and the communities for whom he originally
composed the gospel. Later, John's Gospel was read in the light of the
creeds that had become normative for Christian faith. In each instance,
reading the text, whether in private or in public, was an event in which
the text and the reader or hearers were engaged in a dynamic interaction,
one in which the text informed and influenced a process of theological reflection (see Figure Six).

Reading the Bible in the process of theological reflection today is also an
event of dynamic interaction between the minister and the text. The quality of that interaction will be determined to a large extent by the concrete
dispositions of the person reading the Bible. Persons who are unaware of
the text's historical setting and worldview will read it ahistorically, that is,
as a text with a life of its own but unrelated to any particular past experience or situation. Those who engage the text with awareness of its historical genesis in the lives of individuals and communities will read it with
empathy and compassion for the human situation in which it came to be
Scripture. These readers will also bring more easily to the text their own
experience, both individual and communal. In both cases the dynamic in-

DEVELOPMENT OF SCRIPTURAL TEXT THROUGH TIME

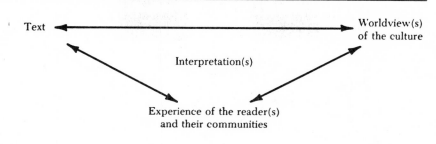

Figure 6

teraction includes several elements: the text and the reader or hearer, each with a definite worldview and each in a particular concrete situation (see Figure Seven).

If Scripture provides paradigms for the minister and, more generally, the Christian, we must still ask: How does the minister *approach* these texts? What must the minister's orientation or stance be toward Scripture?

This approach is perhaps best described as one of intimacy rather than mastery. For the biblical scholar or church historian the pressing long-range goal of their study is a mastery of the languages, cultures, and historical situations which contribute to a reconstruction of what our Tradition is and how it was formed. Such mastery is the lifelong goal of these scholars, a goal rarely attained completely. Persons in ministry most often have neither the background nor the time or interest to attempt such mastery. In fact, they do not need to "master" Scripture. What they do need is enough familiarity to be at ease with the Bible and the skill to bring what they know to bear in the process of theological reflection. This approach of a critical familiarity we may name intimacy.

By intimacy here we do not mean a mystical or nonintellectual approach. Rather, a *more-than*-intellectual grasp of Scripture is envisioned, a grasp which is informed by serious academic study but which "knows from the inside." Faith and understanding are complementary aspects of this relationship. The professional minister is invited to this more-than-scientific mastery of these texts as part of the intimacy invitation extended by

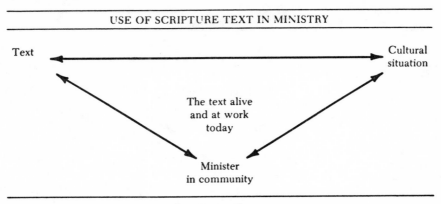

USE OF SCRIPTURE TEXT IN MINISTRY

Text ⟵──────────────────────⟶ Cultural situation

The text alive
and at work
today

Minister
in community

Figure 7

Jesus Christ to all his followers: "No longer do I call you servants, for the servant does not know what his master is doing; but I have called you friends, for all that I have heard from my Father I have made known to you" (John 15:15). Jesus has called us, he has called us friends, and he has called us to work as his friends. We may never be so comfortable with Scripture that we lose consciousness of this "called" dimension. But we must respond to that call, we must learn to become friends, we must work toward appropriate intimacy with the Word.

The first practical step toward intimacy is getting to know Scripture. The contents of Scripture are, to some degree, already known by the minister and opportunities must be created frequently for rejuvenating and developing that knowledge. But what is important at this stage is getting to know what Scripture is, how it is put together, and thus how to make proper use of its diverse images and stories in pastoral reflections.

This befriending moves between a participation in faith in the biblical writings and an informed, critical understanding of them. Befriending goes beyond a scientific or scholarly grasp of these texts, but also goes beyond an amateur selection of individual passages which seem to fit the mood of an occasion. In seeking to befriend the texts of the Scripture, ministers allow themselves to come under the spell of these texts and experience their own lives being interpreted by them, while simultaneously retaining a critical posture toward the texts as cultural and linguistic products. This, of course, involves considerable tension—as does any act of befriending or intimacy. Ministers cannot avoid this potentially creative tension between participation and criticism, a tension in which the participation of the believer does not obstruct or dissolve criticism and historical and literary criticism does not destroy participation.

To clarify our understanding of the minister's stance toward Scripture, it may be useful to reflect on the different levels of participation involved in the process of befriending classical music. Initially, we participate in the music by listening uncritically to a favorite concerto or symphony. At this point we project onto the music what we want it to mean. But as participation grows, so does our desire to understand the music more critically. So we take time to study the history of music, the development of particular composers, the structure and forms of different types of music, and the themes in this particular composition. We push the music itself away from us and set it at a distance so we can look at it with a more objective and critical eye. In doing so we might suspend for a time our more intimate and total participation, but only so that we might later be able to participate in the music with an appreciation formed and informed by critical understanding.

Participation in the Scriptures, as the first step toward befriending them, can happen in different settings. The minister simply reads the Bible out of interest or for enjoyment. Certain writings are more attractive than others. Some may even be experienced as repugnant. But through reading the Bible and attending to these personal reactions the minister gains an initial familiarity. This familiarity is enhanced when the minister reads the Bible or hears it read in a liturgical context, whether in the Eucharist or in other worship events.

A deeper level of participation is modeled by the use of Scripture in communal prayer. In charismatic prayer meetings, within the family, and in religious congregations, Christians—convinced that common prayer, rooted in Scripture, is a privileged place to meet the Lord—gather to read and reflect together on the Bible.

The meditative reading of the Scripture is still another way to befriend the Bible. This *lectio divina* constitutes a principal activity of traditional monastic life, reinforced in the communal experience of attending to Scripture readings in the daily celebrations of the Divine Office. Methods for the practice of *lectio divina* can be learned easily and many in ministry find this style of prayer helpful. This prayerful exercise demands the full attention and active cooperation of the minister, since it approaches Scripture not merely with the intellect but with the full personality.

Ignatian contemplation may also assist the minister in befriending

Scripture. In this type of prayer one begins by reading the biblical narrative, then recalling and reconstructing the scene in one's imagination. Involvement grows as the person in prayer gradually enters the biblical scene—seeing the persons, hearing the events, even becoming a participant in the drama. In grace, the person in prayer becomes more deeply aware of the events and how these are a part of his or her own life now. Indeed, Christ himself comes forward to the minister, presenting himself in the mystery being contemplated. What is sought in this contemplation is a deep-felt knowledge of the Lord, a knowledge like that gained through personal contact, shared work, common struggle, and intimate heart-to-heart conversation. Befriending the Scriptures in contemplation means befriending the Lord. Because of the attention needed for this type of prayer, it may be better suited for a time of retreat than for one's regular style of prayer in the midst of a usual daily schedule of activities.

As one participates in the Bible in these and other ways, questions will arise that call for a more critical understanding than is available in the prayerful processes of participation. It is the response to these questions that moves the minister into the creative tension between participation and criticism, essential to the process of befriending the Bible as a resource in ministry. Moving from participation to criticism means, as we have said, attending to the text at a distance sufficient to guarantee a more objective and disinterested view. The move is often experienced to involve deprivation and alienation, especially if the prior experiences of prayerful participation have been deeply enriching for the minister. Criticism may seem to threaten the intimacy that has been gained; hence it is resisted. But these feelings can be overcome by the desire to understand the Bible on its own terms and by the conviction that this criticism will, ultimately, enhance one's participation.

These critical questions about a biblical text concern its historical setting and religious milieu, its literacy structure and overall movement, the process of its formation, its dominant themes and world-construct, and the detailed exegesis of particular passages. Not all these questions need be addressed at the same time. Nor should the minister expect to have all this information actively available all the time. But once having spent time gaining this information, the minister values it and can retrieve it when desired. We now have available the tools through which ministers can gain and refresh this critical understanding of the Bible: the *Jerome Biblical Commentary, The Interpreter's Dictionary of the Bible, Dictionary of Biblical Theology,* and journals such as *Bible Today.* In education for ministry today (both initial seminary training and continuing education), time is well spent in acquainting and reacquainting ministers with the use of these resources.

For the Christian minister this movement between participation and criticism is explicitly informed and influenced by faith. As Christians we believe that the Bible, as the Word of God, is a privileged medium through which God may choose to communicate something to us, as we reach decisions about practical pastoral matters. This faith commitment determines how the minister participates in the text. It also influences how the minister attends to the task of critical understanding. As Krister Stendahl has remarked:

> The believer has the advantage of automatic empathy with the believers in the text—but his faith constantly threatens to have him modernize the material, if he does not exercise the canons of descriptive scholarship rigorously. The agnostic has the advantage of feeling no such temptations, but his power of empathy must be considerable if he is to identify himself sufficiently with the believer of the first century. Yet both can work side by side, since no other tools are called for than those of description in the terms indicated by the texts themselves.[11]

What will happen when I as minister befriend the Bible through a creative tension between participation and criticism? It is impossible to predict; once the minister enters into this process the outcome simply cannot be controlled. Sometimes, nothing seems to happen. At the end of a busy day I turn to the Bible, with much on my mind, full of concerns and worries. My effort to be attentive expresses my desire to befriend the Bible and my faith that, through it, I remain in contact with God. But distractions abound and I am unmoved.

At other times a deeper degree of participation, now critically informed, may take place. I am pulled into what I read, as my attention, my thoughts, and my feelings become engaged. All else fades to insignificance as I am led to know and love God in and through the text before me. When such a "Word event" may happen is uncontrollable and unpredictable, since it happens by God's activity. We create the climate for it in the ways we befriend the Bible. But it is God who invites us to such a deeper and more meaningful relation.

A critical study of the Scriptures which includes a dissecting of these sacred texts can be an alienating experience for the believer. Paul Ricoeur speaks of the "desert of criticism."[12] Many a minister and seminarian has entered this desert of text and form criticism not to emerge with faith intact. Yet this discipline and desert are necessary for ministers who would have understanding, as well as faith, inform their pastoral reflections. Beyond this desert lies a "second naïveté" (Ricoeur) toward which we journey all our lives and where participation and criticism mutually illumine our relationship with the Scriptures.

By growing in intimacy with the Scripture through the ongoing dialogue between religious participation and critical understanding the minister gains the familiarity and skill needed to use the Scriptures well in concrete pastoral situations.

Modes of Attending to Scripture

The conversation with the Bible in this model of theological reflection can begin with a moment of free association in which the minister uses memory and imagination to return to Scripture. This first moment of attending is characterized by an open participation in the texts, as the minister follows whatever associations suggest themselves. For example, a current pastoral concern for the "factions" within the parish can lead to an association with Paul's concern for the "factions" in the church at Corinth (1 Cor. 1:10–17). But the connection may also be experienced at the level of images and symbols, that is, as less rational but every bit as real. The same "factions" might, for example, remind the minister of the struggle between light and darkness in the Gospel of John. Finally, the relationship may be experienced without concepts, images, or symbols but in one's religious consciousness. The minister should be sensitive and open to all three possibilities.

The second moment involves a more disciplined and critical attending to the texts suggested by free association. The minister pushes the text far enough away from the present pastoral concern for it to be examined on its own terms. We offer here one design for how this reflective examination might proceed.

Design for the Critical Examination of a Text in Ministry

Read the passage very carefully, or even *write it out* in sense lines to determine the major divisions of the passage, to get a feel for its overall movement, and to determine the key words and phrases.
· What are the major divisions in the passage?
· What are the key words and phrases?

- What rhetorical or literary techniques are used—questions, antitheses, repetition, etc.?
- What is the overall theme?
- What is the movement of thought?

Situate the passage in its literary, historical, and liturgical contexts. By *literary context*, we mean its place in the particular writing of which it is a part:

- What comes immediately before and immediately after this passage?
- How does this passage fit into the total literary work, the letter, or the gospel?
- What light does its literary context throw on the meaning of the passage?

By *historical context*, we mean the concrete circumstances in which the passage was composed:

- What are the historical circumstances—the time, the place, etc.—in which this writing was composed?
- What were the author and the community for whom this was written experiencing? How did they feel toward each other?

By *liturgical context*, we mean the Church's use of this passage in prayer and worship:

- Where does this passage appear in the Church's prayer?
- What are the changes, additions, and alterations to the text in the liturgical context?
- What light does the liturgical context throw on the meaning of this passage?

Finally, it is important to *clarify* images, words, or phrases which may remain obscure by consulting one or more commentaries (for example, *The Jerome Biblical Commentary, The Interpreter's Dictionary of the Bible*).

- What words and phrases need explanation?
- Where do the commentators agree and disagree about the meaning of these images, words, and phrases?
- What opinion do you choose to follow? Why?

Scripture in the Assertion Stage

The role of the Bible at this stage of a pastoral reflection is clarified by recognizing that the sacred texts are themselves a composite of assertions. The plural voices we find in Scripture are not just incidentally different views that have survived due to a lack of editorial polish. The differences are real; at times they are intentionally in contrast with each other. Sometimes, the intentional contrast is simply complementary; at other times it is confrontational. The Priestly Writer of the creation story in Genesis, for example, is both intentionally preserving the earlier Yahwist's view on the nature of evil and the relationship between God and humankind (as presented in the story of the Flood) and proposing a complementary view of each. Major differences in theology and in the historical situation in which this later account was formulated led the Priestly Writer to significantly different, but not contradictory, understandings. The author of Job, on the other hand, intentionally and vociferously challenges the theology that characterizes Deuteronomy, Proverbs, the Wisdom psalms, and the prophetic understanding of retribution.

Later, Jesus and the early Church, while retaining the Hebrew Scripture as sacred, nonetheless undertook from the outset a critical interpretation of these texts. While they recognized in the Old Testament the life-creating Word of God, they took the stance that not everything there was of equal importance, not everything was to be understood by Christians in the same way it had been understood in the Jewish community, not everything was to be incorporated by the Christian group as definitive of their relation with God. They exercised a critical discernment in the way they incorporated their tradition. This assertive stance may be recognized in the confrontation of statements attributed in Matthew to Jesus: "You have heard that it was said [followed by a citation of the old law], but I say to you . . ." (Matt. 5:21, 27, 31, 33, 39, 41).

Thus the Bible is not a book of answers waiting to be matched to contemporary questions, but a set of sometimes complementary, sometimes conflicting, assertions about God among us and about our response to this presence.

A second aid to understanding the role of Scripture in pastoral reflection is to recall how these texts functioned in Christian history. This history is, in fact, the record of Christians' assertive interpretations of the Scriptures in the light of specific cultural and religious concerns. The councils of Nicaea, Chalcedon, Trent, Vatican I, and Vatican II reflect these changing concerns and the Church's assertive response to them. In every age the sacred texts are interpreted in the light of our understanding of our own lives—the meaning of suffering, redemption, sexuality, freedom, grace. If the New Testament portrays Christ as both suffering and glorified, Christians have at different times in history stressed one of these aspects over the other—not because only one is true and the other false, but because one feature seems so important at the time. Such a stress is an assertion: a definite interpretation of Scripture in the light of a specific, limited concern.

Both the Scriptures as an assertive composition and the assertion of our religious history teach us how we may approach the Bible assertively in our pastoral reflections. Such a practical reflection will always entail a selection, a stressing of *some* passages of Scripture. This is done most critically when we are aware of the historical conditions in which these passages were composed and how they are balanced or even challenged by other texts in Scripture. With such critical awareness we are protected from merely selecting passages which buttress our own unreflective convictions or seem, in a contemporary translation, to give clear answers to complicated problems.

When we assertively and critically set some Scriptural passage in relation to a contemporary cultural problem or personal experience, we can expect the sacred texts to illumine human action. In this interaction we should also expect these texts themselves to take on new meaning. St. Paul's allusion to the Christian ideal of mutuality in which "there is neither slave nor free, there is neither male nor female" (Gal. 3), means something very different today than it did two hundred years ago when American Christians held very different opinions about slaves and the role of women in society. The Scriptures are not a "closed book" with a fixed univocal meaning. On the contrary, as a living revelation, these texts continue to surprise and seize us as we attempt to respond faithfully to ever-different cultural and personal challenges. One way to remain open to this continuing revelation is to continue to assertively grasp and question this source of wisdom.

Scripture and the Decision Stage of the Method

At this stage also the reflecting minister and local community learn from the Church's history—the pastoral decisions of councils, regional churches, and local parishes that have shaped this history. A greater awareness of a contemporary community's contribution to this rich history and Tradition will follow on a more accurate portrayal of this history—the two millennia of the Christian Tradition seen not as an unbroken, logical unfolding of certain doctrines, but as, in fact, a series of hesitant decisions and partial insights, not unlike those of the contemporary Church.[13]

An example of pastoral decisions shaping our Tradition is the decision in the twelfth century to require celibacy as a condition for ordination to priesthood in the Roman Catholic communion. The Church, in response to cultural and religious challenges of the time, sought guidance in Scripture (Christ's own unmarried status) for this decision. Scripture did not *prove* the rightness of this decision, but *guided* it; the decision arose in the reflections of the Church and it was the Church that made this decision.

This reminds the contemporary Church, whether as parish or other reflecting community, that at the decision stage the minister and the community become *actors* in the Church. At this stage they move beyond the role of passive listeners or mere recipients of the Church's historical decisions. By their own pastoral decisions they participate in the actions by which the Church assertively responds to the world. But this stage is possible only if the reflecting minister and community have carefully traversed the earlier stages: critically attending to Scripture and Church history and asserting these sources of information against contemporary personal and cultural challenges. Careful attending and assertion will generate insight and suggestions, but it is the reflective minister and community that must give these insights life in practical decisions.

At this stage of pastoral decision the reflecting community must *act*, aware as it acts that it is part of a larger Church, and also aware that its own decisions and actions must remain open to revision and change.

The theological skills required at this stage are not those of scriptural analysis, but those abilities which allow a clarification of the community's sense (*sensus fidelium*) of a pastoral question, so that the decision culminating a reflective process may be a corporate decision. Skills of planning are also required at this stage in order that religious insight and conviction may find concrete and effective expression. We discuss these skills in greater detail in Part III.

Finally, it is useful to recall that our reading of and listening to Scripture does influence our decisions about our personal and collective lives. The challenge of a method of reflection is to bring this influence to critical awareness, making it both more conscious and more critical. A developing confidence and competence in the use of Scripture in our lives can make us "critical participants" in these revealing texts. The more thoroughly we befriend this profound source of wisdom, the more powerfully and accurately can it contribute to and shape the reflections and actions which guide our Christian lives.

Notes

1. "Biblical Theology, Contemporary," in *The Interpreter's Dictionary of the Bible* (New York: Abingdon, 1962), 1:425.

2. Thomas Aquinas Collins, O.P., and Raymond E. Brown, S.S., "Church Pronouncements," in *Jerome Biblical Commentary*, ed. R. E. Brown, J. A. Fitzmyer, and R. E. Murphy (Englewood Cliffs, NJ: Prentice-Hall, 1968), 2:631–32.

3. Raymond Brown finds at least three "different religious groupings" within the developing Johannine community in " 'Other Sheep Not of this Fold': The Johannine Perspective on Christian Diversity in the Late First Century," in *Journal of Biblical Literature* 97 (1978):5–22.

4. For the biblical perspective, see the articles, "Exodus," "Redemption," and "Salvation," in X. Léon-Dufour et al., eds., *The Dictionary of Biblical Theology*, trans. P. J. Cahill, et al., 2nd ed. rev. (New York: Seabury, 1973).

5. "Israel had been enslaved in Egypt and was to be held there, but its God had wonderfully delivered it from bondage and saved it from the power of the Egyptians. There is no doubt that the concrete statement in this confession is based on a definite historical occurrence and it is not difficult to discern the circumstances in which it took place." Martin Noth, *The History of Israel*, trans. P. Ackroyd, 2nd ed. (London: A. & C. Black, 1960), p. 112. See also John Bright, *A History of Israel* (Philadelphia: Westminster, 1959), pp. 110–12.

6. The interpretation of a rescue as being due to the favor and causality of one's God was long since a traditional religious category in the culture in which Israel was born. "The notion of a God who saves His faithful is common to all religions," "Salvation," in Léon-Dufour, *Dictionary of Biblical Theology*, p. 519. In the "Prayer of Lamentation to Ishtar," the Babylonian goddess receives this request: "I pray to thee, O lady of ladies, goddess of goddesses. O Ishtar . . . , secure my deliverance. . . !" And the Egyptian god, Amon-Re, is addressed: "If I call to thee when I am distressed, thou comest and thou rescuest me. . . . Thou art Amon-Re, Lord of Thebes, who rescues. . . ." J. Pritchard, ed., *Ancient Near Eastern Texts*, 3rd ed. (Princeton: Princeton University Press, 1969), pp. 384 and 380.

7. The development of the exodus traditions is interwoven with the development of the Pentateuch as a whole. The stages important for our present discussion include: (a) the (probably) oral epic of national religious traditions from the eleventh century, B.C. (i.e., from the period of the twelve-tribe league after the Exodus [*ca.* 1280 B.C.] but before the monarchy [*ca.* 1000 B.C.]); (b) the Yahwist's written account probably from the time of Solomon (960–922 B.C.); (c) the Elohist's written account usually dated to the ninth century B.C.; and (d) the Priestly Writer's reworking of these traditions in the sixth century B.C. See M. Noth, *A History of Pentateuchal Traditions*, trans. B. Anderson (Englewood Cliffs, NJ: Prentice-Hall, 1972), esp. pp. 8–45; and F. M. Cross, *Canaanite Myth and Hebrew Epic* (Cambridge, MA: Harvard University Press, 1973), pp. 293–325.

8. The Jewish historian, Josephus, in the late first century A.D., recasts the Exodus narrative in partly similar, partly yet-more-imaginative imagery (Josephus, *Jewish Antiquities* [Loeb, vol. 4, trans. H. St. J. Thackeray], 2:320–49), though he maintains that "I have recounted each detail here told just as I found it in the sacred books" (2:347).

9. Because the event was so significant for the existence of the people and so characteristic of their saving God, the classic account, already clothed in assorted imaginative details, was subsequently adapted and used (Josh. 3–4) as the libretto for a liturgical celebration (reenacted yearly as the crossing of the Jor-

dan at the shrine of Gilgal) commemorating the event of crossing the Red Sea. That liturgical text, available to the Deuteronomistic Historian in the seventh century B.C., was finally reused as a "historical" episode, forming a link in his history—no longer the link between Egypt and the desert, but transferred to "the people crossing the Jordan into the promised land."

10. "The Relation of the Gospels to the Moral Life," in D. G. Miller and D. Y. Hadidian, eds., *Jesus and Man's Hope* (Pittsburgh: Pittsburgh Theological Seminary, 1971), 2:111.

11. "Biblical Theology, Contemporary," in *The Interpreter's Dictionary of the Bible* (New York: Abingdon, 1962), 1:422.

12. Paul Ricoeur, *The Symbolism of Evil* (Boston: Beacon Press, 1967), p. 349.

13. See Thomas Kuhn, *The Structure of Scientific Revolutions* (Chicago: University of Chicago Press, 1970), especially the "Postscript" of the 1970 edition, for discussion of the similar inclination of scientists and Christians to explain their respective histories as peaceful and logical developments without disruptions or revolutions.

·3·

EXPERIENCE AND REFLECTION IN MINISTRY

A Definition of Experience

The word *experience* is so vague and all inclusive as to be almost useless. Is there any activity, fantasy, or memory that is not, in some sense, experience? If all things are or can be reduced to experience, the word loses any specific meaning or usefulness.

Yet the word survives. In fact, it flourishes today in theological discussion. Titles ranging from Richard R. Niebuhr's *Experiential Religion* and John Smith's *Experience and God* to Rosemary Haughton's *The Theology of Experience* attest to considerable interest. The role of experience in theological method is likewise much discussed with Tillich, Lonergan, Kaufman, and Tracy each assigning it a significant if differing place.[1]

In the following pages we will outline the meaning and role of experience in this tripolar model of reflection in ministry. At the outset, however, it may be useful to define how the word will be understood here. The pole of experience in this model refers to that set of ideas, feelings, biases, and insights which a particular minister and community bring to a pastoral reflection. Experience thus embraces not only ideas or "understandings" but a wide range of rational and extra-rational convictions, hopes and apprehensions which are brought to a specific pastoral question.[2] Second, such experience refers to the *individual's* experience, not "common human experience." Third, it is assumed that such individual experience is not simply idiosyncratic (though part of it will stand out as quite special to this person or community), but will show the strong influence of one's culture and religious tradition. Though such experience is powerfully shaped both by one's cultural and religious heritage, it is addressed at this pole of the reflection as the experience of *this* person and community.

In this chapter we will further elaborate our use of experience in theological method, clarify the notion of experience by observing how the Christian Tradition itself comprises distilled interpretations of human experience, examine the role of experience in this method of reflection, and discuss questions of access—how we might most effectively approach this volatile and challenging part of reflection in ministry.

The Meaning of Experience in This Model of Reflection

Theological reflection in ministry is most often reflection on a particular concern—our community's care for its senior members; a question of divorce and remarriage; our parish's responsibility to those in our neighborhood who are poorly housed. Such reflection originates in, and is motivated by, certain experiences in the community which invite us to a more careful consideration and more effective expression of our Christian values.

Theological reflection has been understood often, especially since Tillich, as a correlation of Tradition and experience, of the received Christian revelation and contemporary personal and cultural experience. More complicated than the matching of Christian answers to cultural questions, this correlation is today seen as an effort of mutual confrontation: as Christian values provide clues to the solution of quandaries facing a culture—whether about social justice, authority, or the meaning of sexuality—so the insights of a culture, developed especially in its philosophy, literature, and social sciences, may challenge the Christian Tradition to become more consistent with its own best convictions. Likewise, our own lives are comprised of experiences which are given direction and meaning by our religious faith and of other experiences which bring our grasp of the Christian Tradition into question.

Well aware that the Christian Tradition is itself the result of many and powerful human experiences, theologians such as Ogden and Tracy have chosen to restrict the term *experience* to those feelings, attitudes, and ideas found in contemporary life which are, in the first instance, pre-religious and generally available. Tracy's "common human experience" is both human in the sense of not-yet-seen-as-religious and is common in that it is characteristic of a culture rather than an individual. These characteristics of experience as pre-religious and nonindividual sharply distinguish Tracy's use of the term from its use in this method of reflection.[3]

The important difference between that experience which is *common* to a culture and that experience which is *particular* to this individual minister and community has led us to distinguish the poles of cultural information and personal experience. These two kinds of experience certainly intersect and overlap, yet it is important for a reflective group to become clearly aware how their own specific experience around a pastoral concern both reflects their culture and departs from it.

The pastoral and concrete nature of this kind of reflection is seen in the attention given both to understanding the "common experience" of our culture—whether about questions of aging, the place of leisure, or the meaning of wealth—and also to determining the specific attitudes, biases, and convictions we as individuals bring to this reflection.

If experience in this method of reflection refers to *individual experience* rather than common cultural awareness, it can also refer to feelings, attitudes, and convictions that are *already* religious. Pastoral reflection is an activity of believers; as such, its task is to explore experiences in their concreteness, be they genuinely religious in nature or not. In this vein, Avery Dulles, in an otherwise favorable review of Tracy's *Blessed Rage for Order*, has objected to Tracy's restriction of *experience* to common human experience. Dulles suggests a third source for theological reflection: "Christian experience, i.e., the kind of ecstatic or peak experience to which the New Testament, for example, bears witness."[4] In a footnote here, Dulles writes: "By 'Christian experience,' I mean experience that is intrinsically qualified by the Christian symbols through which it is communicated and expressed." Dulles' concern for Christian experience can be satisfied, we believe, in our move away from a two-pole correlation in which experience is made to signify cultural awareness. Our model of reflection acknowledges that personal experience can overlap with cultural information. It can also intersect with the Christian Tradition. Much of our individual experience has been profoundly shaped by the Tradition; such experience is already Christian. (It is important to note that, in this context, "already Christian" does not necessarily mean transformed and sanctified. Our experience may also be shaped by restrictive or negative interpretations within our religious heritage as, for example, concerning sexuality or the role of women in the community. Though such restrictive interpretations are not the proudest part of our heritage, they are parts of the Christian Tradition that have shaped our present experience.) In a sustained reflection in ministry we learn how our own experiences, as composites of religious and cultural values, both provide insights toward pastoral decision and also represent our own narrow interpretations of Christian faith and values.

As a category of reflection, experience overlaps with Tradition in another important way. The lives of adult Christians, with their decades of experience in living a Christian life, are a small but significant part of the larger Christian Tradition. As a believer, my life and experience represent one of the ways Christianity has been lived. In its alternation between sin and faithfulness, between times of deep, authentic faith and periods of confusion, my own life is not unlike the larger Tradition itself. My own experience, though it represents a very partial perspective of Christian life, is itself part of the Christian Tradition. An individual Christian life or the life of a believing community stands in the interval where past and future meet. It is here that the Christian Tradition enters the present and is transmitted to the future. The limited life experience of this believer and this community is critiqued and shaped by the Tradition, but the Tradition is also challenged and altered by the life experience of contemporary believers.

A failure of religious education in the past has been to so focus on the movement of salvation in Jewish and early Christian history as to neglect the salvation history of *this* person and *this* community. Apprehensive about the value of individual experience, we have ignored the experiential details of how God has been leading this individual or this community. Attention to such particular experiences need not detract from the goal of educating Christians in their rich heritage. Rather, it can verify for believers that Christianity's central images of death and life, of failure and recovery, describe their own salvation history.

To discuss the overlap of individual experience and Christian Tradition is to return to the notion of "the sense of the faithful" (*sensus fidelium*). In a theological milieu in which individual experience is seen as threatening and disruptive (of authority and control), this category will enjoy little favor. When faith communities such as parishes are understood largely as passive recipients of the Church's official instruction rather than as generators of belief and Christian action, the notion of a *sensus fidelium* will have little room to develop. This notion itself points to the expectable vitality of a believing community, its own particular "sense" about Christian life and how Christian conviction is to be expressed in the world.[5] Such a notion is admittedly dangerous; it can be used to justify a group's wrongheaded pursuit of its own goals to the neglect of the larger Church. Yet it seems a necessary category of Church life today because it acknowledges the need for each community to be critically in touch with its own hopes and ambitions. The ideal is that this "sense of the faithful," when carefully examined and purified, will contribute to the larger Church through both support and challenge. The path to a revitalized *sensus fidelium* lies in the development of methods by which a community can become more critically conscious of its own experience: how this experience has already been "Christianized" and how its limited insights can contribute to the "Christianizing," the purifying, of the Tradition itself.

The Christian Tradition as Experience

For some Christians their own experience of life feels very distant and different from the stories and events which constitute the Christian heritage. My life feels ordinary and ambiguous compared to the miracles, revelations, and other striking events in the Scriptures and early Christian history. This distance makes religious reflection a more difficult task than it need be.

It can be useful here to recall an element from the discussion of Sacred Scripture in Chapter Two: the Judaeo-Christian Tradition recorded in the Old and New Testaments and developed over the past two millennia of our religious history originates in particular human experiences. A band of slaves fled Egypt, wandered years in a desert, and eventually their descendants found a home in a land to be called Israel. These many human experiences were just that for some of these ex-slaves—human experiences of escape, confusion, and survival. Others of these people saw the experiences differently: these experiences meant something special. Within the pattern and direction of these experiences they perceived a protective presence (*shekinah*) that came to be called Yahweh, God of Israel. The richly evocative words *exodus, Sinai,* and *promised land* interpret these ambiguous experiences as religious and Yahweh-shaped. Of the many different things that the Israelite communities experienced, certain happenings seemed of special significance, seemed to reveal God's presence and purpose in their lives. These critically remembered and interpreted experiences lie at the origin of the Judaeo-Christian Tradition. In fact, a tradition, religious or cultural, can be described as an amalgam of "critically remembered and interpreted experiences." Certain experiences—of discovery, failure, survival, celebration—deeply impress a people; as these experiences are recalled, further celebrated, and interpreted, they begin to form a tradition, a way of self-understanding.[6] Such a tradition is religious when these experiences are recognized as shaped by forces beyond ourselves, as revealing God's grace and love. (Another important part of the "traditioning of experience" is the gradual distillation into dogma of beliefs about these experiences; the logical conclusion of this process is reached in the rigid ordering of doctrines which substitute for and effectively conceal the experiences on which they are based. The self-purification of a religious tradition principally entails the struggle against this substitution of the clarity of dogma for the ambiguity of the experience of the Holy.)

Another example of experience becoming tradition may be useful. On the road to Emmaus two people (as recorded in Chapter Twenty-four of St. Luke's Gospel) had "an experience" of Christ's presence among them. Though it was known that Jesus had died, his presence was suddenly and powerfully experienced by these persons—both in a conversation with a stranger and in the breaking of bread in friendship. As with most such significant events, it took some reflection to clarify the ambiguous happening: "Were not our hearts burning within us!" This "tradition"—this handed-on understanding of Christ's continuing presence among us—is rooted in a human, ambiguous experience. This part of our faith has its force, its truth, both in the Christian belief that it happened and in its being repeated in our own life experiences. (If it took the gift of faith to discern the meaning of such an experience, it was, nonetheless, a human experience of companionship not so different from contemporary experiences which may or may not be revelatory.)

The Christian Tradition can be seen as a constellation of human experiences which have been recognized as revealing God's presence in and care for the world. The persuasion and continuity of such a tradition is grounded in its ability to illumine and resonate with the human experience of each new generation. This occurs not in the reduction of the events of the Christian Tradition to "just human experiences," but in the recognition of the possibility of finding in our own ambiguous, confusing and ordinary life experiences these same graceful revelations which created and move the Christian Tradition.

But the Judaeo-Christian Tradition is not simply the critically recalled and celebrated experiences contained in the Scriptures. It is likewise composed of the experiences—insights, decisions, biases—which describe the practical handing on of this faith over the past centuries. The Council of Chalcedon, the twelfth-century decision for priestly celibacy in the Western Church, the Protestant Reformation, and the Second Vatican Council are a few of the experiential moments through which the Church has interpreted itself in an effort to be faithful in handing on the faith. This extension of Tradition reminds us that it includes not just Scripture and not just the best moments in this sacred history, but all the events of remembering, celebrating, and transmitting. The Christian Tradition is both sacred and human; it includes both the graceful insights and the graceless biases that constitute our religious history. To admit the human, limited side of Tradition is not to deny its gracefulness and its privileged role in the continuing self-revelation of God. The task of theological reflection, confronted with such a Tradition, is necessarily twofold: to recover and to overcome.[7] Mindful of our Tradition's sacredness, we do well also to be aware of its ambiguity and unfinished character. In such a context the Christian Tradition appears less different from and alien to our own life experiences. Theological reflection in ministry challenges us to listen well to the ambiguity and richness in both kinds of experience.

Experience: Its Role in the Model of Reflection

The decision to distinguish a third and separate pole of experience in this model reflects an increased awareness of its influence in pastoral reflection. Historical and philosophical methods of reflection, which are addressed more to insight than to action, have most often sought to skirt the experience of the reflectors. For instance, in most theological reflection on the nature of the Church, understandings of Christian community from our religious tradition are set against philosophical, sociological, and other cultural orientations about human life together. Rarely does it seem germane to include one's own experience of belonging or alienation in the local Church. Such information would seem to prejudice the objectivity of the discussion. Yet even in such an "objective" discussion, which has as its goal a better understanding of the Church in today's society, the influence of the personal attitudes and (not always clearly acknowledged) convictions about community of those doing the reflection may be significant. If this is true in a reflection which intends to be more historically or philosophically oriented, it is especially true for a pastoral reflection. As a minister and a reflective community consider questions of the shape of the Church today, it becomes very important for them to be critically aware of their own past experiences of Christian life together—whether positive or negative, whether in the family, the parish, or in the broader life of the Church—since these experiences will influence (if not always consciously) their reflections and judgments about the future possibilities for Christian life together.

The role and importance of experience has been suspect in Catholic theology for a long time. Theologian Anne Carr begins an examination of experience in Karl Rahner's thought with the observation:

> One of the striking aspects of Roman Catholic theology today is the discussion of a new, fundamental source for theological reflection. In addition to Scripture, tradition in its historical and dogmatic aspects,

and philosophy, human experience itself has become an explicit source in Catholic theology.[8]

Previous to this new interest, it has often been argued (if wrongly) that, as all revelation occurred in Jesus Christ and in the apostolic era, it remained for contemporary Christians only to allow their experience to be shaped and healed by that (finished and clear) revelation. Such an idealistic and rigid view of the Christian Tradition ignored the historical, unfinished and human aspects of this heritage. It likewise ignored the methodological importance of God's continuing presence and action in human life. It is especially this last belief—that God acts always and everywhere in human life—that reminds us that a method of reflection in ministry and theology must be adroit at attending to this presence not only in the confines of Christian doctrine and Tradition, but in the perhaps more surprising arenas of cultural activities and individual human experience.[9]

The conviction that guides this renewed interest in the role of contemporary experience in theological reflection is that the religious truths received in the Christian Tradition can also be discerned in contemporary life. The patterns of grace and revelation illumined in an extraordinary and exceptional fashion in the Scriptures are also visible, to the disciplined observer, in our own lives. This orientation to the relationship of experience and the Tradition is similar to Rahner's method of "connections by correspondence." "Theology is not to be deduced from experience, rather, the correspondence between dogma and experience is to be discerned."[10] Such a belief allows Christians to listen confidently to the three different sources of information noted in this model; it is the same God who acts, if ambiguously, in all three contexts. Further, such an orientation realizes that the Tradition enjoys a special authority over our lives. But this privileged position is not meant to replace or substitute for the authority of our own life experiences. These experiences have their own authority. Human experience is not passively transformed by the revelation transmitted in the Tradition; it is transformed in dialogue with this Tradition. If the religious authority of this experience is not independent of the Tradition, the experience nonetheless demands to be heard for its own information concerning the interplay of a person and a community with the Holy. Because human experience is already open to the gracious activity of God, it, along with the Tradition, "could be a genuine source for theologizing, an equal partner in the dialogue with the objective word of revelation. Each would be a corrective of the other."[11]

In Catholic life in North America this increase in attention to experience is clearly related to the liturgical renewal. Bringing the liturgical vocabulary into the vernacular and involving the participants more thoroughly in the celebration heightened Catholics' experiential engagement in the Eucharist. Another important change associated with the Second Vatican Council was a refocusing of attention on the role of the individual believer's conscience. The work on this reunderstanding of Catholic theology, pioneered by John Courtney Murray,[12] has reminded us that mature Christian faith results not from a passive obedience, but from an assertive and personal choice of Christian life and responsibility.

A further instance of the renewed trust of American Catholics in their own religious experience is seen in their response to the promulgation of the papal encyclical, *Humanae Vitae,* in 1968. Many American Catholics found that the Church's judgment about artificial birth control did not accord with their own experience of the responsible use of contraceptives. A crisis of authority ensued which, in the history of Catholic pastoral reflection, heightened the need for special, critical attention to personal religious experience. No longer was the weight of personal experience to depend solely on its interpretation by official Church teaching. After years of judging their own experience in light of formal Church teachings and traditions, many Catholics were aroused to an exuberant interest in their own particularity and individuality as believers. Such a switch, radical for many, only heightens the need for effective means of attending to personal experience.

If there still exists apprehension about giving attention to individual experience, there is greater concern about placing it at the starting point of a reflection. Must not theological and Christian reflection always begin in the gospels and the life of Jesus Christ? To many, it not only seems more appropriate to begin a reflection at the pole of Tradition, but there is a special fear about beginning in experience. Such attention to individual experience, it is argued, will overwhelm and unbalance a reflection: enthralled by their own experience, individuals and communities will let this unduly sway their decisions. Our experience in employing this method over the past decade has shown otherwise. Rarely does increased awareness of personal experience seem to lead Christians away from their Tradition: more often it leads them toward it. Ministers and communities rarely have a very explicit awareness of their own personal convictions and biases about a specific pastoral concern—be it the issue of homosexuality, or how Christians are to celebrate in worship, or the relation of their parish to questions of social justice. When given an opportunity to reflect on any of these questions, they are quickly impressed with the limitations of their own ideas and convictions and turn to their Tradition for clarifying insights.

Many theologians today argue the need to begin theological reflection in experience as a way to avoid having the symbols and formulations of the Christian Tradition substitute for personal reflection and choice.[13] If it is important to know what we *should* feel and think, it seems more imperative at the outset of a reflection to be critically aware of what we *do* feel and think. Adult responsibility in faith demands that we confront the issues of both how this critically grasped experience affirms the Church's official position on a pastoral question and how these two may be in conflict. On several pastoral issues today we can expect some conflict between individual experience and the Church's recent Tradition. We can also expect that this conflict will not necessarily disrupt our faith but may challenge and quicken it.

Access to Our Experience

Having explored the question of what individual experience is and why we need to attend to it, it is necessary to examine how we are to apprehend it. The question of access to experience is related to the meaning of this pole of theological reflection. If *experience* refers merely to what I consciously *now think* about a pastoral concern, the question of access is quite simple: I take note of these ideas and continue with the rest of the reflection. In this method of reflection, however, *experience* includes feelings as well as ideas, along with those biases and convictions of which I am only vaguely aware. As I come to the question of how this parish should understand itself and what its goals should be, I am influenced by my many past experiences of Christian life together—successes that give me hope for this group but also, perhaps, difficulties and failures that make me apprehensive about cooperation and sharing. In a reflection on the role of women in sacramental leadership I can expect to be deeply influenced not just by the Church's Tradition and by my reading of the cultural trends, but also by my past experiences with women, especially around questions of authority, leadership, control, and sexuality.

This method of reflection in ministry attempts to gain access to different levels of our experience on any specific pastoral question. Since these levels of experience go well beyond the rational (what I can more quickly recall as what I think about this question), we need extrarational means of access to this experience. Extrarational refers to the various feeling and imaginative states that, along with our more cognitive stance, constitute the wide range of human experience. The word *extrarational* is used to suggest that these parts of our experience are complementary to the more cognitive or rational part of our life. The word *extrarational* also points, as the words *irrational* and *nonrational* do not, to the retrievability and positive value of such feelings and images in pastoral reflection.

To reflect, for instance, on our lives as ministers in the Christian Church today, we need to recall the Church's Tradition (or better, Traditions) of ministry. These are expectations that accompany our religious heritage. We need also to become critically aware of present-day demands of ministry—the needs specific to contemporary American life and this culture's understandings of leadership and authority. But such a reflection best begins, we would argue, with a clear sense of who we think *we are* as ministers. Before examining what the Tradition asks of me (I have hopefully been attending to that during my years in ministry), or needs for effective forms of service in contemporary society, it is very useful to listen carefully to my own images and biases about myself as minister. We are interested here in the kind of exercise that Tracy describes as "a 'consciousness-raising' exercise that frees me to be attentive to my experience."[14] An extrarational approach to such information, one which we have found effective in a variety of learning settings, is to invite participants in the reflection to do a sketch—a picture, symbol, any kind of drawing—depicting how they see themselves in ministry. (A subsequent and complementary exercise is to have the persons then do a sketch of how they feel they are seen by the people to whom they minister.) When executed at leisure in a nonthreatening environment, such a simple exercise can tap into surprising and not ordinarily available parts of our experience of ourselves. Such exercises can be educationally valuable—revealing to us feelings, enthusiasms, and doubts of which we were hitherto unaware. These extrarational means of gaining access to our experience are frustrated and misused when we force from them clear, "rational" conclusions; they are meant to suggest and hint rather than to explain or solve. We consider other means of access to the extrarational aspects of personal experience (particularly the exploration of feelings and the use of guided fantasy) in our discussion of education for ministry in Chapter Eleven.

Several of the tools of access to experience which we have found useful have been developed initially within the personal growth and "human potential" movements. These movements have been under serious attack in recent years for the excessive individualism, even narcissism, of some spokespersons and adherents. In our own discussion of the importance of personal experience in the processes of pastoral reflection we are aware of this criticism, exemplified in the religious challenge of the 1975 Hartford Appeal and in the social analysis of historian Christopher Lasch's popular, if simplistic, *The Culture of Narcissism.*

The Hartford Appeal, signed by a number of Catholic and Protestant theologians, presented thirteen "themes" in American culture which, in their judgment, contribute to a "loss of a sense of the transcendent."[15] The statement of the sixth theme, "to realize one's potential and to be true to oneself is the whole meaning of salvation," is an oblique condemnation of the human growth movement. A limitation of the Hartford criticism is its neglect of the more intriguing theological question of the relationship between systematic efforts to "realize one's potential" and God's plan of salvation. Theologian Gregory Baum, one of the critics of the Hartford Appeal, objects to its presupposition of a "radical separation of God and the world": "The Appeal does not recognize the possibility that present in life itself and in history is God's redemptive action, which we must seek out with the help of the Gospel and with which we must identify ourselves."[16] A theology which is convinced of an intimate connection between human development and religious growth will have to construct careful means of attending to contemporary human experience.

In *The Culture of Narcissism*, Lasch attacks assertiveness training, parent effectiveness training, and other forms of human relations skill training as simply pandering to individualism and the desire to manipulate others. Lasch seems to identify *all* efforts at understanding and sharing feelings with the worst possible motivation. It is critical—and the task of such critics of culture—to distinguish parts of this movement that are narcissistic in design and strategy (and which receive much attention in the popular media) from other efforts which are grounded in truer values. Lasch's jeremiad concludes with a plea for citizens "to create their own 'communities of competence.' "[17] Such communities, in American society and in the Christian Church, will depend on the competence which comes with a skillful attending to our own experiences, feelings, and insights.

Critical clarity about our ideas, biases, and our only partly conscious hopes and doubts is necessary if we are to become effective ministers in today's Church. Theological wisdom and cultural savvy will not avail if they are not complemented by a deep, experiential awareness of our own and our community's feelings and convictions. Experiential learning methods and techniques which explore our feelings can, indeed, be employed for selfish and narcissistic purposes. But these methods and techniques, when rooted in a Christian value system, seek to assist the revelation of us to ourselves—a revelation about sin and grace, about God's continuing presence within us. In short, when we as Christians look into and attempt to clarify the murky pool of our lives, we expect to see not just our own reflection, but signs and hints of God's action. Such an anticipation can rescue our effort from narcissism and make systematic reflection on personal experience a truly religious task.

Notes

1. Since this chapter is not a discussion of fundamental theology, but of pastoral or practical theology, it will suffice to recall the general orientation toward experience of each of these theologians. Tillich, as we saw in Chapter One, used *experience* to signify the milieu or medium in which theological reflection occurs. (See his *Systematic Theology* [Chicago: University of Chicago Press, 1951], 1:40f.) Lonergan's transcendental method operates through stages of "experiencing . . . understanding . . . affirming . . . (and) deciding" (see his *Method in Theology* [New York: Herder and Herder, 1972] pp. 13–15). Although Lonergan locates experiencing at the beginning of his method, he gives little attention to the practical challenges and perils of "experiencing one's experiencing. . . ." Kaufmann, in his discussion of method in theology (see *An Essay On Theological Method* [Missoula, MT: Scholars Press, 1975] understands experience as located at the conclusion of a reflection: it functions as a final check on the accuracy of the reflection. Tracy, as we shall discuss further, interprets experience as those pre-religious, publicly available understandings which are revealed in the language, ordinary and scientific, of a culture (see pp. 43f. of *Blessed Rage for Order* [New York: Seabury, 1975]). This pluralism of theological methods reminds us that *theological reflection* is an analogous term. To pursue a more philosophical method in a pastoral context is both uncritical and unproductive.

2. See David Tracy's discussion of this expanded understanding of experience in his article, "The Particularity and Universality of Christian Revelation," in *Revelation and Experience*, Edward Schillebeeckx and Bas Van Iersel, eds. (New York: Seabury, 1979), pp. 109–110.

3. Reflection in pastoral theology begins with experience as already, in part, religious and Christian. Without the philosophical task of fundamental theology of examining *whether* this experience is religious, pastoral reflection seeks to discern *how* it is genuinely religious and Christian and how it is to influence a pastoral decision. Philosophical and pastoral reflection are simply different; difficulties follow when one attempts to substitute one for the other.

4. *Theological Studies* 37 (June 1976):308.

5. This interpretation of the *sensus fidelium*, in stressing the individuality and agency of a community's sense of faith, departs from the more passive un-

derstanding offered in the document on the Church of Vatican II. In *Lumen Gentium*, #12, the *sensus fidelium* is presented as representing uniform and universal accord: "Thanks to a supernatural sense of faith which characterizes the People as a whole, it manifests this unerring quality when 'from the bishops down to the last member of the laity,' it shows universal agreement in matters of faith and morals." Despite this stress on uniformity, the document acknowledges that not only does the sense of the faithful "cling without fail to the faith once delivered to the Saints," but it also "penetrates it more deeply by accurate insights, and applies it more thoroughly to life" ("Dogmatic Constitution on the Church," in Walter M. Abbott, ed., *The Documents of Vatican II* [New York: America Press, 1966], pp. 29–30). This clinging-penetrating-applying is an excellent description of the dynamic of theological reflection in ministry.

6. Apparent here is the influence of Clifford Geertz's definition of religion as a cultural system. See Geertz's *The Interpretation of Cultures* (New York: Basic Books, 1973), especially Chapter Four. While influenced by this attractive and comprehensive orientation toward cultural and religious traditions, we share Peter Berger's reservations about the tendency of such "objective" definitions to foreclose on the possibility of transcendence; see Berger's "Some Second Thoughts on Substantive versus Functional Definitions of Religion," *Journal for the Scientific Study of Religion* 13 (June 1974):125–33.

7. Karl Rahner elaborates this dual challenge in his outline of christology's task regarding the confessional statements of Chalcedon in his "Current Problems in Christology," in *Theological Investigations* (Baltimore: Helicon, 1961), 1:149–54. This dual task arises from the fact that the Christian Tradition is not simply God's appearance in human history, but is also the result of human efforts of interpretation and transmission of this revelation.

8. See Anne Carr's "Theology and Experience in the Thought of Karl Rahner," in *Journal of Religion* 53 (July 1973):359. The articles in *Revelation and Experience* (cited in Note 2 above) explore the dichotomy that developed in the Christian Tradition between (a supposedly finished) revelation and on-going (but not revelatory) human experience.

9. Catholic theologians address this question in terms of a theology of ongoing revelation: see Avery Dulles's "The Meaning of Revelation," in Joseph Papin, ed., *The Dynamics of Christian Thought* (Villanova, PA: Villanova University Press, 1970), pp. 52–80; and Thomas O'Meara's "Toward a Subjective Theology of Revelation," in *Theological Studies*, 36 (September 1975):410–27. David Tracy, in his article in *Revelation and Experience*, suggests the expanded understanding of experience that allows the recognition of revelation as experiential: "For those, however, whose notion of experience is sufficiently wide to encourage an exploration of intense, old and new religious experiences, and whose notion of hermeneutics is sufficiently sensitive to the intrinsic relationship between intense personal experience and its genre-expression in classical texts, events, and persons, then the seemingly tired and merely conceptual category 'revelation' becomes authentically experiential" (p. 115).

10. See Carr, "Theology and Experience in the Thought of Karl Rahner," p. 375.

11. Ibid., p. 376.

12. See his introduction to, and the statement of Vatican II on, "The Declaration on Religious Freedom," in Walter M. Abbott, ed., *The Documents of Vatican II* (New York: America Press, 1966), pp. 672f. See also John Coleman's "Vision and Praxis in American Theology: Orestes Brownson, John A. Ryan and John Courtney Murray," in *Theological Studies*, 37 (November 1976):3–40.

13. Irish theologian Enda McDonagh argues for experience as the starting point for moral investigation in his *Gift and Call* (St. Meinrad, IN: Abbey Press, 1975):8. See also Thomas O'Meara "Toward a Subjective Theology of Revelation," cited above. Peter Berger, though not a theologian (to which he happily confesses), also argues for experience as the necessary starting point of a reflection on religion in his *The Heretical Imperative* (New York: Doubleday, 1979), p. ix. Berger's book pursues a method which intends to inductively "uncover and retrieve the experiences embodied in the tradition" (p. xi).

14. Tracy, *Blessed Rage for Order*, p. 65.

15. See *Worldview*, Summer 1975, for the statement of the Hartford Appeal and commentaries and criticisms by a number of religious thinkers.

16. Ibid. p. 11.

17. Christopher Lasch, *The Culture of Narcissism* (New York: Norton, 1978), p. 235. Lasch's uncritical condemnations of assertiveness training, parent effectiveness training, and human relation skills appear on pp. 65–66, 166–67, and 182–86 respectively.

·4·

CULTURAL INFORMATION
IN THEOLOGICAL REFLECTION

To read the signs of the times, to hear the voices of the age—in these evocative images of Vatican II the community of faith has been challenged to renew and strengthen its dialogue with the culture in which it lives. The model of pastoral reflection which we explore in this book incorporates this challenge, seeing cultural information as an indispensable component in theological reflection in ministry.

The relationship of a culture—its biases, insights, and convictions—to a religious tradition and so to theological reflection is a complex and intriguing one. Not content with a simple and antagonistic juxtaposition of Church and "world," most Christians today recognize culture as an ambiguous environment which not only represents demonic and evil forces in life but also—in part, because Western culture has itself been so powerfully shaped by Christianity—provides tools and opportunities to the Tradition for its own self-examination and growth. The ambiguity and challenge of a culture's contribution to theological reflection can be glimpsed in the question of sexuality. In American culture's fascination with pornography we can see its negative influence on our understanding of sexuality. On the other hand, contemporary psychological insight—from Freud through Erikson and Horney—offers the reflective Christian insights that can deepen and enrich an understanding of sexual maturing. Thus, out of the pole of cultural information both pornography and psychology provide data for pastoral reflection on sexuality. These sources in the culture are to be consulted, their information set in dialogue with insights from the religious Tradition and from ministerial experience, as the believing community moves toward pastoral decision making and action. In this chapter we will discuss several understandings of the contribution of cultural information to pastoral reflection. Our consideration shall focus in particular on the social sciences as vehicles for understanding the culture.

Webster's New World Dictionary defines the word *culture* as "the concepts, habits, skills, arts, instruments, institutions, etc. of a given people in a given period."[1] For sociologists, culture designates the social context of a group or a people, "including all the material and nonmaterial products of group life that are transmitted from one generation to the next."[2] More simply, culture is the way of life of a social group.

The definition offered by theologian Don Browning highlights components of culture which most directly influence theology and ministry. For Browning, culture means "a set of symbols, stories (myths), and norms for conduct that orient a society or group cognitively, affectively, and behaviorally to the world in which it lives."[3]

Information arising in such a milieu constitutes the third pole of the model of theological reflection. The contribution of cultural information in pastoral reflection may be explicit, as when an understanding from the culture reinforces or challenges a religious insight. (The active debate in religious circles over the United States Supreme Court decision concerning abortion is a current example of such a reflection. In an earlier decade the debate over United States involvement in Vietnam offered a similar example.) Or the influence of culture on religious reflection may be more implicit, functioning through convictions or biases of which one is unaware.

In distinguishing among these potential sources of religious information (Tradition, experience, culture), we recognize the significant interplay and overlap among them. Religion and culture cannot be simplisticly dichotomized: God does not abide unambiguously in the Christian Tradition nor Mammon in the culture. In this model of reflection, culture and religious Tradition are understood to overlap in two significant ways. The American culture is deeply influenced and shaped by the Christian religious Tradition; Christian values and images survive even in the most secular aspects of American culture. Second, God's presence and action in the world is not restricted to the Christian Tradition. As God shapes and abides in all of creation, this same God can be discovered in cultural as well as in explicitly religious life. The Christian minister today must be sophisticated enough, to be sure, to know the difference between religious values and cultural values, as well as to recognize areas of congruence. One goal of our method in pastoral reflection is to make more explicit the generally implicit influence of the culture on pastoral decision making and ministerial action. When cultural influences remain simply or chiefly implicit in pastoral practice there are at least two detrimental effects. First, implicit cultural influences cannot be evaluated adequately in the light of the properly religious values and goals of Christian ministry. Second, cultural influences and information that remain only implicit also cannot be used to full advantage to contribute to ministry and religious action.

In our initial discussion of the tripolar model in Chapter One we noted that the pole of cultural information represents not a realm of unredeemed nature, but a mixed environment, partly antithetical and partly complementary to Christian life. As a mixed environment, cultural information must be dealt with. It cannot be ignored or, perhaps more exactly, it is ignored only to the detriment of Christian ministry. It is only by dealing with culture as an explicit factor in theological reflection in ministry that the community of faith is in a position to recognize and overcome the negative effects of culture and to harness and use its complementary forces. It is also only when alert to the voices of the age as they sound in the culture that the community can hear the call to judgment that can arise in the culture as it challenges the Church to be aware of how its structure has drifted away from the gospel norm or how its practice is less reflective and more superficial than it should be.

Our discussion thus far has suggested at least three postures from which the conversation between the religious Tradition and cultural information might begin: (a) the religious Tradition challenges the culture; (b) the religious Tradition is challenged by the culture; (c) the religious Tradition uses the resources of the culture in pursuit of its own religious mission.[4]

The first stance displays Christianity in its prophetic role: in the light of the revelation it has received, the Christian Tradition convicts the world of sin and calls it to repentance and conversion. It calls to account those institutions and values which, oppressive and false, deny the life of the Spirit. Here, the religious Tradition may lead the believer and the community of faith to take a stand over against the culture, to dissociate themselves from it even at the risk of culture's sanctions.

The second stance is reflected in the self-examination to which the religious community is invited by developments within a culture. Thus the civil rights movement in the United States has confronted Christians with facts of personal and institutional racism within the Church. The women's movement challenges the religious Tradition to examine its language and structures for evidence of implicit and explicit sexism. Movements for liberation in the Third World challenge the Church to examine its support of, and even identification with, colonialism and capitalism.

These cultural movements—themselves often deeply influenced by religious convictions—challenge Christianity to self-examination and reformation.

In the third stance the religious Tradition uses the resources of the culture in pursuit of its own religious mission. It is this orientation to the potential contribution of cultural information to theological reflection in ministry that we shall pursue further here.

Our focus on this third stance does not indicate that this is the preferred or "best" attitude for ministry. All three orientations represent authentically Christian responses to the question of how the Church is to live in the world. All three must be represented for a full appreciation of the ambiguous presence of the divine in the human realm. We concentrate on this "instrumental" relationship to explore more directly the possible contributions of cultural information to the active practice of Christian ministry.

In the discussion of cultural information as a component of theological reflection in Chapter One, we listed four sources through which this information can be sought: philosophy, political interpretation, the social sciences, and other religious traditions such as Islam or Buddhism. In this chapter we will focus on the social sciences as a source of cultural information particularly relevant to contemporary Christianity. Our concern will be to examine how the social sciences can serve as resources to the religious Tradition, assisting the achievement of its mission and ministry.

Pastoral reflection begins, as theologian John Shea notes, in the questions that people ask about "what is creative and destructive in their interpersonal lives and the systems in which they live."[5] The social sciences can be a valuable tool for ministers and the community of faith in their efforts to understand these forces and to respond effectively to them. The social sciences do not, taken alone, give answers to the community of faith. It is our conviction that information from the social sciences must be in a dialogue of mutual clarification and challenge with the historical religious Tradition and with the experience and insights of the contemporary believing community if it is to have something constructive and life-giving to contribute to the life of the Church. But the social sciences contribute to the pastoral conversation both a perspective and a fund of information which are indispensable in contemporary ministry. Here, we will explore three ways in which the social sciences may contribute to theological reflection in ministry.

Social Sciences and the Intellectual Perspective of the Age

In every era of Christian history, theology has found itself in dialogue with
the dominant intellectual categories of the time. In this long dialogue,
Greek philosophy, especially that of Plato and Aristotle, has spoken loud
and persuasively. In this century the development of the social sciences
has provided a new and significant conversation partner for theological
reflection. Carr notes that Karl Rahner argues, especially in his later work,
"that theology may find its most significant dialogical partner not in philosophy but in the natural, psychological, and social sciences which shape
man's self-understanding in the present."[6] Don Browning stresses the contemporary function of the social sciences as "coordinating models," analogous to the pervading myths and theological images that supported a sense
of shared meaning in previous cultures. These models give shape to the
basic intellectual and emotional orientation of our culture. "They give
certain members of the society (for instance, its intellectual elites) kinds of
maps which orient them to their worlds, tell them what to trust, what to
hope for, and how to get what they have come to believe is good."[7]

Avery Dulles, too, recognizes this new conversation partner for theology. He notes the emergence and importance in contemporary theology of
what he characterizes as the "secular dialogic," the "attempt to achieve
new insights through a kind of dialogue between traditional Christian
faith and the aspirations and insights of contemporary secular man."[8] If
these aspirations and insights of contemporary culture are an appropriate
conversation partner for theology, then access to the social sciences becomes imperative for the reflective minister.

We can give examples here of two areas of social science theory and research that touch on contemporary "aspirations and insights" that are
especially relevant in ministry today: the nature and possibility of the
human person, and the structure and dynamic of human community. Religious questions about vocation, personal morality, and spirituality will be
necessarily related to the surrounding culture's philosophical and psychological persuasions about human life and development.

More specifically, the growth of developmental psychology over the
past several decades has made available to theological reflection a clearer
awareness of the differing challenges encountered over the lengthening
life span of adults today. This delineation of specific challenges in the psy-
chosocial maturing process represents a significant contribution to a contemporary Christian spirituality of adult growth and holiness.[9] Here, the
role of such cultural information becomes clear: it can neither be allowed

to *determine* the shape of Christian spirituality (this happens, for instance, when cultural ideas overwhelm theological conviction, producing a short-lived fad or religious fashion), nor can such information be ignored in the pursuit of a "pure" and unchanging understanding of religious growth.

Another significant contribution to theological reflection in ministry may be drawn from sociology's inquiry into community. Pastoral reflection is almost always concerned with the style of our life together—its potential and its specific challenges. Sociological theory and research concerning contemporary forms of community can contribute to theological reflection by pointing to specific problems of community life today and by suggesting strategies of clarification and conflict resolution which facilitate the formation and growth of community.[10] Here again, this sociological information is neither simply to replace inherited models and convictions about Christian community nor is it to be ignored in an effort to safeguard the uniqueness of the Church.

Social Sciences and the Self-purification of the Church

The social sciences may serve as resources to the Church's self-understanding, in this way assisting the self-critical function of the Church. The analytic stance of the social sciences can provide for religious reflection another point of view, another place to stand in understanding the Church's activities in society, in bringing to light its presuppositions and in evaluating its effects. Thus, the social sciences are a resource to the self-purification of the Church. In his *Religion and Alienation,* Gregory Baum, a theologian who has undertaken a disciplined dialogue with the categories and insights of classical sociological thought, discusses one way in which the social sciences can serve as resource to the self-corrective task of the religious Tradition. A basic insight of classical sociology concerns the distinctions among subjective intention, concrete action, and objective effect. The insight is that social actions (and institutions) have objective, observable social effects and consequences.

Religious action, religious language, religious dogma, and religious institutions exist in and interact with a social world. In the perspective of the social scientist they too have "structural consequences" in the "objective order." The important distinction here is that between the intention or motive of a religious action (subjective) and the consequence or effect of this action (objective). Religious structures (decisions, laws, dogmatic formulations, liturgical symbols) influence other structures and individuals in ways that may well be different than those who plan and undertake them may have wished. An effect of increased sociological sophistication is to enable the religious person to be aware of the objective consequences of religious action and dogma. These structural consequences—that is, concrete effects on individuals or on social relations or on cultural consciousness—occur apart from, and sometimes in direct opposition to, the motivation or intention or goals or hopes or values of those who set the action in motion.

To understand religion in terms of its explicit values is not to understand it incorrectly but to understand it partially. "Religion," as Baum notes, "has a social impact which may be hidden from the theologian."[11] The religious Tradition can draw upon this sociological insight in its attempts to remain faithful to a properly religious mission in the midst of changing historical and social circumstances. The community can thus examine the effects—on individuals and society—of its actions and structures, with particular care to discern what are the unintended, unanticipated, and even undesirable effects. For example, the establishment of seminaries to upgrade the quality of professional ministry in the Church (religiously positive motive) may also reinforce the gap between clergy and laity (religiously negative effect). The Church's stress on the importance of marriage and family life (religiously positive intention) may result in the neglect of any effective ministry to unmarried, widowed, separated, or divorced persons (religiously negative effect).

Baum discusses this self-corrective function of the religious Tradition as critical theology. The word *critical* does not designate a new content area for theology; it is rather an orientation or approach that should characterize contemporary theological analysis in a variety of different content areas. A critical stance in theological analysis is one concerned with the structural consequences of dogma and religious practice as well as with orthodoxy of belief and purity of motivation. Critical theology, often using the methods and findings of the social sciences, will attempt to discern what are the consequences for individuals and society of certain religiously motivated actions and institutions and then to evaluate these consequences in light of gospel values. It is possible for religiously correct motivation to lead to an action that has religiously negative effect. Leaders in the religious community are at least naive and probably even negligent if they do not make use of this insight, widely available in the culture from the social sciences, to understand and evaluate their own activities.

Mature sociological awareness, one which has itself moved beyond the temptations of reductionism, can assist the community of believers to be accountable for the structural consequences of its religious belief and be-havior. Often the methods and findings of the social sciences will be useful tools in this examination, enabling the religious Tradition to discern the objective social effects of its religiously motivated action. But this analysis does not reduce the full meaning of religious action to its social conse-quences. Rather, it moves to understand and evaluate these social conse-quences against the gospel criteria of its mission in the world. The goal of this evaluation is not to legitimize religious action by reference to socio-logical categories nor, even less, to "demythologize" religion action as "nothing but" its social consequences. Rather, the goal of this use of the insights of sociology is to help the Church bring its action more in line with its intentions, its values, its mission, by assisting the Church to see and to address the structural contradictions that beset it. In this analysis, sociological insight (such as the distinction of intention and consequence) may focus the inquiry and sociological tools may be used to gather infor-mation; but it is the gospel which provides the criteria against which the adequacy of religious dogma and structure will be judged.

Social Sciences Provide Tools for Ministry

Thus far we have discussed primarily the ways in which the *theoretical perspective* and *defining categories* of the social sciences may serve as re-sources to the religious Tradition. The *methods* and *findings* of the social sciences are valuable as well. Van Campenhoudt discusses this role of the social sciences: "When a pastoral decision has to be made, the appeal to theology is not enough, for today, more than ever, all decision making re-quires a precise, scientific knowledge of reality, and it is not the role of theology, but rather that of the social sciences, to provide us with such in-formation."[12] There are several examples of ways in which the community of faith may take advantage of the methods or findings of the social sci-ences to better carry out its ministry. First, the empirical methods of data gathering and analysis can be used to provide accurate information about a situation or issue that faces the Church. Thus, statistics concerning pop-ulation changes, or information about the incidence of unemployment, or an assessment of the needs experienced by recently divorced parents can contribute significantly to the shape of an effective ministry.

Second, the religious Tradition can define a problem according to its own criteria and then use social science research methods to test a hy-pothesis or to achieve a more accurate description of the problem. The so-ciological and psychological analysis of the priests of the United States, commissioned by the Roman Catholic bishops in the early 1970s, is an example of such use of the research methods of the social sciences.[13]

Third, the religious Tradition can adopt the techniques and tools developed in the social sciences for use in pursuit of its own goals. Thus, religious persons have become trained in and use therapeutic techniques developed in the psychological disciplines, skills of management and planning developed in organization development, and skills of small group interaction and problem solving developed in the communication disciplines.

Finally, the social sciences can provide information and interpretation on questions that are of independent interest to the religious community. It can be useful for the minister to see how a particular question appears in a secular view, how it is understood and evaluated by the social scientist—not necessarily in order that the minister will see it that way, but because seeing a complex problem from another point of view can often enhance one's understanding. Thus, the minister will have an even better appreciation of the question when it is understood in the Christian perspective.

Conclusion

So far we have discussed several advantages to theological reflection in ministry of dialogue with the social sciences. To learn from and to influence the contemporary situation which helps constitute the Church alive today, the community of believers first needs to experience and to understand this situation. The interpretive categories, research methods, and findings of the social sciences are important tools in understanding the contemporary situation. But it must be stressed that what the social sciences provide for the community of faith is not answers but access to resources. Determining the shape of the contemporary Church remains, under the influence of the Spirit, the task of the believing community. In this task it is the criteria of the gospel, not the social sciences, to which the community remains accountable.

The caution to Christian ministers regarding the use of the interpretive categories and helping techniques of these psychotherapeutic disciplines in pastoral counseling sounded by Cobb and Browning is instructive here.[14] Browning calls for a realization that the therapeutic practices and psychological interpretations are themselves immersed in particular "cultures," with value assumptions and ideological commitments that are not necessarily congruent with Christianity. This immersion is not so total that these resources remain useless to the mission of faith. But believers, ministers, and theologians must be sophisticated in their use. An early step in such sophistication is a dialogue of mutual exploration and critique between the religious Tradition and the psychotherapeutic perspective, one which searches for the areas of both overlap and antagonism.

What is said here of the therapeutic disciplines might also be said of the Marxian analysis of society. There is much that is valuable here both to challenge and to reinforce the Christian vision, but there is not immediate equivalence. Dialogue and critical evaluation are required, along with a systematic critique of the assumptions that stand behind the interpretive categories of Marxism.

Thus, the community of faith must be sophisticated in its use of the social sciences, whether it be its theoretical perspective, its methods, or its findings that are being used. But this critical sophistication is necessary in the religious Tradition's use of any ancillary knowledge—philosophy and financial management techniques as much as the social sciences. To use well the resources of the social sciences the community of faith must be able to draw upon them critically. Believers, ministers, and theologians must be aware of the assumptions, even biases, from which the paradigms and findings of the social sciences result. They must appreciate the circumscribed context in which the findings of the social sciences have validity; they must acknowledge that the interpretive categories available within the social sciences are partial. Aware of these limits, the believing community will be better able to dialogue with and to distill the resources of the social sciences in the service of the religious mission of justice and meaning.

Notes

1. *Webster's New World Dictionary of the American Language*, college ed. (New York: The World Publishing Company, 1964), p. 359.

2. G. A. Theodorson and Achilles G. Theodorson, *Modern Dictionary of Sociology* (New York; Crowell-Apolla, 1970), p. 95.

3. *The Moral Context of Pastoral Care* (Philadelphia: Westminster Press, 1976), p. 73.

4. The history of the discussion of the relationship of Christianity to culture is a long and rich one. Questions raised by Augustine in *City of God* have remained relevant across time, to be taken up again in this century by Paul Tillich in *Theology of Culture* (New York: Oxford University Press, 1959), by Reinhold Niebuhr in *Christ and Culture* (New York: Harper, 1951), and by others. Recently, the work of Latin American theologians such as Gustavo Gutierrez in *A Theology of Liberation* (Maryknoll, NY: Orbis, 1973) and Juan Luis Segundo in *The*

Liberation of Theology (Maryknoll, NY: Orbis, 1976) has urged a more radical interpretation of Christianity's role in transforming culture.

5. "Doing Ministerial Theology," in D. Tracy, ed., *Toward Vatican III* (New York: Seabury, 1978), p. 184.

6. Anne Carr, "Theology and Experience in the Thought of Karl Rahner," in *Journal of Religion* 53 (July 1973):373.

7. Browning, *The Moral Context of Pastoral Care*, p. 73.

8. "The Apostolate of Theological Reflection," in *The Way*, supplement 20 (Autumn 1973):115.

9. For one effort to engage the dialogue between developmental psychology and the categories of a traditional Christian understanding of the human person, see Evelyn Eaton Whitehead and James D. Whitehead, *Christian Life Patterns: The Psychological Challenges and Religious Invitations of Adult Life* (New York: Doubleday, 1979).

10. Examples of this dialogue between contemporary sociology and Christian understandings and aspirations of community can be found in several chapters of *The Parish in Community and Ministry* (New York: Paulist Press, 1978), edited by Evelyn Eaton Whitehead, as well as in her article "Clarifying the Meaning of Community," *Living Light* 15 (Fall 1978):376–92.

11. *Religion and Alienation* (New York: Paulist Press, 1975), p. 2.

12. Andre G. Van Campenhoudt made this observation in his address to a symposium in the United States on the local church in 1975. This address, *The Local Churches*, is available in mimeographed form from Prospective in Brussels, Belgium.

13. The findings of these studies appeared in Eugene C. Kennedy and Victor J. Heckler, *The Loyola Psychological Study of the Ministry and Life of the American Priest* (Washington, D.C.: National Conference of Catholic Bishops, 1971); in "American Priests," a report of the National Opinion Research Center prepared for the United States Catholic Conference (Chicago: NORC, 1971); and in Andrew Greeley, *Priests in the United States: Reflections on a Survey* (New York: Doubleday, 1972).

14. See John B. Cobb, Jr., *Theology and Pastoral Care* (Philadelphia: Fortress, 1977) and Browning, *The Moral Context of Pastoral Care.*

Part III

A Method for Theological Reflection in Ministry

The dynamic that moves a reflection in ministry is threefold: attending, assertion, decision.

Attending is a Christian virtue through which we patiently discern the voice of God wherever it reveals itself. This virtue encompasses a range of specific skills—from the ability to read accurately a scriptural text to the ability to listen carefully to the movement of the Spirit in this community of faith.

Having listened to the Word, we are called to witness to it. Our witnessing occurs among a variety of believers. This skillful testifying to the different religious information that arises in the Christian Tradition, personal experience, and our culture is best described as assertion.

A mutual and respectful assertion of beliefs and insight can be expected to generate decisions for action. Thus, in a final stage of decision making the faith community moves to express its conviction in service to and in challenge of the world.

In Part Three we discuss in some detail this dynamic of theological reflection through which the ministering community moves from insight to action.

ATTENDING—THE INITIAL
STAGE
OF REFLECTION

Our intention in this volume is to identify both a model and a method of theological reflection in ministry. In the discussion of the model we have indicated that theological reflection in ministry must include information drawn from three sources of potentially religious information—Christian Tradition, personal experience, and cultural information. Thus, we describe a tripolar model. In this section we turn to a discussion of the method—how the minister and the community of faith may go about using the religious information from these sources in the process of reaching decisions about pastoral action. We have sketched this method in the overview chapter. Here, we will develop in greater detail the three stages in the dynamic of pastoral reflection. Our discussion of each of these three essential stages of the reflective process will include a description of the basic skills that are involved and a consideration of their use in theological reflection in ministry.

Attending in the Process of Reflection

Any process of reflection necessarily begins in attending. Theologically, we must listen to the Word before witnessing to it. Faith is a response to revelation; our initial posture is the receptive one of attending to this saving message.

The peculiarly contemporary challenge in theological and pastoral reflection concerns the focus of our attention: To what are we to attend? What are the different styles of listening appropriate to different sources of religious information? Christians today are challenged by a variety of sources demanding their attention. Increasingly, religious attending is seen less exclusively as a question of listening to the Scriptures and the ongoing witness of the Christian Church. These remain the central focus of Christian attention, to be sure. Complementing these, however, are sources within our culture and our own changing adult lives. Christians and, especially, professional ministers are searching for ways to listen more carefully and effectively to these sources of information.

This increasing interest in an ability to listen has accompanied a gradual shift in Christian self-understanding. Contemporary believers seem more acutely aware of themselves as *seekers* than as *possessors* of truth and grace. Such modesty has long been an insight (if not always a practice) in the Christian Tradition. The increased visibility of other religious traditions coupled with our own recent and profound experiences of change within the Christian Church have made us more alert to our status as learners. We are called to listen continually and carefully to God's surprising presence in human history.

This shift in self-understanding deeply affects the professional minister and the style of ministerial leadership. The minister today is seen less exclusively as the one who *brings* God and more as one who helps *discern* God, already present. The minister is a skillful attendant to the movements of God wherever these appear. The word *attendant* captures well this shift in the stance of Christian leadership. Ministry is moving away from a more authoritarian and hierarchical style in which a minister is one who "molds and rules" (the language of Vatican II in its *Constitution on the Church,* #10). The shift is toward a style of "servant leadership" (Greenleaf, 1978) in which the minister is an attendant—one whose role is to listen for the Lord's presence and to assist other believers in their own attentive response to God's movement in their lives.

This shifted theological vision requires of ministers a new self-definition and a new asceticism, as their central role in the community of faith is seen to involve a capacity for creative listening to complement the traditionally more highlighted roles of preacher, decision maker, and judge.

Interpersonal Skills of Attending

Over the past two decades we have come to an increasingly comprehensive understanding of the elements of effective communication between persons and within groups and large organizations. The disciplines of psychology and counseling have contributed to this understanding of communication skills, as have the management and organization sciences. In this chapter and that which follows, we will examine the skills required for effective interpersonal communication and then explore the relevance of these attitudes and behaviors for the larger conversation that is theological reflection in ministry.

An initial stance for any conversation is that of the listener. The listener is one who pays attention; paying attention is a receptive, but not a passive, attitude. To listen well is to listen actively, alert to the full context of the conversation—the words and silences, the emotions and ideas, the situation in which the conversation takes place. Communication theorists speak of this larger awareness in terms of skills of attending. Attending is the first act in communication. If I cannot pay attention it will be difficult for me to listen; if I do not listen it will be difficult for me to understand accurately and to act effectively.

Attending begins in an attitude of openness which enables me to set aside my own concerns and turn myself toward you. But attending does not end in this openness. Its object and its proof is that I respond to you with understanding, that is, with both accuracy (I have heard correctly what you have said) and with empathy (I am aware of what it means from your own point of view).

The two basic components of attending are thus the ability to listen actively and the ability to respond with accurate understanding (Egan, 1976). Skills of active listening are those which enable me to be aware of the full message. This includes my being alert to the words of the message and to their precise nuance. But equally and often even more important are the nonverbal factors involved. In personal conversation these nonverbal elements include posture, tone of voice, eye contact, timing, gestures, and emotional content. In written communication, too, there are aspects of context that are important to my understanding of the full message. The tone of the writing (scholarly or popular, argumentative or conciliatory, analytic or inspirational), the format in which it appears (there are crucial differences among a handwritten note, a mimeographed flyer, and an engraved invitation), the timing of its publication—all these may reveal information of even more significance than the words I read.

To listen actively, then, calls for an awareness of the content, feeling, and context of communication.

To respond accurately also requires a range of skills. First among these is empathy, the ability to understand another person's ideas, feelings, and values from within that person's frame of reference. This initial stance is prejudgmental. Empathy does not mean agreement; it does not require that I accept the other's point of view as my own or even as "best" or "right" for that person. The goal of empathy is to understand; as such it precedes evaluation. Evaluation and decision are not necessarily secondary in communication, but they are subsequent to accurate understanding.

A second skill for accurate response is paraphrasing. I show you that I understand your world from your point of view by saying back to you the essence of your message. To paraphrase is not merely to parrot, to repeat mechanically what you have just said. Rather, I show in my restatement that I have really heard *you*, that I have been present not just to your words, but to their wider meaning for you. In such sensitive paraphrasing I go beyond a simple assurance to you that "I understand" by offering a statement of what I have understood. You are then able to confirm that, in fact, I have understood you or to clarify your message so that my understanding may be more accurate. In either case, I have demonstrated my respect for you and for your message. It is important to me that I understand what you say, and it is to you that I come to check my understanding.

These, then, are the skills of attending: to listen actively, alert to the content, feeling, and context of communication; and to respond accurately, demonstrating that I have understood its meaning from the communicator's frame of reference.

We have thus far discussed these skills of attending in terms of their use in personal communication. But their relevance in ministry and pastoral reflection goes beyond the strictly interpersonal situation. The model of reflection we discuss here calls the minister and the community of faith to the use of these skills in pastoral decision making. Let us examine now how these skills are relevant to the processes of theological reflection in ministry.

Attending in Theological Reflection

The first stage of the pastoral reflection method is attending. The attitudes of listening and response, discussed by communication theorists as the skills of attending, are relevant as one approaches the three sources of religious information in the tripolar model. Active listening and accurate response are the skills required of the minister (and the community) who wishes to explore the contribution of each of these sources of information to the processes of pastoral decision making. The attitudes and behaviors of attending come into play, analogously, in attempts by ministers to assess the religious significance of information from each of the poles of the model of theological reflection we discuss here. For a reflective ministry, ministers must attend well to their own experience—in both the personal and professional spheres. The reflective minister is self-aware, having begun the lifelong process of self-knowledge and self-acceptance which marks both maturity and sanctity. Such self-awareness is the basis of that gradually developing confidence in the validity of my own (however partial) perceptions which is the mark of adult maturity. This maturity includes a recognition of, even comfort with, the ambiguities of my own interior life. Knowing the contradictions and confusions (as well as the convictions) that mark my own soul, I am able to stand with others in their pain and doubt and joy. And as I stand with them, I learn of the movement of God in the world today.

As I come to a mellow, even peaceful, awareness of how unfinished is my own grasp of truth, I need less to defend against persons and experiences which might hold new or challenging information. I am open to the truth that may reside, half-hidden, in my own and others' ongoing experience.

Such openness is a goal of Christian piety; it is a requirement of effective, reflective Christian ministry. My exploration of the world within can be enhanced by tools of listening and response. I can adopt a more "listening" stance in prayer, feeling less the need to fill my mind and heart with words and images, attempting rather to empty my heart and "wait on the Lord." Keeping a personal journal may help me chart the movement of the Spirit in my own life. In it I may keep track of how I spend the time and energy of my ministry, noting the persons, ideas, issues, and situations that enliven me to generous service and those that frustrate or frighten me. Or I may note my dreams or the images that come to me in prayer and reverie. These and other efforts to listen to myself are, we would argue, basic tools for a reflective ministry.

The attitudes and skills of attending enable the minister to learn from the experiences of others as well as from his or her own. The first (though not only) stance of the minister as she or he approaches another person is to listen well—for the word which God has already spoken in this person, for the word of gift or need that the person brings, for the word of challenge or confirmation that this person's experience holds for the religious Tradition. The communication skills of attentive posture, sensitive paraphrasing, and empathetic response can enhance the minister's presence and effectiveness in the myriad interpersonal situations of ministry—preaching and teaching, counseling and consoling, advocacy and planning, problem solving and conflict resolution. And it is in these experiences in their personal and professional lives that Christian ministers can listen for the religious information that will enrich their pastoral decision making.

Christian ministers are challenged today to develop more critical attending skills not only at the personal level, but also in regard to their religious Tradition and culture. Academic theology has become enormously more sophisticated in this century in its means of accurately attending to the sources of the Christian Tradition. The art and science of hermeneutics remind us that the interpretation of any document begins in critically attending to both text and context. In biblical studies, text criticism and form criticism alert us to the significance of the various contexts, the "life situations" in which the sacred texts were composed. Historians of Christianity teach the minister, likewise, to attend both to the decisions of Chalcedon, Augsburg, and Trent and to the cultural contexts of these ecclesial events. The reflective minister must also be able, in a more immediate setting, to discern the signs of the times (an imperative we discussed in Chapter Four) and to attend effectively to "the sense of the faithful," this community's grasp of the Tradition (as we saw in Chapter Three).

The third source to which a minister must attend is the culture and its various speakings: the media, the social sciences, the dominant cultural philosophy, the technology it prizes. The reflective minister pays attention to these cultural sources, expecting to find information that will influence pastoral decision making and even, in grace, to hear the word that the Lord speaks in this cultural context. Not every minister will be comfortable in dialogue with each of these cultural sources. Not every pastoral decision will require or benefit from information from each source. But the process of theological reflection in ministry will characteristically include information drawn from cultural sources. And the reflective minister will expect to develop some degree of personal competence in approaching the sources of cultural information.

Our colleague, John Shea, has written of this reemergence of listening as an element in theological reflection. In his "Doing Ministerial Theology" (1978) he discusses four ways in which the dynamic of listening and response is a part of the theological responsibility of contemporary ministers.

Many people today have only nonreligious language in which to speak of their ultimate questions and experiences. Ministers, then, need to be able to hear these religious dimensions of the secular vocabularies of the age—vocabularies of personal development, of justice and political reform, of ecological concern, of artistic expression, of belonging and community. They need to be able to recognize and respond to these religious experiences implicit in apparently secular concerns, sensitive to the ways in which these correspond to the traditional images in which Christianity has understood itself.

Second, ministers are called upon today to assist the larger community of faith in its transition from one theological self-understanding to another. In the Catholic community this is often seen (though, no doubt, too simplisticly) as the movement from a pre-Vatican II to a postconciliar theology. Similar transitions are being experienced in many Protestant circles as well. To assist these transitions ministers will need to listen well to the explicit religious questions (often expressed in the categories of an earlier theology) that arise among believers, to discern the deeper values of faith that these questions touch, and to respond in a manner that reflects both theological accuracy and respect for the immediate religious tradition which grounds the question.

Third, the minister must be able to hear the assumptions and presuppositions that lie behind the religious programs and pastoral decisions that are currently in effect. Alert to these underlying categories—even prejudices—of thought and value, the minister can assist a community of believers to come to more critical awareness of the frame of reference which guides their actions. These assumptions can then, themselves, be examined in the light of the gospel and subsequently reinforced or altered in order that the Church's action be consonant with its deepest understanding of its mission.

The fourth listening task of ministry today, as Shea sees it, is to discern this ongoing relationship between faith and action, the creative links between the Christian story and the concrete activities—individual initiatives, programs, institutions—which the community of faith undertakes in the world. If the third listening task invites a critical examination of the current "established" shape of ministry, this fourth invites an equally critical exploration of the new forms of Christian action that may be demanded as the Church moves into its future.

Attending as a Ministerial Asceticism

This new emphasis on attending as part of the pastoral reflection process can be described in terms of a religious discipline or asceticism. The skilled attentiveness in which reflection begins and on which it is grounded is itself an ascetical exercise in self-emptying. As Jesus Christ "emptied himself, taking the form of a servant" (Philippians 2:7; "servant" as attendant), ministers skilled in pastoral reflection empty themselves to allow space for revelation. Such a movement of emptying applies whether the person is attending to a scriptural text, a social movement, or stirrings within the individual's own life. This spirituality of *kenosis* (emptiness), little emphasized in an action-and-achievement-oriented culture such as ours, is required of every Christian. Such a spirituality, we have suggested, is exercised not only in prayer, but in the specific, learned behaviors through which we can more effectively empty ourselves of our own agenda at the first stage of a reflection. By our "own agenda" we mean those convictions and prejudices, hopes and distractions, which usually accompany us and can short-circuit the reflective process.

Attending, as experts in the helping professions insist and as our own experience confirms, is a very active and intense endeavor. A significant part of the challenge of attending, whether to a text or to another person, is this emptying out of our own agenda (our plans for this encounter or our fears about this issue) and a suspending of interpretation and judgment until we have thoroughly *heard.* The more we think we know about a person or a text as we begin a listening process, the less likely we are to really hear. Knowing in advance what this text *must* mean or what *this kind* of person needs, we likely fail to listen fully. When this happens our interpretations shape our listening; these prejudgments then function as prejudice.

A common event in counseling situations further illustrates how attending can be aborted. A counselee (or even a friend in conversation) will often initiate a discussion by sharing a concern that is not really the deepest question at issue. This "presenting problem" functions to test the waters, to see if the risk of sharing a deeper concern can be taken. An unskilled counselor or minister may rush in to solve this initial problem without continuing to listen for any deeper concern. Asceticism for the professional minister as listener requires a self-emptying which allows attending to be accurate and unprejudiced.

A special maturity is demanded in such ascetical attending. Listeners must have sufficient self-trust and self-confidence to set themselves aside for a time. Psychologically, this is possible only for those persons who know they will survive this period of receptivity. Such maturity allows us to listen nondefensively, relatively empty of our own needs and prejudices and genuinely open to the new and unexpected.

The spiritual discipline or asceticism required for skillful pastoral attending must be supported by an ascetical life style—a mode of living and working in which the professional minister is not *regularly* overbusy, tired, or distracted. (In Chapter Ten we continue this discussion of an "asceticism of time.") The hectic life style of many in ministry today works against pastoral reflection. Instead, it fosters fatigue and distraction, inhibits skillful listening, and disrupts effective reflection. The method of reflection outlined in this book involves suppositions not only about education for ministry, but also about spirituality and personal maturity.

Finally, the spiritual discipline which allows room and focus for effective listening can assist the professional minister to deal with the expectation (among one's parishioners and within oneself) that the minister be the "knower"—the person who has answers and can take a stand. Such a role is, in part, required of a minister, but to complement this role the contemporary Christian leader must learn the style of discerner and facilitator, a role which stresses listening, receptivity, and shared responsibility in discovering God's actions among us. Increased skill at attending to God's movements will help ministers be more comfortable with their own partial knowledge, more alert to "the signs of the times," and better attendants to the Christian community.

Additional Resources for Attending Skills in Ministry

Robert R. Carkhuff and his associates have been at the heart of the contemporary interest in systematic understanding of the behavior involved in effective interpersonal communication. His early *Helping and Human Relations: A Primer for Lay and Professional Helpers* (New York: Holt, Rinehart and Winston, 1969) is a classic in the field. The Human Resource Development Press currently publishes a range of materials useful to skills development in ministry; see, for example, Robert R. Carkhuff, R. M. Pierce et al., *The Art of Helping III* (Amherst, MA: Human Resource Development Press, 1977).

The work of Gerard Egan is central in the development of skills and skills training. In his *The Skilled Helper: A Model for Systematic Helping and Interpersonal Relating* (Monterey, CA: Brooks/Cole, 1975), we find a model for understanding the "helping" relationship that is relevant to many of the roles of the minister. Along with the accompanying workbook, *Exercises in Helping Skills* (Monterey, CA: Brooks/Cole, 1975), this book provides a systematic introduction to skills of listening, response, and confrontation. In his *You and Me: The Skills of Communicating and Relating to Others* (Monterey, CA: Brooks/Cole, 1977), Egan treats much the same material, but in a more popular style. This book can be used with groups of adult Christians interested in improving their skills of communication in their own lives and in ministry.

Other approaches to skills for effective listening include: Lawrence M. Brammer, *The Helping Relationship: Process and Skills* (Englewood Cliffs, NJ: Prentice-Hall, 1979); K. Bullmer, *The Art of Empathy* (New York: Human Sciences Press, 1975); A. P. Goldstein, R. P. Sprafkin, and N. J. Gershaw, *Skill Training for Community Living* (Fairview Park, NY: Pergamon Press, 1976); and A. Ivey, *Microcounseling: Interviewing Skills Manual*, 2nd ed. (Springfield, IL: Charles C. Thomas, 1977).

·6·

ASSERTION—A VIRTUE
IN PASTORAL REFLECTION

Assertion, in our life of faith and in pastoral reflection, represents the act of witnessing to the Word that we have heard. Aware of God's Word and its impact on our life, we feel called to announce this good news and to challenge others to hear and accept it.

There are different ways to bear such witness and a variety of means for sharing our conviction and insights. In Jesus' life, for example, his initiating the conversation with the Samaritan woman at the well is one kind of assertion; his driving the money changers from the temple is of quite a different kind. A consideration of assertiveness, as an interpersonal and theological skill, addresses the question of how the Christian effects this sharing. Assertiveness guides Christian witness so that it is neither weak and self-effacing (a nonassertive witness) nor intolerant (an aggressive witness). Assertiveness becomes a necessary theological skill as we recognize that our witnessing takes place in a context of others' convictions and insights and is itself a product of our own ongoing search. Not possessed of any final or absolute understanding, we must remain open and listening even as we witness. A witnessing that is closed to new information is not assertive, but disrespectful and intolerant.

The challenge, then—interpersonally and theologically—is to find a balance by which we can present our own insights and beliefs forcefully, without forcing them on others.

Two characteristics of the contemporary life of faith underscore the importance of assertiveness in theological reflection in ministry. The first is a keen awareness of religious pluralism. More and more today we realize that the differences between our beliefs and those of others are not simply the result of ignorance or deceit. The pluralism we experience among us reveals the partial (but real) access that each of us has to the truth. As we saw in Chapter Two, biblical scholars and Church historians remind us that this pluralism is not just a contemporary experience. The Christian witness of faith has been pluriform since the beginning, its diversity again a sign of the richness of its good news for humankind.

In the face of this religious pluralism—both within and beyond each community of faith—skills of assertion become especially crucial. Genuine religious dialogue can occur only when our values and beliefs are shared forcefully and respectfully with those whose lives are guided by other religious insights and convictions. Ecumenical dialogue is vitiated when participants can maintain neither a truly attentive nor an assertive posture. Dialogue requires more than stating our truth, pausing politely, and then restating it. Dialogue in this latter mode functions not as a mutual exploration, but as an attempt (usually fruitless) at indoctrination.

A second characteristic of the contemporary life of faith adds to the need for assertiveness. This is the reflective Christian's need to be not only a child of God, but an adult in faith. Mature Christians properly remain children of God throughout their adult lives. This child-parent relationship symbolizes the life we draw from God as well as our continuing dependence upon God's graciousness. Yet, as adults, Christians need to become more than heirs of the Christian Tradition, more than recipients of its riches. They need to participate in its handing on. And to participate fully as adult believers, they need to grow into full ownership of and responsibility for their faith. The Tradition *becomes* these adults as they accept it personally and become engaged in handing it on.

To achieve such a mature stance in faith, we need an assertive adult relationship with God. Adult intimacy with God demands assertiveness—a searching and challenging response to God's ambiguous presence in our lives. A model of such assertiveness is Jacob wrestling with Yahweh (Gen. 32). To struggle and "contest" with God is, to be sure, to enter into a threatening relationship. It is religious assertiveness, a virtue gradually developed in adult life, that gives us the courage to stay with the struggle "to the breaking of the day." With this strength of religious maturity we are able to wait upon the Lord's presence without falling into either extreme—a childish and nonassertive passivity or rebellious rejection. In this sense, assertiveness is both a skill required for theological reflection and a necessary virtue of Christian maturity.

Our discussion of assertion will begin in an examination of the interpersonal skills and proceed to an exploration of assertion as a stage in the method of theological reflection in ministry.

Assertion as an Interpersonal Skill

An ability to insert myself effectively into the larger world in which I live is one sign of adult maturity. This capacity for engagement beyond myself is key to success in love and work, in cooperation and conflict. It is this capacity for mature interaction that we call assertiveness. I am assertive when I go out to other people—to undertake an action, to offer my help, to express an idea or feeling, to meet my needs, or to defend my rights. Assertiveness marks many of the ordinary transactions of daily life: I invite you to join me for lunch; I close the door to keep out the noise from an adjoining room; I call to check on an error in my bank statement; I suggest a plan for how our ministry team might proceed. In each of these ways I take some personal action that influences my world or shapes my environment.

Assertiveness involves both attitudes and behavior. An assertive attitude depends on my appreciation of my own experiences, needs, and purposes. My experiences, needs, and purposes exist in a context of those of other people, to be sure. But a conviction that my own perceptions and goals are of value is basic to mature assertion.

To clarify the assertive attitude, it may be useful to distinguish it from two alternatives. If my characteristic attitude is that my own needs and views must always give way to others, that the value or validity of my own experience is not sufficient to merit consideration or preference in the face of other people's, my stance may be described as nonassertive. If, on the other hand, I function from the conviction that my own needs and views must always take precedence, my stance is more characteristically aggressive. The assertive stance is found along a more flexible middle range. I am basically convinced that my own needs and views are of worth. I am therefore willing to make these known, to express and pursue them with other people. These other people will themselves have ideas, needs, and purposes. My pursuit of my own goals acknowledges and respects this social context.

An assertive attitude can be expressed in a range of behavior. In many instances you and I can pursue our purposes in harmony, either functioning autonomously or in cooperative effort. In some circumstances, however, our purposes or needs will be in opposition. These situations of disagreement and potential conflict are the test of the assertive stance. In the face of conflict, the nonassertive person leaves the contest or "gives in." The aggressive person always moves to insure that his or her position shall win out. An assertive attitude permits more flexibility. There may be instances in which an assertive person will choose to set aside his or her position. In some other instances there may be a need to hold firmly to a position even in the face of valid and significant opposition. But the more characteristically assertive stance is to acknowledge the validity of both positions and to negotiate toward some mutually acceptable compromise, one which respects the core values of both parties even as it requires mutual accommodation.

An assertive attitude, then, involves self-awareness, self-disclosure, and self-worth. *Self-awareness:* in order to pursue my own needs and purposes I must be aware of what they are. I must *know* what I have experienced, what I think, how I feel, what I need, what I want to do. This knowledge is not likely to be full and finished; one indication of a nonassertive stance is an unwillingness to act until I am completely sure. Self-awareness is rather an ability to know where I am now, to be in touch with the dense and ambiguous information of my own life.

Self-disclosure: I am able to express my ideas, my needs, my purposes. This requires both skill and will. In terms of skill, I must be able to state my position. I must have the words to express myself appropriately so that I may be understood. This may bring up a question of vocabulary: Do I have the right words to express myself accurately in a variety of different situations? In some situations, using a technically correct theological term may be of critical importance to expressing my goal or my vision accurately. A woman in ministry, for example, may feel the need to speak of her work in explicitly theological terms in order that its pastoral relevance can be better appreciated by herself and others in the Church. To share myself with a friend or with my spouse I will need a well-nuanced vocabulary of feelings, one that goes well beyond "I feel good" and "I feel bad." There may well be other vocabularies important to my effectiveness in the daily tasks of my ministry—as a preacher, counselor, and planner. Many of us can improve our ability to function assertively by acquiring the vocabulary which enables us to express ourselves more appropriately in the various important contexts of our personal and professional lives.

A related skill of self-disclosure is concreteness—my ability to be clear and specific in communication. Self-disclosure can be thwarted by a retreat to speaking about "most people"; "everybody knows . . ." instead of "I think that . . ."; "most people want . . ." instead of "I want . . ."; "people have a hard time . . ." instead of "it is difficult for me to. . . ." To be clear in communication I will need to be able to speak in the first person, to say "I," to acknowledge my own ideas and needs and values. In addi-

tion, I need to be able to make statements that give specifics about my experiences (the concrete things that happen to me), my actions (the particular things I do), and my feelings and emotions. To tell you that "things
are going well for me in the parish" is to share some information, but not
very much. Communication goes further when I share specifics of the situation: "Over the past months I worked closely with the officers of the parish council in planning a lay leadership retreat that they conducted last
weekend. I enjoyed the give and take of the planning sessions and I felt
good about being able to work with them as peers in the retreat itself."
Again, to tell you "I really feel discouraged in my ministry" is a start. But
this self-disclosure becomes more concrete when I can describe the events
and actions that discourage me.

Self-disclosure requires will as well as skill. I must actually speak up,
express myself, communicate my ideas or values. Often this part of assertion is directly related to my sense of *self-worth*. Beyond knowing my own
insights, needs, and purposes, I must value them. This need not mean that
I am convinced that they are "the best." It means, rather, that I take them
seriously as deserving of examination and respect—from myself and from
others as well. My perceptions of myself and of the world have worth and
weight. By valuing them myself I contribute to the possibility of their
being appreciated by others.

The skills of attending discussed in the previous chapter and those of
self-disclosure considered here make assertive dialogue possible. With
these skills we are able to communicate accurately to one another and to
listen well. To sustain this assertive dialogue additional skills are important. We must be able to tolerate the ambiguity that arises as we attempt
to hold several (partial) perspectives in tension and we must be able to
deal with conflict.

Conflict is one of the dynamics of communication about which our rhetoric can be misleading. When we discuss the values of communication it is
most often upon the experiences of harmony and cooperation that we
dwell. Our focus on these positive aspects is understandable, even fitting.
But it can be misleading, leaving the impression that effective communication must avoid all disagreement, anger, or competition. The truth, of
course, is that such conflict is one of the inevitable and expectable elements of normal human communication. Whenever persons are in dialogue over a period of time, especially if matters of some importance are
involved, we can expect that differences will arise, disagreements will develop, and discord will emerge. The challenge of effective communication
is not to do away with all conflict or, worse yet, to refuse to admit its pres-

ence among us. The challenge is rather to develop ways by which we can deal with the conflict that will, expectably, develop as we attempt to stand in dialogue on issues about which we are each vitally concerned.

Skills of conflict resolution begin in the realization that conflict is normal and in the conviction that it need not always work against our shared purpose. Beyond this, conflict management requires skills of confrontation. Confrontation is used here with a meaning broader than negative interpersonal exchange. Skills of confrontation enable me to give (and receive) emotionally significant information in ways that invite further exploration rather than self-defense. My ability to confront others effectively, that is, in ways that lead to further communication, is enhanced when I am able to speak descriptively rather than judgmentally. Judgment is not irrelevant in communication, but premature judgment is likely to short-circuit the process of exploration and mutual understanding. Other skills that make effective confrontation more likely are the ability to accept feelings of anger in myself and in others and to show respect for other persons as I disagree with or challenge them.

These interpersonal skills necessary for mature assertion carry over into the dialogue which marks theological reflection in ministry.

Assertion as a Stage in Theological Reflection

When we have carefully attended to the information arising from Tradition, culture, and our own experience concerning a specific pastoral concern, we must bring the data into contact. This encounter may be a relatively peaceful one in which these data confirm and further illumine each other. But this meeting may also be a tense and challenging event. Whatever the style of encounter, the success of this meeting depends on each source being allowed fully to assert itself, however much this challenges the other partners in the reflection.

The trilogue that this assertion stage instigates supposes some mutuality among the partners. This mutuality is not a strict equality; the Christian Tradition and its information enjoy a position of privilege and priority in theological reflection. As Christians we believe that this revelation (even as shaped by centuries of interpretations and misuse) is normative: it reveals in a unique and exceptional fashion God's will for us and for human history itself. Yet the Tradition pole of this model of reflection itself represents an assertive and often tense relationship: Scripture as interpreted by believers in specific historical and cultural contexts; Church history as guided both by God's unfailing presence and human, fallible decisions. Karl Rahner's formula for the theologian's twofold task regarding Tradition—to preserve and to overcome—highlights the ambiguity of the assertive stage of reflection. In a theological reflection in which cultural and personal influences on a specific concern are acknowledged and in which the plural interpretations of a rich and varied religious Tradition are attended to, this stage of assertion will provide the opportunity for "preserving and overcoming" the Christian Tradition. Whether we are addressing the question of social justice (and different forms of slavery and oppression) or the shape of Christian ministry (and the changing role of the laity), the assertion stage allows and demands that we respond both to the revelation we find in our Tradition and the human, culturally influenced expressions which have shaped our Christian past. In this model of reflection the Tradition is seen neither as merely a human product nor as an undiluted divine deposit in human history. Its being both divine and human makes theological reflection continually necessary and exciting.

The benefit for contemporary ministry of a theological reflection involving an assertive engagement of information from these three sources is highlighted when we consider the alternatives. A return to our tripolar image makes this clear. In a reflection in which Tradition simply interprets experience, without consideration of cultural information (whether through neglect of the exegetical sciences on the interpretation of Scripture or of psychological understanding of the human person), the conclusion will be fundamentalistic. Second, in a reflection which is simply a dialogue between cultural information and individual experience, the conclusion (and, of course, the reflection itself) will not be specifically Christian, although it may be "religious" in the sense that it reflects cultural or "civil" religious themes. Finally, a reflection which is essentially a dialogue between the Christian Tradition and cultural information (whether philosophy, philology, or science), to the neglect of personal experience, will tend to yield conclusions of a more theoretical nature. Ministerial decisions arising from such a reflection, overlooking—as they do—the experience of the persons involved, suffer the likelihood of being arcane, sterile, or simply irrelevant.

We can note other ways in which the mutuality necessary for theological reflection can be lost. An individual or a community can be so influenced by its own experience (as, for example, in the awareness among some women of the patriarchical and misogynist tendencies in the history and current life of the Christian Church) that they feel forced to reject the Tradition. Impressed by these negative experiences, these persons may be unable to listen to the Tradition in its other (and sometimes contradictory) testimony on women, personal worth, and human liberation. Thus, they

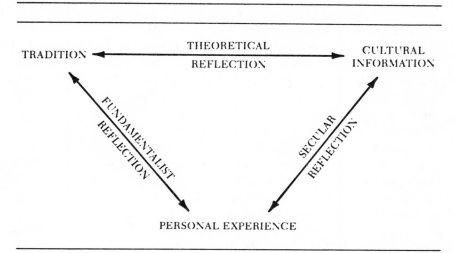

Figure 8

break off the dialogue, the theological reflection, concerning women and Christianity.

But the dialogue can be broken in other ways as well. A person or a community may be so impressed with a teaching drawn from the Tradition (as, for example, the recent Vatican official statements concerning the moral evil of contraception) that the testimony of married Christians—their experiences of marriage, sexuality, and parenthood—seem irrelevant. Assertive dialogue is not possible in such a situation. Attending only to one source of information (Tradition), and listening to only part of the information available there (focusing exclusively on the statements concerning contraception and neglecting the Tradition's conviction of the importance of personal conscience), the reflection fails.

In our first example it is experience that aggressively disrupts the assertive conversation of theological reflection. In the second, Tradition functions as the aggressor. Culture, too, can be an aggressor in theological reflection, especially when its influence goes unrecognized. A powerful and painful example of this is found in the history of Christian missions. For centuries well-meaning European and American missionaries brought with them not only the gospel but Western cultural values and prejudices as well. Only recently have we become aware of the cultural imperialism implicit in many of our best missionary efforts. If the unwitting influence of our cultural biases undercuts many of our missionary efforts, the contemporary awareness of this influence awakens a more careful theological reflection on means of sharing the good news of Christianity with those of non-Western cultures.

We began this chapter with a discussion of two factors in contemporary Christian life that highlight the need for assertion in theological reflection today: our growing awareness of religious pluralism and the increasing maturity of Christian laity. A third factor is significant as well: the understanding of ministry as a corporate endeavor, a task shared within the community of faith. When the minister stands alone, in an autonomous role as sole authoritative leader within the community, there is less need for attitudes of assertion and skills of interaction. But when, as today, the reflections and decisions which shape the Christian community are seen as necessarily collective, as growing out of a greater mutuality and consensus, assertion becomes a crucially important virtue. This virtue of assertion and its attendant skills stand at the heart of the processes of ministerial decision making, to which we now turn.

Additional Resources for Assertive Skills in Ministry

Robert Alberti and Michael Emmons and their colleagues at Impact Publishers have made important contributions to the literature of assertion theory and skills. Their *Your Perfect Right: A Guide to Assertive Behavior* (San Luis Obispo, CA: Impact, 1974) was an early work on this topic. Since then, Alberti has edited *Assertiveness: Innovations, Applications, Issues* (1977) and Stanlee Phelps and Nancy Austin have published their influential *The Assertive Woman* (1975), both published at Impact. *The Assert Newsletter,* published quarterly, is an up-to-date resource on assertiveness technique and research.

Valuable work on assertion skills also appears from Research Press in Champaign, Illinois. Of significance here are: A. J. Lange and P. Jakubowski, *Responsible Assertive Behavior: Cognitive/Behavioral Procedures for Trainers* (1976); Sherwin B. Cotler and Julio J. Guerra, *Assertion Training: A Humanistic-Behavioral Guide to Self-Dignity* (1976); R. P. Liberman, L. W. King, W. J. DeRisi, and N. McCann, *Personal Effectiveness: Guiding People to Assert Themselves and Improve Their Social Skills* (1975).

Additional resources that avoid the superficiality and extremism of some assertion literature are: B. G. Berenson and K. M. Mitchell, *Confrontation: For Better or Worse* (Amherst, MA: Human Resource Development Press, 1974) and S. A. Bower and G. H. Bower, *Asserting Yourself: A Practical Guide for Positive Change* (Reading, MA: Addison-Wesley, 1976).

Finally, a resource useful in the review and critique of assertion literature is C. Kelly's chapter, "Assertion: The Literature Since 1970," in J. W. Pfeiffer and J. J. Jones, eds., *The 1977 Annual Handbook for Group Facilitators* (LaJolla, CA: University Associates, 1977), pp. 264–75.

·7·

DECISION MAKING—
GOAL OF REFLECTION IN
MINISTRY

J. Gordon Myers

The purpose of theological reflection in ministry is "to allow faith perspectives to influence personal and social life" (Shea, 1978). The end product it pursues is not religious insight but insightful religious action. The process of reflection will, characteristically, bring about a deeper appreciation of the religious tradition and the ambiguous power of its history and its symbols for life today. This deeper appreciation leads to a "traditioned awareness," a religiously sensitive understanding out of which religiously effective action can flow. The critical test of any method of theological reflection *in ministry* is not simply the quality of the insight to which it leads but the quality of the ministerial action which is its fruit.

Decision Making in Ministry

We turn now to the third stage of the method of theological reflection in ministry—the stage of decision making. It is in this crucial stage that we make a move often neglected in more academically based theological reflection—the move from insight to action. How does the insight we have gained from consulting the three sources of religious information, listening attentively to their ambiguous data, engaging in an assertive dialogue of mutual illumination and critique—how does this insight influence choices and lead to action? We suggest that it does so through processes of decision making and planning. In this chapter we shall outline one method of decision making that may be useful in moving the minister or the ministerial team through theological insight to pastoral action.

It is, of course, not only at this final stage of the method that decision is required. All along, choices are made: what issue to consider, what sources of information to consult, how to consult, when has there been "enough" consultation. But we focus on decison making here as those processes that bring theological reflection to practical, corporate action.

We also do not mean to suggest that the earlier stages of the method bring one to a clear insight from which pastoral action is "deduced." The stages are not that distinguished; often the insight becomes clear only in and as the decision is made.

Ignatius Loyola, himself an advocate and model of reflection in action, observed that the problem is not so much in making a decision, but in getting ready to make a decision. The model and method of theological reflection discussed in this book is, from one point of view, designed to bring believers to this readiness for decision in a fuller and more complete fashion. The tripolar model alerts us to where we should look for religiously significant information. The two early moments of the method—gathering the religiously significant information in the attending stage and evaluating it in the assertion stage—bring us to a readiness to plan. In the third stage this readiness is moved into concrete decision and practical action.

A conviction that undergirds our method of theological reflection is that the important and complex pastoral issues of our day are most effectively resolved through the corporate reflection and joint action of Christians who, while possessing different skills and life experiences, act out of a shared faith. We believe that the current shift from the minister as solitary decison maker to the ministry team or leadership group will continue. This shift is hastened by new awarenesses in both theology and the management sciences.

The challenge of communal action is alive in the Church today. Christians who are unhappy with the impersonality and bureaucracy of official Church life seek out informal groupings of like-minded believers with whom they can share their religious life and hopes. Parishes experiment with neighborhood subgroupings in an attempt to nourish a sense of belonging and mutual commitment among members. Women and men in ministry establish collaborative work teams and peer-support groups. Religious congregations stress anew the value of their life in common as a sign of the gospel promise of community and struggle to make this sign a practical reality in their local houses and institutions. Denominations attempt to develop structures to encourage the exercise of shared authority and collegial responsibility among bishops, ministers, and people. And theologians work to develop an ecclesiology that takes seriously the implications of the Church's understanding itself as the people of God.

Acting collaboratively for the sake of others is an acknowledged value in management circles as well. There is growing evidence that leaders, acting as lone decision makers, become increasingly inadequate in proportion to the complexity of the task before them. In addition, decisions that are "handed down" are often met with suspicion or indifference—attitudes that may contribute to a serious lag in implementation. Commitment to a decision grows in proportion to direct involvement in the problem-solving and planning process. We will work harder and more creatively to implement decisions that we have helped to make.

Yet our conviction of the necessity of collaboration in ministry is cautioned by our experience. For many, the ideals of community and collaborative ministry, once a source of renewed enthusiasm, have now become a source of frustration. The goal of community can seem distant from the facts of Church life one experiences; the task of communal action too monumental; the gap between the rhetoric and the reality too broad to be bridged. Many religious persons who have given themselves generously over the past decades to the effort of collaborative ministry come away now with a sense of frustration, failure, and confusion. The words of a colleague in ministry express it well: "Maybe I'm just tired, or maybe I'm getting old, but for me these days real collaboration seems a very distant goal. People are so different in what they expect from one another; communication and planning takes so much time. Sometimes I feel that I have been lied to! Team ministry may be good as an ideal, but there is so much confusion in the effort. Community may be a great image of the Kingdom, but I'm not sure it is a possibility in the life of active ministry today."

This experience is not unique among ministers today. Lacking the methods, skills, and strategies which might enable us to translate our religious values into concrete group action, we find ourselves with new vision and heightened expectations—but with few tools of implementation. Combine high expectations of the success of collegial decision making with little previous experience or skill in coordinated action. Add very complex and value-laden issues of faith and justice. For many in ministry, the result is the atrophy of both motivation and effectiveness. The collegial venture collapses.

Ministering persons coming together today to plan pastoral action on a particular concern are vulnerable to poor performance. This vulnerability is demonstrated by the following four-phase movement characteristic of many pastoral planning groups of good will.

Case Study I—When Collaboration in Ministry Fails

University General Hospital is a large urban hospital with a dozen or so full-time chaplains representing a variety of denominations. Due to the hospital's central location, the emergency ward offers care to a large and growing number of women victims of the crime of rape. However, there exists no pastoral counseling component to the ward's medical services. The chaplains, skilled in basic one-to-one life-coping skills, look forward to gathering together as a problem-solving unit to establish a pastoral care program designed to offer assistance to these women.

Phase One

We join the chaplains at one of their initial gatherings. They are for the most part unskilled and inexperienced at group problem solving and pastoral planning. Their identity as a group and a corporate understanding and acceptance of their task remain unclear. Basic assumptions concerning expectations and the feasibility of their project go untested. This vagueness causes some anxiety, yet their excitement with this new pastoral venture cushions the initial tension. The enterprise is begun.

The chaplains continue their meetings together. After just a few sessions they begin to uncover the complexity of their situation. They still have not articulated a clear goal nor arrived at a common acceptance as to whom they wish to minister: The individual woman? Her friends and family as well? Some chaplains wish to include local neighborhood clergy in their planning effort. Others suggest that politicians and law enforcement representatives join in. Needs and solutions are prematurely and inappropriately mixed. The result is confusion and a series of false starts.

The task is indeed multifacted and value-laden. The chaplains experience themselves as distant, not connected either to one another nor to the vital data needed to resolve their pastoral dilemma. Questions concerning the needs of women victimized by rape are not asked. Essential psychological and sociological information from the culture is not collected. Important religious information remains unavailable.

The chaplains' identity as a working group continues to be clouded. This confusion is reinforced by the absence of a structured plan of action. These factors combine in an acceleration of stress. The earlier enthusiasm which tempered anxiety initially now gives way and new questions emerge: Will we fail? Will we be embarrassed by our efforts? Will our plans be accepted by our colleagues and superiors in the hospital setting? Trust in self and in the group's performance and achievement begins to erode.

Phase Two

Their confidence shaken, the chaplains begin to look outside the planning group for working models of successful team performance. They hope that their own feelings of incompetence can be overcome by fixing attention on positive reference groups working on similar issues. Too often, this does not prove useful. They find no positive reference groups. Rather, the chaplains discover that other pastoral care teams are similarly confused, or so different in their composition or context that their models do not "fit" the current problem. Having lost touch with their own resources, and discouraged by the absence of "answers" outside themselves, they sense that failure is imminent.

This fear of failure has a debilitating effect upon the group. Members report feelings of doubt, deficiency, and difficulty in imagining a future program of pastoral care. The chaplains feel disempowered and draw back from group participation. Confidence erodes further. The group becomes aware of its poor performance; working together becomes a high risk endeavor; further isolation results. Questions of relatedness now require serious attention within the group. Public embarrassment is a real possibility.

Phase Three

The situational strains now become interpersonal conflicts. Anxiety is high. Normal coping skills freeze. The group begins to attack the designated leader and, then, one another. The response within the group to the emergence of this interpersonal conflict can lead either to escalation or repression. With escalation, members of the chaplains' group begin to adopt entrenched positions. Communication moves from concrete and specific language to abstract and global generalizations. The communication process then becomes distorted by win-lose manipulations that destroy attitudes of trust and cooperation and replace these with suspicion, exploitation, and coercion.

With repression, the conflict is denied. The group takes on a social weightlessness characterized by boredom since it must avoid approaching any issue or question that may bring the conflict to the surface. Members act flat and listless; the group is only indifferently productive. The feelings of frustration and anger that cannot be dealt with in the group itself are often displaced onto other persons and situations in members' lives. The effort to fix blame for the group's difficulty can result in scapegoating. Soon there is a movement to return to a more traditional autocratic style of leadership and decision making. The group now wants a leader who will decide for them.

Phase Four

At this point the chaplains are no longer a problem-solving and planning team. Much of their potential for effective ministerial action has been destroyed. They have identified themselves as inadequate to accomplish their given task. Frustration and anger yield to despair. Distress within the chaplains' group spills over into more general hospital care situations and experiences. Thus, the cycle of distress continues at a broadened level.

We can diagram this four-phase cycle of team breakdown.

CYCLE OF TEAM BREAKDOWN

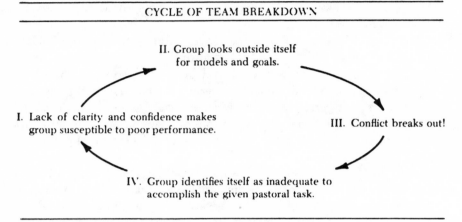

II. Group looks outside itself
for models and goals.

I. Lack of clarity and confidence makes
group susceptible to poor performance.

III. Conflict breaks out!

IV. Group identifies itself as inadequate to
accomplish the given pastoral task.

Figure 9

Two themes emerge here: privacy and vagueness. The former was demonstrated by a deepening separateness within the chaplains' pastoral planning group and an increasing distance between them and the data most needed to resolve the pastoral issue being pursued. The chaplains became reclusive, sealed off from essential cultural resources, the richness of the Christian Tradition, and the present lived-faith experience of one another.

The theme of vagueness emerged as they had no plan of action, no problem-solving methodology. Task identity and decision-making processes remained unarticulated. Essential resources went unnamed. The chaplains' group was adrift from the beginning. Anxiety grew out of control. They became a casualty. Their pastoral mission failed.

Case Study II—A Strategy for Decision Making in Ministry

St. Philip's Church is a medium-sized parish in an urban setting in a large American city. A strength of the parish is its ability to gather together reflection groups made up of core staff leaders and parish members. These groups commit themselves to a process of reflection and planning in order to enhance the pastoral life of their local church.

One such pastoral working group has been meeting regularly for several weeks. Their task is to design and implement a pastoral plan focused on the needs of older persons in the parish. Earlier sessions have been devoted to exploring various sources of information concerning life in the mature years. There are senior parishioners in the planning group and other elder members of the parish have been consulted. Group members have read in gerontology, they have discussed their own hopes and fears of aging, they have contacted others engaged in ministry among seniors, they have read prayerfully in Scripture, they have consulted other religious resources. We join them now in the decison-making stage of their larger reflective process.

Preliminaries—The Organization of the Working Session

At the outset of this planning session the group has found it useful to choose a convenor rather than a chairperson. This, they have found, helps them to avoid the trap of casting only one person in the leadership role. Instead, the convenor encourages the leadership to emerge and, perhaps, to shift spontaneously over the course of the meeting.

It is the task of the convenor to note the various responses the group makes as it moves through the stages of the planning strategy. Group members have used this process previously in their efforts in pastoral collaboration; the convenor is able to count on their knowledge of the stages of the process and their willingness to hold themselves to the discipline of the strategy.

Step One: Identifying and Defining the Pastoral Concern

Group members know from experience that a vaguely stated pastoral concern leads to an abstract and, therefore, ineffective plan of action. Their prior reflection together on the questions of mature age has enabled them to agree now on a concise and clear statement of pastoral concern.

> *Pastoral Concern as Stated:* "How to enable the older persons of St. Philip's Parish to live in greater awareness of the religious significance of their own lives."

The group is now in a position to move more deeply into an analysis of the question, identifying concretely and specifically the elements that are a part of the initial concern. Again, as a result of their earlier work at the attending and assertion stages of the method, they are able to identify a dozen or so underlying needs. After discussion, these are combined into the following three statements, judged to represent central challenges to religious significance in the mature years.

1. The need to gain a sense of self-worth independent of economic productivity and social role:
   "I am more than what I do."
   "My personal worth does not depend solely upon my usefulness to others."
2. The need to interpret the significance of my own life:
   "Of what use has my life been to myself and others?"
   "What are the meanings inherent in my own life story?"
3. The need to come to terms with the changes and losses of mature age:
   "I tire more quickly and cannot get around as much."
   "So many of my cherished friends and companions have died. I feel alone and abandoned."

The convenor gains acceptance of these three need statements and then assists the group to rank the needs to determine upon which the group will focus initially. The group agrees, after some brief discussion, to start their planning efforts with the second statement: the need to acknowledge and appreciate the meaning of one's own life. The remaining need statements are held for subsequent planning sessions.

The first step of the planning process is now complete. Group members have agreed on an issue of pastoral concern, identified three important needs that underlie the concern, and chosen to focus on one of these needs in particular. In the process they have avoided some of the usual traps into which groups fall at this early stage. They have avoided confusing needs with possible solutions—"older people need more inexpensive vacation trips"; "the seniors in the parish need more social activities based in the parish hall." These are really tentative solutions articulated as needs. The group has also avoided making accusations of blame: "I don't think most people in this parish really care about us old folks"; "the pastor has too much say over how parish funds are spent."

Step Two: Formulating Goals—Imagining a Preferred Future
At this stage the group determines its goals, based on a vision of the future, a future in which this need has been met adequately. The convenor asks

them to imagine St. Philip's Parish five years from now, acting at its best in assisting elders in the process of finding and celebrating the meaning of their lives. There are several ways in which these images of the future can be elicited. For our example here, the members spend twenty minutes or so in quiet, noting the various images, symbols, hopes, and actions that express for them a preferred future for older persons in the parish. These individual contributions are posted on large newsprint sheets so that they can be shared at a glance by the whole group. A discussion of these individual images then follows in order to clarify them and make them more concrete. These individual contributions are then grouped in categories and set into general goal statements using the formula, "By 1986...." Goals that are somewhat complex may be specified more exactly by listing subgoals as well. Statements of anticipated outcome help to give substance

---

GOAL STATEMENT

By 1986 St. Philip's Parish, acting as a Christian community, will assist senior parishioners to affirm and respond to the religious significance of their own lives by:

Subgoals	Anticipated Outcomes
A. fostering a process of "life review" culminating in the religious reminiscence of those in mature age.	1. Eighty percent of the senior members of the parish have participated in communication skills training courses. 2. Fifty percent of the senior members of the parish are involved in life style support groups. 3. A particular methodology for theological reflection upon one's life is used throughout the parish (demonstrated in sermons, used in adult study groups, etc.). 4. Fifteen percent of the yearly parish budget goes directly to the maintenance of these educational and "life review" activities for senior members.
B. Developing and practicing those symbolic and ritual actions which, empowered by God, enable the liberation of older persons from the biases of the "American Way."	1. Parish liturgies will take place twice ayear to ritualize the retirement passage for both the retiree and spouse. 2. During three "Elder Sundays" a year, senior parishioners will share reflections upon their lives with the parish community as a whole. 3. Home visitations, prayer, and discussion groups will be meeting throughout the parish. 4. There will be a regular weekly home liturgy program for those senior members who cannot get out.

Figure 10

to the goals and move, as well, toward concrete objectives that can be used later as criteria for evaluation.

With the statement of these general goals, the planning group has set its direction. In the next step they give time to an articulation of the religious rationale that substantiates their work.

Step Three: Statement of Mission

Step Three involves a further reflection upon the goals, in order to identify the values that these goals are meant to express. These value statements are then brought together in a coherent formulation which serves the planning group and the parish as a statement of mission. In the case under consideration here, the mission statement could read, in part, as follows:

> The Christian community of St. Philip's Parish believes that with mature age can come new possibility for spiritual growth. It is in the Christian of advancing years that a lifelong experience of faith and the psychological resources of maturity can combine in an affirmation of the spiritual significance of life. We commit ourselves, therefore, . . .

Step Four: Setting the Year's Program Agenda

The planning group now takes each goal statement, along with its anticipated outcomes, and formulates programs. The programs are the specific activities and identifiable means through which the goals will each be achieved. An initial movement in such program development involves the group in a process of brainstorming, an attempt to generate as many possible alternative means to achieve each desired goal. The goal of the brainstorming phase is to stimulate creative approaches to the goals at hand.

In a typical brainstorming session each goal, in turn, is written on a large newsprint sheet, prefixed with the phrase "how to":

> "How to foster a process of 'life review' culminating in religious reminiscence for those in mature age"

Group members are then invited to suggest ways in which this might actually be achieved at St. Philip's over the coming year. In order to encourage creativity in these initial suggestions, steps are taken to minimize the group members' fear of the rejection or negative evaluation of their ideas. During this brainstorming phase, critical judgment is suspended. This means:

BRAINSTORM . . . . . Nobody says no.
BRAINSTORM . . . . . Nobody says "that will never work."
BRAINSTORM . . . . . Nobody says "that is a dumb idea."
BRAINSTORM . . . . . Nobody says "that has already been tried."

A premature movement into evaluation should be avoided at this point. All ideas are welcome; each suggestion is noted.

As the brainstorm segment moves to a close (a time limit or an end to creative ideas in the group), members work for a clearer understanding of the suggestions that have been made. They continue to suspend critical judgment; the goal here is rather to gain clarification or to note similarities among the suggestions.

After this period of clarification, there is movement into evaluating the options. The processes of critical judgment now come into play. The planning group has suggested a range of possible actions to achieve a particular goal. Further inquiry has clarified these options. Now the group moves to evaluate the suggestions in order to select those most useful. They apply the following criteria to each of the action items:

· Will this action clearly and directly contribute to the achievement of the goal?
· Is the action feasible in light of internal and external constraints—that is, are time, money, resource people, facilities, etc. available?
· Does the action item have "reach" and challenge to it? Will it take us beyond where we are already?
· Is the action congruent with our mission statement?

Usually, some additional discussion and clarification are required at this point, as the group builds on the initial suggestions until they become programs that can be implemented.

Step Five: Final Shaping of the Program Agenda for Implementation
The concrete recommendations for action, designed to move toward the preferred future articulated in the goal statements, are reaching final statement. In this step the members of the planning group bring the action recommendations into final form and address themselves to the question, "Who is to do what by when?"

At this stage in the process, the use of a pastoral planning worksheet can assist the group to focus their attention upon the final details of the shaping process. At the top of the worksheet the particular goal upon which the group is working is written. The second line on the worksheet consists of four headings, each designating an important element in implementation:

Column 1, "Action Recommendation." In this column, the particular plans of action intended to achieve the goals stated at the top of the worksheet are listed.

Column 2, "Necessary Collaboration." This column identifies those team efforts required to achieve the plan. These interpersonal or intercommittee arrangements should be agreed to prior to listing.

Column 3, "Measures of Achievement." In this column are listed the evidence or data which will publicly verify the accomplishment of the stated program.

Column 4, "Remarks." This column can be used in a variety of ways. For instance, the names of those responsible for the particular program can be listed here.

With the completion of the set of worksheets, one accompanying each goal of the planning group's program, the program agenda is complete.

Step Six: Establishing a Schedule for Ongoing Assessment

It is a reasonable expectation that some adjustments will be required in the program as it unfolds. Original recommendations and plans should remain open to influence by new information and by learnings generated in the operation of the program itself. Therefore, the planning group sets a schedule of evaluation meetings over the program year. As these dates near, it may become clear that one or another of them is not necessary. But early scheduling helps to assure that evaluation will be taken seriously and that the program will remain flexible and accountable to the mission statement and the goals.

In this discussion of the planning effort at St. Philip's, we have described a structure for group planning that has proved successful in a variety of ministerial and educational settings. Clearly, there are other strategies and planning designs that can be used to good effect. Our goal here has not been to identify this strategy as the sole vehicle of pastoral planning but to exemplify how the skills and strategies being developed in management disciplines can function as resources in pastoral decision making and, thus, in the larger processes of theological reflection in ministry.

PASTORAL PLANNING WORKSHEET FOR 1981–82

Goal I. Subgoal A. "By 1986 St. Philip's Parish, acting as a Christian community, will assist senior parishioners to affirm and respond to the religious significance of their own lives by: (A) fostering a process of 'life review' culminating in the religious reminiscence of those in mature age."

(1) *Action Recommendation*	(2) *Necessary Collaboration*	(3) *Measures of Achievement*	(4) *Remarks*
To conduct three weekend communication training workshops involving one hundred senior parishioners.	Adult education committee and parish budget committee	Proper assessment of communication needs established; workshops conducted; evaluation by participants.	J. P. Burns responsible
To develop and implement "life-review" programs facilitated by the elders for other elders and their families.	J. P. Burns, adult education committee, and local seminary faculty team	Ten trained elders have each facilitated five "life-review" programs; evaluation of effectiveness made by participants and local seminary faculty team.	L. T. and B. D. Roy responsible
To purchase a parish van, equipped with special rigging for elderly passengers, for the exclusive use of this project.	Parish budget committee and L. Jones (purchasing agent for parish)	Van purchased and in operation. Following equipment installed: armchair seats, special lift for easy entrance and exit, emergency health equipment, air conditioning.	Brenda McCarthy and Alice Jones responsible

Figure 11

Additional Resources for Decision Making in Ministry

The work of Robert Carkhuff, available from the Human Resource Development Press in Amherst, Massachusetts, is germinal in this area of theory and skills, as in others. Especially useful are his *The Art of Problem-Solving* (1973) and *How to Help Yourself: The Art of Program Development* (1974).

Gerard Egan's contribution to the specification and description of the stages of the decision-making process is found in *Change Agent Skills: Model and*

Methods for the Renewal of Systems (Monterey, CA: Brooks/Cole, in press) and in the accompanying workbook.

Recently, there have appeared several useful handbooks that give step-by-step analysis of the processes of group decision making. Significant among these are: Harry Fagan, *Empowerment: Skills for Parish Social Action* (New York: Paulist Press, 1979); R. Kaufman, *Identifying and Solving Problems: A System Approach* (LaJolla, CA: University Associates, 1976); L. Sperry, D. Mickelson, and P. Hunsaker, *You Can Make It Happen* (Reading, MA: Addison-Wesley, 1977); D. J. Warren and R. B. Warren, *The Neighborhood Organizer's Handbook* (Notre Dame: University of Notre Dame Press, 1977).

Two additional highly recommended resources are James M. Hardy, *Corporate Planning for Non-Profit Organizations* (New York: Association Press, 1972) and Alvin J. Lindgren and Norman Shawchuck, *Management for Your Church* (Nashville: Abingdon Press, 1977).

PART IV

Reflection in Ministry—
The Method in Action

"Everybody talks about theological reflection, but how is it done?" In Part IV we present three different instances of this method of ministerial reflection in action.

James Young, in a very personal style, reflects on his own journey toward a ministry to divorced and remarried Catholics. Peter Henriot uses the method to examine the relative absence, and then the recovery, of the notion of social sin in recent Catholic awareness. James Whitehead explores a question of contemporary spirituality—the use of time in the development of a Christian life style.

In these examples of reflection on three different aspects of Christian life and ministry—divorce, social justice, personal sprituality—we hope to demonstrate both the utility and the flexibility of this approach to theological reflection in ministry.

·8·

DIVORCE AND
THE CATHOLIC TRADITION

James J. Young

The American Catholic community has only recently been forced to reflect theologically about divorce and remarriage, because there was very little divorce among Catholics until the mid-1960s. The Christian Tradition that Christian marriage should be a commitment by man and woman "for better, for worse; for richer, for poorer; in sickness and in health; until death do us part" was largely accepted and lived out by Catholics until the social upheaval of the sixties began to tear American marriages apart. Historically, the Catholic Church had worked mightily through its parishes, schools, and helping agencies over the past hundred years to help millions of dislocated immigrants find economic and social stability in this alien land; that determined strategy seemed to have borne great fruit during the American familistic period of the 1950s when Americans were marrying at the youngest ages in the century, having the largest families, experiencing the greatest economic security, and divorcing at very low rates.

Then it all seemed to begin to unravel. First one heard of a friend's marriage breaking up, and then another, and then another, until by the early seventies it seemed there was an epidemic of marital instability, as much among Catholics as the population at large. Social researchers continue to puzzle over the reasons for the rise in the divorce rate in the sixties and seventies. It was obviously a time of social change touching deeply every aspect of American life, and at such times of social unrest there are always those who fix on the theory of moral decline, spreading degeneracy, weakened moral fiber, a widespread rejection of traditional values. Other observers began to speak of the institution of marriage undergoing escalated change in an overwhelmingly industrialized society.

They saw marriage influenced by new human concerns about friendship and fulfillment. Some spoke of a crisis of rising expectations in marriage and pointed out that widespread divorce did not indicate a turning away from marriage, but that the evidence suggested large numbers of people abandoning what they saw as unsatisfactory relationships and searching for more fulfilling partnership in marriage. Whatever the causes, divorce has now touched every American family, and the whole discussion has become intensely personal for most Americans and especially for Roman Catholics.

The Reflection Begins

Divorce and remarriage among Catholics became a focus of concern for me not so much by personal choice as by the fact that divorced Catholics came to me for help. I had come to Boston's downtown Paulist Center in 1971 after some marriage counseling study and work in Chicago. (I had studied community mental health at the University of Chicago, and was interested in nonprofessional helping approaches, and especially the ways in which the Church's ministry could be more closely attuned to mental health concerns.) Three women who approached me saying that "the Church should do something for all of us divorced Catholics" were my first encounters with these hurting, searching divorced Catholics. This contact began a process of theological reflection for me which has continued for over a decade.

Attending to My Own Experience

My own reaction to the overture of these three women was, at first, reluctance. I realize now that I was deeply influenced by a "sickness" model that had been part of my counseling training, which immediately typed these divorced persons as "sickies" or "broken wings," the kind of people you could expect to be demanding but not easily helped. Yet I was very much a post-Vatican II pastor, convinced that the Church should reach out to the neglected and suffering. I don't think I had ever heard the word *divorce* in my seminary classes, and I think I assumed that, on this issue, as on so many others, the Roman Catholic Church was hopelessly outdated. The personalistic theology of the times had influenced me greatly and I felt the Church should act to relieve the guilt and alienation the divorced experienced. Early on I believed that the Roman Catholic Church should change its discipline on divorce and remarriage and bless the second marriages of divorced Catholics. Looking back, I can see now my early response was largely structural and legal, assuming that changing law to permit second marriage would salve the pain of the divorced. I obviously undervalued the Roman Catholic Tradition; similarly, I undervalued the depth of divorce pain in assuming a new marriage would relieve it. Even though I was an unmarried person myself, I recall that I saw very little value in a single existence.

Two persons entered the process at this point and forced me to reflect more deeply and suspend some of my preconceived notions. The first was Dr. Bob Weiss, a Harvard researcher and an expert on divorce. He read about our group in the newspaper and called seeking to find out what was going on. Bob was involved at that time in developing an educational group-support model through Harvard's Laboratory for Community Psychiatry as a way of providing help for divorced persons independent of the traditional therapeutic models. Weiss believed that most divorcing persons were normal people caught in a time of severe situational distress, who might even be said to look "sick." He believed the sickness model of some of the traditional helping professions would only reinforce their own loss of self-esteem and increase their dependence on others. He saw the need for new approaches to challenge the health and competence of the average divorcing person by offering them insight, concrete strategies for change, and group support at a shaky time of transition. His "Seminars for the Separated," an eight-week adjustment model, grew out of this concern, and he and I soon discovered that, although we came to the divorce issue from distinctly different backgrounds, we shared a general outlook about the potential of the divorcing person. Weiss also became my mentor, directing me to the serious sociological and psychological literature on the issue, and became a ready consultant as I attempted to understand better this complex phenomenon. He was most valuable in reinforcing some of my basic helping instincts while broadening my horizons about the complex issue of divorce.

The second important person to enter the picture was an experienced canon lawyer, Father Jack Finnegan, then Professor of Canon Law at Pope John XXIII Seminary in suburban Boston, and a judge of the Marriage Tribunal of the archdiocese of Boston. Jack was known to some of the people who came to our group from his tribunal experience, and became a ready speaker at our meetings and a valuable ally. Jack began opening up for me the richness of the Catholic canonical tradition, and he gave me wider bearings in the changing canonical and theological response of the Church to marriage and divorce generated by the Second

Vatican Council. Bob Weiss and Jack Finnegan remain important resources to me to this day.

When I first became involved in this ministry, people would often ask
me, "Father, were your parents divorced?" "No," I would say, "my parents had a very happy marriage for forty-three years before my father died
in 1974." I feel now that I was deeply influenced by the success of my parents' marriage, and this helped me accept the Christian ideal of perma-
nent marriage as something humanly achievable. I also have two married
sisters and a married brother, and all of them continue to have lasting first
marriages. I began to appreciate, too, that even though I was very much
an enthusiastic proponent of the more pastoral Church of Vatican II, I was
also a deeply traditional Catholic in my bones—someone who loved the
Catholic people and their long-standing approach to being a Christian in
the world. I began to discover that I was by disposition much more a re-
former than a revolutionary. I was concerned in helping divorced persons
find peace and a place within the Catholic community. I also had a keen
realization that change in the Church could not be brought about instan-
taneously by actions or demonstrations of power. I recognized that the
Church and the Catholic people change slowly, and that I was in for a
long involvement on this issue. I can recall, after about two years, grasping
the increasing complexity of the issue for myself and the Catholic community, experiencing the deep resistance change in this area engendered, and
realizing that change would be slow in coming. My theological reflection
was deeply influenced by this realization because it introduced some real
patience into my reflective process.

I also became keenly aware that I was being deeply affected by the divorced persons I was meeting. They were lively, critical, deeply religious,
searching. They gave me a real sense of a creative *sensus fidelium* at work
on this issue, and my continuing dialogue with them kept me grounded in
the real and prevented me from getting trapped into academic blind
alleys. They offered continuing support to me as their minister, and continuing challenge. I also began to be enriched by the professional pastoral
experience of many other priests, ministers, and other helping profes-
sionals. I was obviously not the only person in the Churches grappling
with this complex issue at the grass roots, and my theological searching
brought me into contact with many stimulating partners in reflection. An-
glican priests, Jews, orthodox church lawyers, feminists, lawyers, journal-
ists—all enriched the varied and ecumenical dimensions of the reflection
for me.

I began to devour everything I could read on the subject. There was a growing body of Catholic literature available, especially by canonists. Monsignor Stephen J. Kelleher made provocative contributions from within the Catholic Tradition by his writings calling for a whole new Catholic approach. I began to learn that the helping professions were no quicker than the Church in coming to terms with this issue, and that serious research was not well supported financially. I discovered how difficult it was to get hard data on the problem. The Census Bureau gave out raw data which required some sophistication to interpret, and there were no data on religious affiliation and divorce. Those of us working within the Churches were usually working from educated guesses about the extent and causes of the problem.

Attending to the Tradition

I began to come to some sense of the long Christian Tradition on the issue. Catholic Scripture scholarship, freed after World War II from a doctrinal straitjacket, opened up for me the real meaning of the divorce sayings of Jesus and the way the early Christian community attempted to be faithful to the Lord's call for radical permanence in marriage, while at the same time compassionately permitting second marriage in certain situations where the good of persons demanded a new marriage. I began to get a better understanding of the patchwork quilt of early Church Tradition; here an Orthodox canon lawyer, Dr. Lewis Patsavos, was extremely helpful. I began to learn about the Catholic canonical tradition, and why the Western Church diverged from the East in the early Middle Ages and developed the discipline forbidding second marriage, which we live with today. Through this inquiry I came to a rich sense of the pluriformity of the Christian Tradition, along with a sense of how little we know of much of this historical development.

After 1950, Catholic theologians, especially Edward Schillebeeckx and Bernard Häring, began to trace the history of marriage theology in the Western Church and began to develop the covenantal, personalist theology of marriage which became the teaching of the Church at Vatican II in the Constitution on the Church in the Modern World (*Gaudium et Spes*). The covenant theology articulated here seemed to project a new vision of Christian married life very much consonant with the modern expectations of a more satisfying interpersonal relationship. The bishops at Vatican II used language such as "the intimate partnership of married life and love" and "the friendship distinctive of marriage," and spoke of a dynamic love relationship growing day to day. Some observers saw the marriage theology of Vatican II as a great leap forward in Catholic understanding, a kind of Magna Carta which it would take the Catholic people several generations to absorb and to translate into new forms of married life.

The description of the marriage relationship as a contract had dominated Catholic marriage theology since the Middle Ages. This was an advance for the time, since it highlighted mutual responsibility and rights in marriage and was a notable advance for women; but today this view of marriage seems to deal too much with the "outsides" of marriage and not enough with the "insides." For people today it is not enough to have a legally correct union in the eyes of the Church and state. Rather, they want a marriage that contributes to personal development and provides them with friendship, happiness, and satisfaction—a relationship that opens them more to their own growth potential, the growth potential of each other, and opens them as well to others around them in their world. In searching to find ways of religiously describing this positive, modern development in marriage expectations, the bishops at Vatican II drew on the most ancient "marriage talk" in its Tradition: the biblical description of God's relationship to the Israelites as a loving husband to his bride—a marriage covenant. The Hebrews had described their God's care for them in all the intimate, touching, beautiful language that husband and wife use in describing a strong marriage relationship. In using the language of married love to talk about God, the Hebrews achieved a richer grasp on the nature of God's love and at the same time saw that the relationship of wife and husband to each other should be like God's relationship to them— faithful, tender, forgiving. God formed a "covenant" with the Israelites, and husbands and wives are asked to form a covenant with each other and with God. God's self-revelation to Israel over the centuries as a loving spouse raised Jewish and Christian expectations of marriage. These decidedly more personalist categories seem to relate much more creatively to our contemporary understanding of marriage than the older more legal categories, helping us describe in traditional biblical language the "insides" of marriage.

Attending to Cultural Information

From anthropology and sociology, I began to get a sense of the radical transformation the institution of marriage was undergoing in our contemporary world. Family historians helped me understand the dramatic impact the twentieth-century idea of companionate marriage had on the institution of marriage. When men and women expected little from their marriage relationships, they were obviously more stable. As moderns began to look for personal satisfaction and fulfillment, their chances of being dissatisfied in marriage escalated. The medical revolution and longer life expectancy suggested to some observers that we were substituting divorce for death—the ordinary solution to an unsatisfactory marriage. Our contemporaries are having a hard time living so long together, expecting so much of each other. Others suggested that our appetite for personal happiness in marriage is outstripping our capacity to attain it. The feminist revolution with its expectation of equality in marriage created exciting new freedom for the married woman, yet also created enormous strain for spouses, producing serious questioning of accepted roles and shaking established ways of relating and dividing tasks.

Movement into the Assertion Stage

One could interpret the profound change in contemporary Western marriage in positive terms, seeing an evolutionary thrust contributing to greater personal development and mutual respect within marriage, or one could see traditional bonds in decay. This analysis prompted me to evaluate how much of contemporary Christian marriage was founded on Christian values and how much was a cultural wrapping. Could marriage be altered in dramatic ways and still be Christian marriage? Some futurists were predicting a kind of serial monogamy for moderns with several different marriage partners adapted to certain periods of one's life. Would moderns still value lasting marriage? Or could the emerging form of marriage give space for a greater realization of personal dignity? Whatever the view, divorce was an index of the coming apart and decline of marriage as we knew it, with divorcing partners searching for new forms of marital happiness.

It began to come clear to me that there were two distinctive ways of dealing with marital breakdown in the Church of Jesus Christ. The Western Church of which I am an heir is restrictive about second marriage, attempting to radically uphold the Lord's call to permanence in marriage by refusing to permit second marriage after divorce. The Orthodox and each of the mainline Protestant Churches accepted the same obligation to institutionally serve the Lord's call to permanence, but then insisted that other gospel values suggested compassion in the case of failed marriage and an acceptance of some second marriages for the good of divorced spouses who could not sustain a life alone. It became increasingly clear to me that both were authentic responses to the teaching of the Lord, with each shaped by distinctive cultural and theological forces. I began to see that it was too facile to say that the Western Church should abandon a thousand years of tradition and readopt the practice of the early centuries, jettisoning in the process a thousand years of canonical development which had obviously borne great fruit in the life of married persons in the Western Church. I also became worried by the prospect of greater Catholic permissiveness on divorce and remarriage leading to more divorce and remarriage. At a time when the institution of marriage was undergoing rapid, profound change, I began to ask myself, "Shouldn't the Catholic Church move slowly?" It should do so not so much to preserve its teaching and authority, but to protect persons reliant upon the Church who need support for their values and personal beliefs in a time of threat.

Assertion Leads to New Insight

Somewhere around this time Jack Finnegan began to insist that the burden of proposing and supporting the permanence of marriage should not be laid upon the ministry with divorced Catholics, but rested rather with the Christian education of the young, marriage preparation, and marriage enrichment. He felt that divorce ministry was by nature a ministry of compassion which had to focus intensely on the personal recovery of the individual, and might have to make certain compromises with teaching and discipline in order to be faithful to the deeper responsibility to reconcile and heal individuals. Yet, because marriage teaching, preparation, and enrichment are not yet strong ministries, it is important to move cautiously as we develop better institutional service of the gospel values. We began to see divorce ministry providing a very needed corrective to the harsh rejection of the divorced in the past in the Catholic community, yet insisting that our service to permanence in this new cultural situation was only beginning to take on the inventive new forms needed to support our values.

Insight Leads to Action

Once I had resolved some of these issues through theological reflection, I surprisingly began to see that there was a great deal we could do for people pastorally after divorce that in no way required a changing of teaching and discipline. I began to see that we had become overly absorbed with legal or structural solutions, while our pastoral care of the divorced was still in its infancy stage. We needed to put much more energy and imagination into developing programs for personal recovery after divorce and support systems to help women and men achieve a new single autonomy after divorce. I recognized that modern society pushed the divorced all too often into hasty remarriages that soon failed, with sad consequence for large numbers of people. I began to see that the Catholic community was uniquely suited to provide a system of support and common values which would help the divorced Catholic achieve the personal recovery they needed before rushing into a second marriage. I also saw the need to support the numbers of men and women who simply did not have the option of remarriage.

The more I began to look kindly at the Tradition and cautiously at the contemporary experience of marriage and divorce, the more I began to get in touch with the ambivalence among the people I was serving. I began to discover that, if one became a strong agent for change, one will gather around oneself those committed to the same vision. But the more I began to grasp the complexity and ambivalence of the issue, the more I seemed to detect the complexity and ambivalence within the people I was serving.

I began to discover that they were deeply concerned about permanence in marriage and that the last thing they would wish on anyone was a divorce. There was no romanticism about divorce among the divorced. They worried about their children and they did not want the Church to back off its traditional service to permanence, especially for their children's sake. Somewhere in this period I had a real breakthrough in my own insight about this pastoral ministry, a breakthrough which I feel was a direct result of so much theological reflection on the issue. I began to see that what was most important to the divorced Catholic was not so much approval for a new marriage but reconciliation to the community and access to Holy Communion. I began to realize anew what a eucharistic people Catholics are, and how the divorced person—often isolated and lonely after the breakup of a marriage—craves the community and belonging which Catholics enjoy at the eucharistic assembly. I saw that, as much as they would like to have Church recognition for their new marriages, they could get along without it as long as they could share that intimate communion with God and with each other which the Eucharist offers Catholics. This reconciliation to the Eucharist of remarried Catholics required no change in teaching or discipline on marriage; rather, it was a fruit of the new eucharistic theology of Vatican II which proposed the Eucharist as primary sacrament of reconciliation. The believing community of the divorced began to teach me that a way of living in the present was possible—offering healing, personal support, and community belonging now—without changing Church discipline and teaching on marriage. I also began to see that, out of this process of reconciliation, with the reinclusion of so many divorced and divorced/remarried Catholics in the community, might emerge a solution which none of us could foresee at this time. I began to grasp the time-conditioned nature of our doctrinal and legal solutions and began to sense the possibility of a future solution that none of us could now fathom.

It became so clear that the pastoral care of the divorced implied no compromise with our traditional values on permanence in marriage, but rather made them even more attractive. So often in the past we had served our values with a harshness and strictness that alienated those whose response was imperfect. I began to dream about the possibility of a community which could lovingly propose permanence and work diligently to hand on the value to the young, support those struggling to build lasting marriages, while all the time reaching out daringly and compassionately to offer Christ's healing to the brokenhearted after divorce. I began to have a sense that we would find some way of providing public Church acceptance of sincere remarried persons, short of the liturgical blessing the Western Church reserves for first marriage, and that such an acceptance would be possible the more we felt confident about our service to permanence and our care of the divorced.

The Stage of Decision Making

Since the mid-1970s, I have made decisions based on this theological reflection which presently position my ministry. An initial decision was to do all I can to expand the Church's care of the divorced. I travel, write, and speak about the shape of this ministry, working especially in training lay leadership and educating clergy and other religious leaders to collaborate with lay persons in this ministry. The models of pastoral care, especially the support group, need continuing experimentation and refinement.

In November 1975, divorced Catholics from about twenty states and Canada gathered at Boston's Paulist Center for a conference on divorce ministry. So many new and exciting developments were occurring all across the two nations that the conferees unanimously agreed to establish a network organization to connect the ministry and facilitate its continuing development. The North American Conference of Separated and Divorced Catholics was born at that meeting. NACSDC promotes education for clergy and laity through regional conferences and a yearly national conference at the University of Notre Dame. It promotes the sharing of resources through its newsletter, *Divorce*, and its own resource packets. It helps facilitate communication among interested Church and secular organizations and agencies. Most of all it concentrates on the development of lay leadership and the emergence of divorced Catholics as ministers one to another in the local Church community. The organization is still based in Boston at the Paulist Center; Sister Paula Ripple, F.S.P.A., serves as its executive director and I serve as its chaplain. Sister Paula and the lay board (fourteen divorced Catholics representing the twelve episcopal regions of the United States, and two representing Canada) continue to give visibility to the needs of divorced persons through the two nations.

In addition, I continue to work closely with other interested groups in the Catholic community, such as the canon lawyers and theologians. I have developed a sense of converging expertise. Presently our divorced-Catholics organization is working with the Canon Law Society of America on a paper on divorce ministry which would sketch the relationship of personal recovery to the annulment process. It deals with such issues as readiness to enter the annulment process and readiness for a second marriage. Through the Catholic Theological Society of America, we are working with Catholic theologians on the eucharistic theology behind the internal forum solution, i.e., the reconciliation to the Eucharist of remarried Catholics whose marriages have not been blessed by the Church. I have also been in dialogue with Catholic Charities and National Family Life, trying to work collaboratively with other interested Church agencies in furthering the development of this ministry. I think such collaboration is possible because we have focused on pastoral care and have avoided getting embroiled in theological and canonical disputes. I have a renewed appreciation of the many-faceted resources and viewpoints on the Catholic community, and the great value in building allies on this sensitive issue.

Five years ago I made a significant decision not to become involved full time on this issue. One does not serve any cause by becoming overinvolved in it, especially when a question is as absorbing as this one and the need is as great as it is around the divorce issue. I took a position in 1975 directing the pastoral program at a theology school, and in 1978 became Director of Formation for the students of the Paulist community. I soon discovered that working with young ministers in a generative, building capacity was a marvelous complement to the healing ministry with the divorced.

Seminary work brought me into touch with positive, idealistic, growing edges in the life of the Church, while the ministry to the divorced so often burdened me with the pain of the Church's inabilities to respond. I found this mix of ministries most mutually enriching.

I began to see myself as a Catholic priest continuing to raise questions and promote discussion about the issues surrounding the Church's ministry to the divorced, rather than becoming the advocate of one solution. I began to see that the process of development, once underway, needed participants theologically and ecclesially well grounded to guide the development, rather than advocates bent on forcing a certain, all too time-conditioned solution upon the Catholic people. I found myself becoming more and more patient, learning patience especially from the divorced people who were such a witness of healing patience to me.

References

Finnegan, John. "Marriage Law," in *Chicago Studies* 15 (1976):281–304.
————. "The Pastoral Care of Marriage," in *Origins* 5 (August 28, 1975).
Häring, Bernard. *The Law of Christ.* Cork, Ireland: Mercier Press, 1963.
Kelleher, Stephen. *Divorce and Remarriage for Catholics?* New York: Doubleday, 1973.
Patsavos, Louis. "The Orthodox Position on Divorce," in James J. Young (Ed.), *Ministering to the Divorced Catholic.* New York: Paulist Press, 1979, pp. 51–64.
Schillebeeckx, Edward. *Marriage: Human Reality and Saving Mystery.* New York: Sheed and Ward, 1965.
Weiss, Robert. *Loneliness.* Cambridge, MA: M.I.T. Press, 1973.
————. *Marital Separation.* New York: Basic Books, 1975.
Young, James J. *Growing Through Divorce.* New York: Paulist Press, 1979.
————., Ed. *Ministering to the Divorced Catholic.* New York: Paulist Press, 1979.

·9·

SOCIAL SIN: THE RECOVERY OF A CHRISTIAN TRADITION

Peter J. Henriot

On May 4, 1969, James Foreman, former head of the Student Nonviolent Coordinating Committee, interrupted regular worship services of the fashionable Riverside Church in New York City. He dramatically read to the congregation and brought to the wider attention of the religious community in the United States the "Black Manifesto," a demand for five hundred million dollars in "reparations" to be paid to blacks in this country for damages from past exploitation by American whites. The drama of this incident raised numerous questions across the nation. *Emotionally:* What were our feelings in the face of such rhetoric and unusual circumstances? *Sociologically:* Where was "brotherhood" and "sisterhood" in the light of such a black/white confrontation? *Politically:* What were the power implications of this demand? *Economically:* Was a demand for so much money realistic, and how would the money be used? *Ethically:* Was it really just to speak of an obligation to pay reparations? *Theologically:* What were the implications of directing this demand to the American religious community?

Many churches and synagogues were not prepared to deal in any substantive theological fashion with this demand. Leaders of various religious groups appeared to fall back on either outright rejection or confused acceptance. Yet, at its deepest level, the "Black Manifesto" raised important issues of conscience on the meaning of community, of repentance, and of social sin.

The vocabulary of social sin began to appear in the religious dialogue of the 1960s on questions of racism, poverty, and war and peace. But this discussion of social sin is something for which many of us were not prepared. As Christians, we belong to a tradition whose roots include the powerful pleas of Isaiah and Jeremiah for social justice. We also live in the memory of Jesus' critique of the injustices of his day and his concern for the poor and the outcast. Yet the idea of social sin was experienced by many in the sixties and continues to be experienced today as alien to this rich moral tradition. In this chapter we will use the tripolar model to trace the re-emergence of this notion of social sin in recent Catholic social teaching and moral theology.

Attending to the Experience of Injustice

Social sin is a category that attempts to recognize and to interpret the structural injustice experienced in contemporary society. This systemic injustice may take several forms:

A structure that violates and oppresses human dignity is unjust. For example, a welfare system which operates as though its premise were that the poor are somehow bad and therefore not to be trusted or given any say in what happens to them is a structure that violates the dignity of the poor. It is an oppressive structure that makes victims out of those who are obliged to follow its patterns and customs. Minimal payments, excessive surveillance, demeaning interviews, a punitive philosophy, the ever-present fear of cut-off of funds—all of these elements of the structure of a welfare system offend human dignity. We would refer to personal action of such a character as sinful. But the action of the structure is even more effective in violating the poor and powerless than is the action of an individual person.

A situation that promotes individual selfishness can be called unjust. For example, zoning and tax systems that allow individual citizens to preserve their privileges at the expense of the poor and the powerless provide situations that support individual selfishness. Such restrictive legislation makes it impossible for the less economically advantaged to seek more desirable surroundings outside of the central city. A tax system which places a disproportionate burden for the public good upon lower- and middle-income people (e.g., through numerous loopholes for higher income brackets) is clearly a system that promotes the individual selfishness of some citizens in our society.

Another example is the financial-income policies widely practiced in this country. Investments are made either to obtain quick gains (profits) or long-range gains in investment value (growth). Both reward persons with capital for steering clear of monetary involvement involving risk or growth of other persons' interests, such as an investment in the poor, in minority banks, in development of cooperative businesses that have slower but more consistent growth cycles when managed properly. Therefore, the poor cannot obtain loans from banks or the government as easily as big interests. Similarly, mortgage payments and insurance are harder for low-income persons to obtain than for richer persons, making it next to impossible for the poor or lower middle classes to enjoy a decent life according to normal standards. Unionized, blue-collar working people are paid low wages in many areas, which do not enable them to maintain any real security. They are constantly afraid of price increases, layoffs, new minority members entering their unions, and of changing neighborhoods, which the financial establishments will see as signs of declining property values (often a self-fulfilling prophecy caused by the financial institutions themselves). Hence, they bitterly resist integrated neighborhoods, low-income housing programs, welfare expenses (which crimp their already limited incomes), union minority training and membership programs. Meanwhile, the more affluent, who have invested capital with appropriate tax write-offs and protection privileges (for the good of the economy, investment must be encouraged), pay proportionately less taxes to social improvement programs when they have much more wealth. These are all interlocking structures that define an environment as unjust.

The complicity or silent acquiescence in social injustice is an act of injustice. This occurs when one is *aware* of unjust structures or situations but refuses the responsibility of trying to change them when capable of doing so. There is no way to ascertain how often this may occur in a society as complicated as ours. Probably, people are ignorant (inculpably) of their indirect participation in arrangements that cause evil to other human beings. An example would be the problem of purchasing farm products produced by large agribusinesses or farmers who utilize farm laborers at below-living wages, who do not provide decent housing or provisions for the migrant farm workers, who lobby in state or federal legislatures against allowing such people to unionize (a right guaranteed by Catholic teachings as early as the encyclical *Rerum Novarum* of Pope Leo XIII). Continued patronage of such producers by buying their products rewards their system of doing things and supports the oppression of farm workers.

These interlocking and pervasive patterns of injustice question the adequacy of Christian moral understanding to the complexities of modern social and economic experience. The Church's attempt to face this challenge has drawn upon both cultural (especially upon developments in current sociological understanding) and theological resources.

Attending to the Culture

The theoretical framework of contemporary sociology recognizes the in
fluence of social realities that goes beyond the individual. Sociologists speak
of the reality of social structures and emphasize that in modern society
these structures—systems and institutions, socio-economic-political arrangements—are highly influential. For example, in their classic discussion of the sociology of knowledge in *The Social Construction of Reality*
(1967), Peter Berger and Thomas Luckmann stress the objective and historical fact of the institutions and structures of society. These institutions
and structures are external to the person and persistent in their reality and
influence, whether or not they are recognized. In order to understand social institutions and structures, it is necessary to understand the process
involved in both their genesis and their maintenance. Berger and Luckmann summarizes this process in three moments of a dialectic:

Externalization—the process by which we superimpose order on our
environment in order to make it more meaningful and more useful.

Objectivation—the process by which the product of our externalization
is experienced as an autonomous reality confronting the individual as an
external and coercive fact. ("That's the way things are"; "That's the way
'they' want it"; etc.)

Internalization—the process by which structural reality is passed from
generation to generation in the course of socialization. (Newcomers and
children are taught how to live by existing ways so they can survive.) "Society is a human product. Society is an objective reality. Man is a social
product" (p. 61).

According to Berger and other sociologists, the structures and institutions of our society are neutral neither in constitution nor in operation.
This is extremely important. Structures and institutions essentially embody value relationships, reflecting the values of those who construct
them. Once created, these structures and institutions in turn influence
these values. A political structure such as a representative assembly, an
economic structure such as a tariff on certain imported goods, an educational structure such as compulsory schooling to the age of eighteen, a
legal structure such as the bail and bond system, a technological structure
such as the modern communications media, familial structure such as a
matriarchy—all of these embody meaning and value and reinforce and
promote the same. As such, these social structures have tremendous
human potential for good and for evil. Properly functional social structures provide greater and better opportunities for human growth available

to all groups in society. Unjust and unresponsive social structures hinder this human growth and freedom, thereby oppressing human dignity.

Attending to the Theological Tradition

Since the 1960s there has been considerable theological reflection on the meaning of sin, reflection which helps to throw light on the issue of social sin we are treating here. Biblical scholarship has shown that, in its more refined scriptural treatment in John and in Paul, *sin* is used in the singular and implies a state or condition. This sin belongs more to the inner person, the actor, than "sins" or acts of "transgression." It is a description of what flows from the character or quality of a person. The theologian Louis Monden (1965) has discussed this by describing sin in terms of "option." Sin is thus seen primarily as a stance, an orientation, a direction that we give to our life, rather than a single act or deed or incident. This stance is manifested and reinforced in the day-to-day actions—or failures to act— that go together to define our lives.

Another theologian, Piet Schoonenberg, offers a helpful insight into the power of sin when he explains how man is "situated" in sin, how sin can pervade our whole being. According to Schoonenberg (1965), this "situation" is integrally related to our capacity to choose freely:

> The freedom of the will does not mean that the will acts without any connection with what the whole person is, does and feels. . . . Modern individual and social psychology makes us realize to what extent the decision of our will is influenced by our way of seeing concrete reality, by the spontaneous reaction of our drives, and, hence, also by the knowledge and motivation which we may receive from others—in one word, by our whole former education and present environment. All of this constitutes the ground on which, and the raw materials with which, our free decision takes shape (p. 111).

In this context, Schoonenberg speaks of the power of bad example, especially its power to obscure values and norms. Each individual, previous to any responsible decision making, has a need for moral formation; without this moral formation, individual virtue is very difficult, if not impossible. A simple and clear example is that of a child born into a family that lives from theft or prostitution, a family in which the norms of honesty and chastity are not observed and where these values are not alive or operative. We are reluctant to say that such a child seriously sins, because he or she has no possibility of making the choice of value. Yet, there still is harm which is done to others by the child, the harm which is done since the child has no chance of growing as a human person in this area of virtue. This situation of sin is perceived by Schoonenberg as analogous to the situation of "original sin." For the wider sin, the "historical sin" of human-kind, is seen as a complex fabric of unjust social structures and many individual sins reinforcing each other. In this way a social milieu or general situation of sin for the whole human family builds upon itself. The social situation of original sin is basically a situation in which individual sinfulness is facilitated.

Theological emphasis upon sin as situation—which at once relates more adequately to the findings of modern biblical scholarship and modern psychology—challenges traditional moral theology to move away from its *act orientation* (described later in this chapter) to an approach of actor orientation. With this understanding, the social implications, indeed the social incarnations, of sin are more readily placed in perspective.

The possibility for social incarnations of sin has been explained well by the Canadian theologian Gregory Baum, who suggests that we take seriously the category of the *demonic*. The demonic means that the evil at work among us cannot be reduced simply to individual human malice. Rather, there are processes and structures among us that multiply evil and spread destruction vastly exceeding the harm that can be done by individual choices. Evil establishes itself profoundly in human history and is perpetuated by forces which, in part at least, seem to escape immediate personal control. Baum (1971) points to the political order and notes that the behavior of certain institutions is not wholly determined by the will of those who belong to these institutions nor even by those who exercise authority over them. Institutions seem to have a life of their own: they can multiply good, with their beneficial effects comparatively independent of personal generosity or the lack thereof; or they can multiply evil, with tendencies adversely affecting the lives of many people with a malice far surpassing the malice of the individuals involved. According to Baum, "The system, the apparatus, the machine does harm and inflicts suffering even against the good will of the men who serve it" (p. 120).

Baum is not directing his remarks against institutions as such but is simply pointing to the social consequences of institutional life and the possibilities of the demonic to transcend individual personal fault. This description of social sin is extremely important in our complex technological society with its highly interdependent domestic and global responsibilities. Poverty, hatred, discrimination, prevention of political and social participation on the part of some in the decisions that make the society we live in—it is to these realities that the notion of social sin must now be applied by Christians who would be apostles of the Kingdom in their own time.

Assertion: The Reemergence of a
Christian Understanding of Social Sin

The reemergence of social sin as a significant category of Christian social analysis involves a dual movement of assertive engagement with the Christian moral tradition. To return to the language of Rahner, it has been necessary to *recover* the deep roots of the Christian awareness of corporate and structural evil; it has been necessary to *overcome* or at least complement several tendencies of recent Christian moral thinking that have contributed to the atrophy of this awareness.

The Underdevelopment of the Notion of Social Sin

The Catholic bishops in attendance at the international synod in 1971 acknowledged this blind spot in Christian life:

> How is it, after 80 years of modern social teaching and two thousand years of the Gospel love, that the Church has to admit her inability to make more impact upon the conscience of Her people? . . . The faithful, particularly the more wealthy and comfortable among them, simply do not see structural social injustice as a sin, simply feel no personal responsibility for it and simply feel no obligation to do anything about it. Sunday observance, the Church's rules on sex and marriage tend to enter the Catholic consciousness profoundly as sin. To live like Dives with Lazarus at the gate is not even perceived as sinful (Preliminary Document to *Justice in the World*, #7).

How can we account for this absence of the category of social sin in moral thinking and the pastoral awareness of many Christians? The "religious" person in our society is often equated with the "morally upright" person. But individual morality is what we focus on, not social morality. An individualistic spirit appears to prevail in both the theoretical framework of Catholic moral theology and the practice of moral virtue. We can suggest several reasons for this.

First, traditional moral theology was act oriented rather than actor oriented. Arising especially out of the practice of the Sacrament of Penance, this has meant a concentration upon concrete actions, specific instances, and individual events. As a consequence, the general quality of the person who performs the acts—his or her orientation, habits and attitudes—has not been emphasized. Traditional moral theology tended to be concerned with the deed performed rather than with the sort of person who performed the deed.

The act-oriented approach does not help to delineate a broad range of responsibility for me as a Christian because, with so much emphasis on what I "should do," there is not enough emphasis on what I "must be." Take the example of an ethic of measuring personal success and deriving great personal satisfaction from the acquisition of material goods (closely related to the traditional concept of the personal sin, "avarice"). A serious evil in affluent circles in the United States today, this attitude is translated into action as frequently through omissions as through acts. There arises a serious social manifestation of excessive attachment to one's personal possessions (shown, for instance, by refusal to support tax reform measures). This seems to be a case of social sin, large-scale hardness of heart, which results from an aggregate of individual self-concern. But the act orientation of traditional moral theology does not provide much assistance in guiding individual Christian consciences here.

A second and related reason for the theological underdevelopment of the category of social sin has been the traditional doctrine of "inculpable ignorance." Traditional moral theology has always taught that a person does not sin if he or she is ignorant of the seriousness of the deed that he or she performs. People would be culpable, or guilty, if they were in fact ignorant through their own fault, for example, if they did not make a reasonable effort to enlighten themselves. But if they were ignorant through no fault of their own—truly inculpable—then there would certainly be no sin involved, even if they did something very seriously wrong in the "objective order." Since it is presumed that individuals can be knowledgeable of individual actions and their consequences, "inculpable ignorance" would not be considered very common among individual actions. But the intricate complexities of the modern social scene would make "inculpable ignorance" much more common and hence social sin much less frequent.

Third, much recent theology in both Protestant and Catholic circles has been influenced by existentialist and personalist philosophies. This has resulted in what Johann B. Metz (1971) has called the "privatization" of theology, a serious loss of the social dimension of the Christian message. As a consequence, there is a significant "apolitical" thrust in theology in general, and in moral theology in particular.

A fourth reason why social sin has not been emphasized seems to be the distinction drawn between *legal* and *moral*. Although the two are often confused, they are definitely not identical, either conceptually or in the practical order. Indeed, it is possible to have something that is completely legal according to all proper laws, but is definitely not moral in the sense that it does not render justice. An example would be a system whereby highly exorbitant interest is charged on loans according to the law, even though it does great injustice to those lower-income persons obliged to pay the interest. Persons who "follow the law" might consider themselves to be highly moral, yet they may fail in justice. This legalistic mentality has frequently prevailed in religious discussions of social justice, hindering the development of a social morality that shows appreciation of social sin.

The Recovery of the Notion of Social Sin

The return to prominence of this category of social sin in contemporary Christian life is the result of influences both in our religious tradition and in our culture.

Certainly the experience of the Second World War heavily influenced European and American theologians to consider the social dimension of theologial thought and Church action. Something much more profound than Rauschenbusch's "Social Gospel" was needed in the face of the war's horrendous moral evil and the complicity of so many "good" Christians. Bonhoeffer's search for a "religionless christianity" and his willingness to face "the cost of discipleship" gave rise in the postwar years to searching analyses of the relationship between the gospel and the modern social order. Key to that search was an emphasis upon structures. Recognition of the power of structures was given in Pope John XXIII's *Mater et Magistra*, in his discussion of "socialization" (#59–67). The relation of structures to sin was subsequently developed in a remarkable passage contained in the 1965 document of Vatican II, *Gaudium et Spes:*

> To be sure, the disturbances which so frequently occur in the social order result in part from the natural tensions of economic, political and social forms. But at a deeper level they flow from human pride and selfishness, which contaminate even the social sphere. When the structure of affairs is flawed by the consequences of sin, a person, already born with a bent toward evil, finds there new inducements to sin, which cannot be overcome without strenuous efforts and the assistance of grace (#25).

What is particularly remarkable about this passage is that it cogently links structures and sin, it stands out in isolation in the total document, and it was not immediately followed by further development of the same theme in other Catholic social writings.

A major advance in the development of social theology came from Protestant thinkers. In July 1966, at Geneva, the World Council of Churches Conference on Church and Society began grappling with the theology of revolution, with the fact of violence in the modern world, and with the Christian's relation to violence. The problem of violence necessarily raises the structural issue, which has to do with the ways of life. When aggregated and considered society's normal ways of doing things, modes of living are called the system or the structures. If the system is oppressing human dignity, then it is itself doing violence to the oppressed. This violence by political, economic, and social structures—despite its seeming legality, its subtle, nonviolent appearances, its projection by the ruling powers as part of the unchangeable status quo—is the situation which provokes a violent defense, the action of revolutionaries who seek to remove the unjust structures.

The World Council of Churches meeting recognized that for many in the world, especially in the developing countries, the question was one of meeting violence with violence. The real authors of disturbance are identified not as those who hunger and thirst after justice, but those who, to protect their privileges, prevent justice by maintaining the structures of oppression.

Two years later, in April 1968, the Beirut Conference on World Cooperation for Development, sponsored by SODEPAX, again returned to the problem of unjust structures.

> And our responsibility is not merely as persons for other people, but also for the political and economic structures that bring about poverty, injustice and violence. Today our responsibility has a new dimension because we now have the power to remove the causes of the evil, whose symptoms alone we could treat before (*World Development: The Challenge to the Church*, Geneva: SODEPAX, 1968, p. 15).

The relationship between these structures of oppression and sin was made explicit at Beirut: "We know the reality of sin and the depth of its hold on human beings, and on our political and economic structures ..." (pp. 16–17). Injustice was seen sometimes to be "so embedded in the *status quo"* that violent revolution might be justified to bring about change (p. 20).

This "opening to violence" was, understandably, a trend which disturbed many Church leaders and theologians. In his 1967 encyclical, *Populorum Progressio,* Paul VI had spoken of the fact that persons "are easily induced to use force to fight against the wrong done to human dignity," especially when "it is a question of manifest and lasting tyranny that damages the primary rights of the human person and inflicts serious harm on the common good of the country" (#31). When the pope went to Latin America in 1968, however, he clarified his position so as to avoid endorsement of violent revolution.

Latin America: Medellin and Gutierrez

In late August and early September of 1968, the Second General Conference of Latin America Bishops met at Medellin, Colombia. The Medellin Conference opened with an address by Paul VI who warned that Christians "cannot be linked with systems and structures which cover up and favor grave and oppressive inequalities among the classes and citizens of one and the same country . . ." (*The Church in the Present-Day Transformation of Latin America in the Light of the Council,* Washington, D.C.: Latin American Bureau, USCC, 1970, 2:31). The discussions referred to those systems and structures as being forms of "internal colonialism" (the domination of the poor classes by the rich classes) and "external neocolonialism" (the domination of the poor countries by the rich countries). Again and again, the power of structures was emphasized and the need to transform them was stressed. Not surprisingly, this very theme has been emphasized in Latin America. For years, the Argentine economist Raul Prebisch had been insisting that the basic problems facing development in the poor nations were structural and needed to be met by changes of structures.

The concluding statement of Medellin was very explicit about injustice embedded in structures: "[The Christian] recognizes that in many instances Latin America finds itself faced with a *situation of injustice that can be called institutionalized violence* . . . violating fundamental rights" (2:78; emphasis added). The realities of this injustice were clearly said to constitute "a sinful situation" (2:71). The general secretary of the conference, Bishop Eduardo Pironio, emphasized: "It is evident that in the Latin American reality there exists a 'condition of sin' that ought to be transformed into a reality of justice and sanctity" (1:112).

The direction of thought on structures and sin, which was being set forth at Medellin, was finding its underpinning in the works of several Latin American theologians who were discussing a "theology of liberation." Foremost among these theologians was Gustavo Gutierrez of Lima, Peru. According to Gutierrez (1970), *liberation* is a far more expressive word, theologically as well as sociologically, than *development*. *Development* tends to be heard primarily in an economic sense and connotes dependence of some people on the assistance of others. *Liberation*, however, emphasizes more of the integral human aspects of the process and immediately connotes the struggle against the asymmetrical power relationships between rich and poor.

The theological importance of Gutierrez's emphasis is clear. In biblical language, liberation is primarily liberation from sin and it is a liberation possible only through the power of God and, in the New Testament, the power of Jesus Christ. To speak of liberation in a social sense, then, is to speak of social sin—and to emphasize the social struggle against that sin. Gutierrez writes:

> Christ thus appears as the Savior who, by liberating us from sin, liberates us from the very roots of social injustice. The entire dynamism of human history, the struggle against all that depersonalizes man—social inequalities, misery, exploitation—have their origin, are sublimated, and reach their plentitude in the salvific work of Christ (p. 257).

The implications for the life of the Christian—and for the Christian Church—are readily evident.

The 1971 synod of Catholic bishops marked an important moment in the development of Catholic social analysis. Traditional Catholic social thought has seen a fairly consistent line of development in the teaching of the Church since the days of Leo XIII. Leo's *Rerum Novarum* set the general tone and style for the body of social doctrine, with its emphasis on basic human rights and its explanation of the traditional scholastic teachings on social justice. Scripture was used by Leo in the form of quotations to bolster lines of argument, an approach common to most expositions of Church teachings at that time. Pius XI's *Quadragesimo Anno*, the many writings and addresses of Pius XII, and two major encyclicals of John XXIII, *Mater et Magistra* and *Pacem in Terris*, followed this same general pattern. These teachings contain a growing receptivity to secular, social science sources.

A new departure in this development came with the Second Vatican

Council's document, *Gaudium et Spes* (The Church in the Modern World), and subsequently with Paul VI's *Populorum Progressio.* Both of these documents revealed an emphasis upon biblical theology rather than a reliance simply on biblical quotations. That is, an effort is made to theologize upon the scriptural teachings on social justice and on the social mission of man in this world. This emphasis upon biblical theology, in the view of many, adds a new dimension to the social teaching of the Church.

This new dimension reached a still clearer expression in the document of the Second Roman Synod entitled *Justice in the World,* of November 1971. Biblical theology clearly provided a central thrust in the preparations for, the debates over, and the final wording of this major document. Thus the bishops of the synod were able to say:

> Scrutinizing the "signs of the times" and seeking to detect the meaning of emerging history, while at the same time sharing the aspirations and questioning of all those who want to build a more human world, *we have listened to the Word of God* that we might be converted to the fulfilling of the divine plan for the salvation of the world (Introduction; emphasis added).

Listening to the Word of God, the bishops said that "the hopes and forces which are moving the world in its very foundations are not foreign to the dynamism of the Gospel, which through the power of the Holy Spirit frees from personal sin and from its consequences in social life" (Introduction). This emphasis by the Synod on the congruence of secular and religious (gospel) forces is highly significant. But even more significant is the stress placed upon the social implications of a scriptural understanding of sin.

The "New" Category of Social Sin

A major theme in biblical theology is, of course, the theme of sin and redemption. It is this theme which the synod document on world justice explicitly picks up and develops in a social content, thereby explicating a new dimension in Church social teaching—the dimension of social sin. While this category of social sin can be found in earlier teachings, it is not found with the explicitness and detail with which the synod debated the topic and wrote of it in its final document.

It is thus possible to trace how the category of social sin evolved from a rather lean theological status to a significant factor in the synod debates, eventually to receive authoritative acceptance in the document, *Justice in the World.*

Since the 1971 synod, there has been repeated reference to the category of social sin and emphasis on the ministry to social structures. The concept of liberation, for example, with its implications for evangelization, was very fully discussed in Pope Paul VI's 1975 letter, *Evangelii Nuntiandi* (#25–37). The liberating struggle to overcome evil in our world today touches on a variety of structural problems, as listed by the pope: "famine, chronic disease, illiteracy, poverty, injustices in international relations and especially in commercial exchanges, situations of economic and cultural neo-colonialism sometimes as cruel as the old political colonialism" (#30).

This recognition that liberation has implications for changing social structures can also be found throughout the final document of the Thirty-second General Congregation of the Society of Jesus (1975). This Jesuit document, which became highly influential for other religious congregations in the Catholic Church, focused attention on injustice "not only personal but institutionalized: built into economic, social, and political structures that dominated the life of nations and the international community" (*Our Mission Today,* #6). In direct reference to the earlier source, the document states that the "cult of money, progress, prestige and power has as its fruit the sin of institutionalized injustice, condemned by the Synod of 1971 . . ." (#29).

One of the clearest expositions of social sin in an official document from the United States Catholic Conference is found in the 1978 *National Catholic Catechetical Directory.* In its chapter on guidelines for teaching the Church's social mission, the directory delineates the concept of social sin and indicates the implications of this doctrine for ministry.

Recent attention to the structural dimensions of social injustice can be found in the first encyclical letter of Pope John Paul II, *Redemptor Hominis* (1979). He addresses explicitly the need for "redemption from sin," a redemption that can only come from Jesus Christ. That he has in mind a redemption which also touches on social sin seems clear from the very strong sections in the encyclical where he speaks of the threats to human progress coming from the disparities between rich and poor nations, the uncontrolled development of technology, the arms race, and the violation of human rights (#15–17). For example, in speaking of the gap between rich and poor, he argues: "So widespread is the phenomenon that it brings into question the financial, monetary, production, and commercial mechanisms that, resting on various political pressures, support the world economy." And he speaks of the "difficult road of the indispensable transformation of the structures of economic life . . ." (#16).

The emphasis which Pope John Paul II would place on the social structural situation in the world in his encyclical was anticipated a few months earlier by the final statements coming from the Third Conference of the Latin American Bishops (CELAM), which gathered in Puebla, Mexico, early in 1979, ten years after the Medellin conference. There were many who feared that conservative reaction to the strong structural emphasis on social sin, which had marked the Medellin meeting, might turn the thrust of the Puebla discussion toward a more personalistic approach in the ministry of the Church. But this was not to be the case.

In its opening chapter, the Puebla document speaks movingly of the situation of inhuman poverty in which millions of Latin Americans live, a poverty which "is not a transitory stage, but is the product of economic, social and political structures." Thus, "this reality demands a personal conversion and profound changes in the structures" (#19).

That the bishops of Latin America still choose to see the structures of injustice in terms of social sin can be seen in a passage in the documents which describes the need for the Church to denounce the evil of capitalism as forthrightly as it denounces the evil of Marxism: "The fear of Marxism impedes many from facing the oppressive reality of capitalism. It can be said that, faced with the danger of a system of sin, one forgets to denounce the fight against the reality imposed by another system of sin. It is important to pay attention to the former, without forgetting the latter" (#51). Elsewhere the bishops point to "sinful situations and structures which, all over the world, enslave so many persons and adversely condemn the freedom of all" (#225).

At Puebla, the influence of several years' refinement in the development of liberation theology became evident. Prodded by Pope John Paul's opening address, the bishops emphasized what they considered to be an authentic conception of Christian liberation.

> There are two complementary and inseparable elements: *liberation from all forms of servitude,* from personal and social sin, and from all that fragments man and society and whose source is egoism and the mystery of sin; *liberation through progressive growth in being,* through that communion with God and people which culminates in the perfect communion of heaven, where God is all in all and there are no more tears (#353).
>
> It is a liberation which is effected in history, that of our people and our personal histories and which embraces the different dimensions of existence: social, political, economic, cultural, and their mutual interactions. Through all of this, the transforming riches of the gospel

should circulate, with its own proper contribution, which must be safeguarded (#354).

This significant section of the Puebla documents clearly shows that there has been no retreat from a perception of and a response to the structural reality which is social sin. The Church's mission of evangelization must continue to include confrontation with these unjust structures.

Decision: From Insight to Action

The Church's reflection on social sin necessarily leads to action. It is not enough to *understand* that social structures can be sinful; the Christian must move from such insight to action—actions to acknowledge and overcome this sinfulness. The call is to social conversion.

It is in the concrete and particular processes of pastoral reflection that the connections between the insight concerning structural evil and actions of social conversion can be clarified. It is only when social structures are recognized as more than simple "givens" in life, only when they are seen as subject to, and expressive of, the influence of personal and corporate choice, that they can be healed. As long as such institutions—corporations, prisons, the Church's own bureaucracy—are seen as neutral means of organizing people and coordinating resources, they cannot themselves be ministered to. But, even with this insight, the task of determining in the concrete situation the means of effective Christian challenge and reconciliation remains complex.

As this concrete pastoral reflection seeks to move from insight to action, it must be careful to avoid a central temptation: a simplistic identification of some one structure as purely demonic or, alternately, as purely redemptive. We may be tempted, after a long period of ignoring the religious significance of social institutions, to move to a quick and thorough condemnation of them. Such a fundamentalist action replaces the need for theological reflection rather than issuing from it. Equally simplistic is the suggestion that some one alternate structure (whether socialist, capitalist, Marxist, or utopian-communal) is itself identified with Christian freedom.

With the insight that social structures can be sinful comes the re-visioning of ministry. Christians are called to care for the world in more than one-to-one relationships. Christian ministry is recognized as including, then, a ministry to structures. Whether these be families, educational institutions, social agencies, or multinational corporations, they await the challenge and healing of Christian ministry.

One result of the Church's current reflection on social sin has been the establishment in parishes, dioceses, and religious congregations of ministry centers focused on issues of justice and peace. There are regional and national efforts as well. Since its beginning in 1971, the Washington, D.C.-based Center of Concern, with which I am personally involved, has participated in numerous programs aimed at organizing more effective responses of justice among people in the United States. Focused primarily on international issues, our efforts of analysis, advocacy, and education take seriously the social, politial, economic, and cultural structures of the contemporary world.

There is action as well in areas of education to justice—in religious education, in programs of spirituality and religious formation, and in education for ministry. In this regard, seminaries and divinity schools are, increasingly, responding to this re-visioning of social life and ministry. The strengthening of field education in Catholic seminaries in the past ten years has meant that ministerial students have complemented their more academic study of theology with exposure to, and experience in, various institutions. When the student's supervision is truly professional, this becomes an opportunity not only to care for indivduals in these institutions, but to reflect on the institution itself—its values, strengths, and failings as a social structure. Again, the importance of theological reflection in ministerial education is crucial. Neither ignoring social structures (as something to contend with only after theological studies are completed) nor simplisticly condemning them, ministerial students are invited to continually relate their theological learnings and religious beliefs to the concrete realities of their social world.

Ministry to systems is gaining greater attention both in schools of ministry and in Christian life generally. We recognize now that ministry to individuals in a family needs to be complemented by an awareness of the family as a system and a ministry to this system's need for conversion. Also, we are recognizing that ecclesiology—the study of the Church—fails if it is limited to historical and philosophical reflection; ecclesiology necessarily includes a study of the Church as a system and institution. The Church is not only the mystical body of Christ, but also a social structure in need of continuing conversion. A growing ministry to systems, one built not only on religious enthusiasm, but on an increasingly sophisticated awareness of how systems work, is a major practical conclusion to the recent and continuing reflection of the Church on social sin.

References

Baum, Gregory. *Man Becoming: God in Secular Experience.* New York: Herder and Herder, 1971.

Berger, Peter, and Thomas Luckmann. *The Social Construction of Reality.* New York: Doubleday Anchor, 1967.

Gutierrez, Gustavo. "Theology of Liberation," in *Theological Studies* 31 (1970):245–58.

Justice in the World. Document of the Bishops Synod of 1971. In Joseph Gremillion, Ed., *The Gospel of Justice and Peace.* Maryknoll, NY: Orbis, 1976.

Medellin Documents. *The Church in the Present Day Transformations of Latin America in the Light of the Council.* Washington, D.C.: United States Catholic Conference, 1970.

Metz, Johannes B. *Theology of the World.* New York: Herder and Herder, 1971.

Monden, Lewis. *Sin, Liberty and Law.* New York: Sheed and Ward, 1965.

National Catholic Catechetical Directory. Washington, D.C.: United States Catholic Conference, 1978.

Our Mission Today. Document of the 32nd General Congregation of the Society of Jesus. Washington, D.C.: United States Jesuit Assistancy, 1975.

Puebla Documents. *Proceedings of the Latin American Bishops Conference.* Notre Dame, IN: Catholic Committee on Urban Ministry, 1979.

Pope John XXIII. *Mater et Magistra.* In Joseph Gremillion, Ed., *The Gospel of Justice and Peace.* Maryknoll, NY: Orbis, 1976.

Pope John Paul II. *Redemptor Hominis.* Washington, D.C.: United States Catholic Conference, 1979.

Pope Paul VI. *Evangelii Nuntiandi.* In Joseph Gremillion, Ed., *The Gospel of Justice and Peace.* Maryknoll, NY: Orbis, 1976.

Schoonenberg, Piet. *Man and Sin: A Theological View.* Notre Dame, IN:Notre Dame Press, 1975.

World Development: The Challenge to the Church. Geneva: SODEPAX, 1968.

A CHRISTIAN ASCETICISM OF TIME

We have suggested in this book that theological reflection is necessary and useful for a creative response to the different questions we face in ministry, whether about community, liturgy, or social justice. But such systematic reflection is also necessary for the development of a spirituality for the minister and the believing community. Changes in the Church and the specific needs and strains of contemporary life demand fresh reflection on our life styles and how these lives can more effectively witness to the presence and power of God in contempoary life.

One way to focus a theological reflection on the question of Christian spirituality is to reflect on how we use time in our life. In the following pages we will attend to three sources of information relevant to such a spirituality: our contemporary experience of time, the Christian Tradition's understanding of time, and the negative and positive contributions of our own culture to the question of time management. By placing these in an assertive dialogue with each other, we will begin to discern the outline of an ascetical management of time which is Christian, contemporary, and practical.

Time and Asceticism
"Make the most of your time."
(Eph. 5:16)

Two scenarios:

A counselor in a city agency, her day is filled with an unending flow of troubled persons. Responding to these people is both exhilarating and exhausting. She notices that she is saving less and less time and energy for close friends and for personal quiet and reflection. How to change this disturbing pattern?

Busy with the different groups that he serves, this priest finds himself beginning to wear down. There is too little time for prayer; he hasn't had a satisfying vacation in a long while; it is becoming increasingly difficult to concentrate on his work. A feeling of distraction, of being scattered is replacing his earlier enthusiasm.

Many adults today, especially, perhaps, those in the helping professions, may find something of themselves and their friends in these portraits. A central and enduring concern for all of us in adult life is how to spend our time: how to manage, within this one, limited life I have, the demands that arise—joyful as well as painful—from the loved ones in my life, from my work, and from my own interior life.

The different and often conflicting invitations in adult life share a common medium: time. As we struggle to love well, work creatively, and still care for ourselves, we can ignore this medium or feel that it is somehow a given, beyond our control. Are there not always and only twenty-four hours to a day? Thus, time itself fails to emerge as a focus of reflection.

Yet the sheer busy-ness of contemporary American life and the seemingly endless demands that assault a responsible adult suggest that we become more aware of those personal decisions and nonpersonal forces that shape the time of our life. Research in developmental psychology (see, for example, George Vaillant's *Adaptation to Life*) argues that adult maturity is related to a person's ability to use time—leisure time as well as work time—well. I will suggest that time management, informed by both psychological and religious insight, is a necessary element in a contemporary Christian spirituality. By the phrase "asceticism of time," I mean taking responsibility for the decisions that shape the time of my life—its loving, working, and reflecting. This will include examination of the forces that currently influence my use of time, meanings of time in the Christian Tradition, and efforts to systematically style my use of time to allow the graceful presence of God to be more apparent in my loving and working. A Christian time management, as an asceticism, will always be understood as a response to grace, to the invitation to become less scattered and less self-centered, and more aware of a presence already here. It cannot mean pulling myself up by my own bootstraps or independently structuring my time just for my own purposes. The delicate balance, as in all forms of religious asceticism, is between becoming strong, responsible agents of our own lives and simultaneously remaining attentive respondents to a presence that precedes our insights and disrupts our plans. Christian history is, in part, the story of our continuing struggle to right this balance: now insisting on greater passivity and dependence on God, now demanding greater personal responsibility in actively constructing a holier (that is, more aware, just, and caring) life. In this theological reflection, which takes its place in the long history of the Christian efforts to draw closer to God in time, we necessarily begin by attending to our experience, religious Tradition, and culture on the meaning and potential of time.

The Attending Stage

Contemporary Christians and the Experience of Time

We begin with a reflection on our own experience of time. Unless we are aware of our own concrete uses of time and some of the forces—internal and external—that influence our decisions about time, our theological reflection remains theoretical or, at best, historical. To begin this practical reflection, to *take the time* to listen to the movement of time in our own busy lives, is already an ascetical act. Practical steps in such a reflection will be outlined in the third stage, in the section "Practical Steps in Developing an Ascetical Life Style." Here I will review some common uses of time that have surfaced in a number of workshops on time; as such, this section represents a composite of *some* Christians' experiences of time.

A pattern repeats itself frequently among those involved in the helping professions and Christian ministry. A career begun with excitement, industry, and selfless service gradually becomes overly busy. The minister or helper begins to feel exhausted; distraction and fatigue start to lower the effectiveness of the person's service.[1] This is a point central to our discussion: an asceticism of time is not merely intended to give adults more leisure or enhance their individual well-being, but is intimately related to their service of others, their *diakonia*, and its effectiveness. This effectiveness is related, I will argue, to their choices about how to use their time. Distress often arises not from doing bad, nor from failing to act, but, intriguingly, from doing too much good. The endless demands of persons and systems in need overwhelm those who do not possess a clear and shrewd sense of their own limits. This sense of limits provides the information for the specification of a person's ministry—how and where one is called to serve—and rescues the person from the uncritical posture of a "general vocation," a ministerial jack-of-all-trades responding indiscriminately to every and all needs that arise.

The practical results of this pattern, so common among Christian ministers, are both painful and destructive. As work and outside demands overwhelm the person's schedule, loved ones receive less and less attention. The minister "just doesn't have time" to spend with spouse, children or close friends. There is no time to fit in a vacation or a day off. Most ironically, a very common result of overwork among ministers is the disappearance of prayer from their lives. Young priests, trained in prayer and its importance, often find themselves setting it aside because of the demands of their ministry.

Such experiences of time are not, of course, purely idiosyncratic, simply individuals' experiences uninfluenced by their religious tradition or culture. Religious rhetoric, inherited from previous periods in the Church when the pace of life was perhaps less harried and compulsive, contributes to this pattern. The idea of being "all things to all people" and the Christian ambition to spend oneself in the service of others, when unbalanced by an awareness of an individual's specific gifts and limits, become naive and lead to exhaustion and ineffectiveness rather than a sustained life of selfless service. A more recent version of these ideals, that "the priesthood is a twenty-four-hour-a-day job," may be more grounded in an overly self-serious and heroic self-understanding, than in a useful ideal of Christian service. This is not to suggest that the priesthood or, more broadly, Christian ministry, is a nine-to-five job. In a very real sense a professional minister is never off duty, just as the professional careers of a policeman or doctor include an extraordinary availability. Yet in another sense ministers, like doctors, must *choose* not to work (the potential work being endless) so that other parts of their life can flourish, for their own sakes as well as to enhance work when they return to it. A contemporary asceticism of time will critically examine the variety of our religious rhetoric about time and self-giving, letting these ideals both inform and be informed by contemporary insight into mature and holy time management.

An influence of cultural values may be evidenced in a person's pursuit of busy-ness as a sign of personal worth. Do we not often enjoy being overly busy and especially telling each other how busy we are? This peculiar value, related no doubt to our Western work ethic and the long-standing conviction about the connection between idleness and the devil, allows us to enjoy the misery of being overextended in our work and daily schedules. Applying with a vengeance Chesterton's quip, "If something is worth doing, it is worth doing poorly," professional helpers and ministers at times choose to be involved ineffectively with many projects, committees, and counselees instead of involved effectively with a few. Do we too quickly identify the ensuing exhaustion with Christian self-giving instead of examining the influence of this exhaustion on the effectiveness of our ministry and on the health of the rest of our lives?

This pattern of self-spending, which appears as a nonascetical variety of self-sacrifice, urges us to explore in some detail the religious uses of time and the shape of a Christian management of time. The understanding of time in the Christian Tradition will provide some clues for the construction of an asceticism of time.

Time and the Christian Tradition

When Christians today reflect on their Tradition's convictions about time, perhaps the first thought that comes to mind, because of its recent popularity, is the passage from Ecclesiastes: "For everything there is a season, and a time for every matter under heaven . . ." (3:1). Apart from this view of time (which in its stress of a strict cyclic regularity has an air of pessimism), a reflective believer might recall the importance of the Sabbath in Judaeo-Christian history—a time in the week of special holiness. Others might begin their reflection elsewhere in the rich Christian Tradition, perhaps in the poignant observation of Augustine: "If no one asks me (about time), I understand it; if I wish to explain it to an enquirer, I do not understand it" (Confessions, XI, 14). Yet another Christian might begin by reflecting on an important aspect of traditional spirituality: practicing the presence of God, trying to live one's time with a keen awareness of God's graceful presence in every moment.

These various starting points remind us of the rich variegation in the Christian Tradition's views of time. God's transforming presence in human history being too rich for any one image or passage to exhaust, the Christian is invited to reflect on the pluriform testimony and the many clues the Tradition provides for a theological reflection on time.

Out of these many possibilities for this reflection, I will choose an orientation toward time discernible in the vocabulary of the Christian Scriptures—the distinction between *chronos* time and *kairos* time. *Chronos,* in classical Greek, translated the experience of time as duration, as chronological progression and continuity.[2] *Kairos* referred to time as opportunity or occasion; it is time which has a special significance or potential—the "right time," a favorable moment, or critical period.[3] It is not surprising that religious persons saw here a distinction between ordinary, secular duration and time as having an uncommon religious meaning, as indicating a period of special grace or vulnerability.[4]

When the Old Testament was translated into Greek in the third and second centuries before Christ, its translators used both words for time, though not with a consistent distinction between secular and sacred time. At different points in these Scriptures,[5] however, *kairos* does indicate a period of special religious concern and vulnerability: the Psalmist prayed, "Cast me not away in the *kairos* of my old age" (70:9). Old age is not an ordinary time, but an especially opportune and vulnerable period of life, a time of grace or despair.

Chronos and *kairos* also appear throughout the New Testament. As James Barr (1962) notes, these words do not consistently distinguish secular and sacred time.[6] *Chronos*, for instance, occasionally refers to times of special religious import, such as the time of the star's appearance over Bethlehem (Matt. 2:7) and the time of Elizabeth's delivery of John the Baptist (Luke 1:37). *Kairos* does more consistently refer to a special time of salvation. Jesus announces the onset of his public career: "The time [*kairos*] is fulfilled and the kingdom of God is at hand" (Mark 1:15). Within this new and different time of salvation is a more sharply focused moment: the crisis of Jesus' suffering and death. "My time [*kairos*] is at hand" (Matt. 26:18). *Kairos* in the New Testament is eschatological time—that critical time of judgment and salvation which is ending the long duration of prior history. Jesus mourns Jerusalem for not knowing the time of its deliverance (Luke 19:44). Paul concludes his letter to the Romans by celebrating the present as a time of salvation, the revelation of a mystery "kept secret for long ages [*chronos*]."

This sense of *chronos* as of a long nonsalvific duration is found in a number of passages in the gospels where human life is described as wounded and unredeemed. In the Gospel of Mark (9:21), Jesus responds to a possessed youth who is brought to him by asking, "How long a time [*chronos*] has he had this?" In Luke's Gospel (8:27), a similarly possessed man is portrayed as living inhumanly (in the wilds and without clothes) "for a long time [*chronos*]." In Matthew's account of this story, the demons object to their exorcism "before the time [*kairos*]" (8:29). In the Fourth Gospel (5:6), Jesus is asked to help a sick person who has lain by a certain pool in Jerusalem "for a long time [*chronos*]." In each instance, *chronos* describes a prolonged duration of sickness, a passage of time in which the person is unwhole. The healing of each of these persons, effected by Jesus' timely entry into their life, breaks this long period of chronic illness.

The *kairos* or end-time brought on by Jesus' entry into human life continues today. John L. McKenzie, in his *Dictionary of the Bible* (1965), describes this meaning of *kairos:* "Each step in the process of time is a *kairos* in the sense that it is a critical time, a decisive moment which hastens or retards the *kairos* of salvation and judgment" (p. 892).

A reflection in systematic or historical theology must continue to nuance this distinction of ordinary and special time, but a pastoral reflection will turn to the practical question of the translation of these time experiences in the life of the contemporary believer. I will attempt this translation below when I bring the tradition and contemporary experience into a mutually assertive relationship.

Cultural Influences on Our Management of Time

As adult Christians our decisions about time and life style are influenced not only by the ideals of our religious Tradition, but obviously by the culture we live in. Cultural convictions about the value of time may, however, become so much a part of us that their influence becomes unapparent; a theological reflection intends to make us more aware of such forces.

In this model of reflection we will expect these influences to be positive as well as negative. Culture is not merely a generator of problems and imbalances that religion is called to correct, but is itself a source of insight and wisdom about human life. In this section I will suggest but a few of these many influences on our own understanding of the time of our life.

An obvious and powerful influence in our culture is its hurried, even frenetic pace of living. American adults seem necessarily busy about many things; we *are expected* to be very busy. We may regret this pace and style of living, but it appears "that's the way life is. . . ." Upon examination it seems that such busy-ness is not just necessary, but at times functions as an important index of our worth. The successful executive is typically portrayed in the media as working a sixteen-hour day. Being busy correlates with being important, being needed. Our theological reflection is effective when we begin to get in touch with the cultural values that impel us to use time the way we do.

But if our culture contributes to a compulsive orientation toward time and work, it also offers clues about a more mature management of time. Recent research in developmental psychology has alerted us to significant shifts in our perception of time as we mature. One example is the change that occurs in our mid-years: we begin to measure time less in terms of time-lived and more in terms of time-left-to-live. In George Vaillant's (*Adaptation to Life*) felicitous phrasing, we find ourselves with "more yesterdays than tomorrows." With time no longer an unlimited resource, a maturing adult may feel the need for a life evaluation, a reorientation of energy and time. This inclination, which is part of our psychological development, may be seen by the Christian adult as an invitation to a more ascetical structuring of time.

Another positive contribution of our culture to a religious asceticism of time is the methods and techniques developed in business management for a more effective use of work time. Davidson (1978) and Lakein (1973), for example, offer simple but concrete procedures useful in restructuring one's time. These and other practical methods, though developed in a thoroughly secular context, give our religious ideals specific means of expression. These management methods are morally neutral in that they can be used solely to increase a company's profits, but may also contribute to a more loving use of one's time. In the section below on a practical asceticism of time, I will look more closely at several of these methods.

The Assertion Stage

Having listened carefully to our own experience of time, to some small aspect of our Tradition's rich testimony about time, and having discerned some of the influences of our culture on our use of time, it becomes necessary to set these insights in dialogue (or trilogue) among themselves. I will do this briefly in the following fashion. First, I will translate the distinction in our Tradition of *chronos* and *kairos* in the light of contemporary experience, and then I will reflect on two common compulsions which may influence our religious use of time.

An ongoing challenge for Christian spirituality is to furnish powerful contemporary translations of its traditional categories of belief and practice. Regarding the question of time we can ask: How are *chronos* and *kairos* experienced by believers today? A second challenge is to describe the contemporary experience of *kairos* not only in terms of God's agency and intervention in human life—though this is a primary and crucial task[7]—but also in terms of our systematic responses to such interventions. An asceticism is concerned with a consistent response to grace. In regard to *kairos,* it will mean the styling of our time in the direction of greater freedom from compulsion and dissipation and in the direction of greater awareness—of ourselves, God, other persons, and our work. By so doing we respond to the scriptural imperative to "redeem the time" (Eph. 5:16).

An exploration of *chronos* and *kairos* in the contemporary Christian's life may be facilitated by distinguishing three modes of living in and experiencing time. These modes—dissipation, concentration, and compulsion—are experienced along a continuum. While these modes of time shift about and are often situation-specific (we use our time differently in different contexts), it is useful to discuss them as distinct experiences.

Dissipation will be used to describe a wide range of experiences of time whose common feature is life or time as pointless or directionless. At different periods of our life we may lose interest in our working or loving, or feel most keenly the boredom or drudgery of time. Life goes on, or slips away, or runs out; but it enjoys no special energy or focus. The hero in Camus' *The Stranger* offers an extreme example of time experienced in this mode.[8] In this mode we feel especially distracted, uninvolved, or unfocused. Life has become a chronic and pointless repetition: "Getting and spending we lay waste our powers. . . ."

This mode of time can be named *chronos*, unholy time, not because we are doing evil, but because it is felt as pointless. When we are in it we squander our time or feel it slipping away; it is time lost.[9]

At the other extreme of the continuum is the experience of compulsion. In this mode time is not unfocused, but obsessively focused. Instead of an absence of energy, we experience here a great deal of energy, but of an unfree sort. Things "have to get done"; projects absorb our attention to the neglect of other parts of our life. We feel ourselves "driven" (in a more traditional religious vocabulary, "possessed"). Compulsions insinuate themselves into our lives in a variety of ways. One person may be obsessed with achievement: getting to the top in the diocese or school system; proving she is as capable as the men on the parish team. Another person struggles compulsively to stay young (confronting directly, if unconsciously, time as enemy, time as leading us to death). In each instance the present cannot be enjoyed or even alertly attended to, for the person is distracted from it by the force of the compulsion. Time obsessed is also *chronos*, for it is unfree time; it is unholy because we are possessed by a contemporary demon, a compulsion which distorts our awareness and compels our energy into unbalanced behavior.

A third kind of time experience, which I will describe under the rubric of concentration, occurs along the continuum between the extremes of dissipation and compulsion. I refer to those periods, brief or enduring, in which we feel especially present and focused in our work and other relationships. We feel present to our friends, have a sense of direction in our work, and find ourselves working hard but not compulsively. Another way this experience is described is "I'm doing what I should be doing." This mode of living is contrasted with not knowing what I should be doing with my life (dissipation) and being harassed by all that has to get done (compulsion). Adult believers, aware of their fragility, recognize this mode of living with concentration and focus as a gift and a grace—it need not have happened—and they are grateful to find themselves living thus. As holy time this mode of living can be called *kairotic*. Experienced as gift, the challenge of Christian asceticism is how to respond in a person's life, career, and daily decisions in a way that gives this experience of time a chance to take root and become more than an exceptional interlude.

Personal asceticism, but also Christian ministry itself, can be described in terms of this continuum. The good news of Jesus Christ gives direction and focus to our life; it invites us out of dissipation toward concentrated loving and working. And this good news also rescues us from the unfreedom of compulsions; it can exorcise ourselves and others of the forces that compel us into unbalanced and obsessive life styles. This double movement—delivering us from a pointless, meaningless life and rescuing us from a compulsive one—describes both the action of God's grace and the effort of Christians to live virtuously in the present and in the presence of God.

The orientation to time followed here departs in an important way from another, very ancient, Christian spirituality of time. Influenced both by Greek philosophy and Manichaeism, Christians have at times succumbed to the temptation to distinguish time as earthly, corruptive, and unholy from eternity as the unchanging, atemporal realm of the real, the incorruptible, and the divine.[10] Despite its historical character and its incarnational theology, Christianity at times describes the experience of God in human life as an atemporal event in which we escape time.[11] The asceticism outlined here understands human time as of one piece. When experienced as dissipated, it is emptied of focus and presence and so of the awareness and point of God; when experienced as obsessive, it is a hostile and unholy medium through which a person is driven. But this same time can be experienced as concentrated, as a medium in which we love and work with special attention. We grow *through* time and it is *in* time that we encounter God and other loved ones who transform us. This time as graceful and *kairos* is the same time but now concentrated, brought into focus so that we experience what was always there—a God who sanctifies our time while inviting us to a future, different time.

Thus the intent of this asceticism of time is not an escape from time, nor deliverance from the corruption of time, the body, and change, but the *saving* of time. The transformation, better, the salvation of time is intended: as we rescue by grace and effort ourselves and others from dissipated and compulsive time, we participate in its salvation; as our time is transformed and brought into focus, it is made holy and our lives as lived in such a milieu share this holiness.

Another assertive and useful dialogue is established when we juxtapose the psychological notion of compulsion (a category of our cultural self-understanding) and the Tradition's understanding of asceticism. Christian asceticism and spirituality can, indeed, be understood as the effort to recognize and overcome compulsion.[12] An unreflective life—whether dissipated or overly busy—is a life in which we are unaware of what drives us. We choose and act, unaware of the forces within and without that shape our actions. Compulsions are, of course, most often hidden, unconscious, and for this reason easily escape the efforts we do make at reflection. An advantage of reflecting on our use of time, on the concrete shape of our daily and weekly schedules, is that it can give us a glimpse of these compulsions in operation. An attentive reflection on time may reveal usually invisible forces at work in our daily life. This is due, in part, to the nature of compulsions; unlike dissipation, compulsions give great focus to our activity. It is this very focus, in its imbalance and urgency, which makes a compulsion visible in a careful review of how we use our time. Such a revelation or discovery is a first step in restructuring our use of time into a less compulsive, more virtuous style of loving and working.

Each adult will discover a different set of forces, needs and fears that influence the use of time. Over the past decade of listening to my own demons and those of other ministers, especially those in the Catholic Church, I have come to identify two very common compulsions at work in our choices about the use of time. The first compulsion originates in a personality trait typical in professional helpers: a strong desire to care for and serve others. This excellent desire edges toward compulsiveness as two correctives lose their force: a keen sense of the person's *specific* vocation (gifts and limits that help define what I can and am called to do), and a realization that the person's efforts at helping and serving belong to a larger process of salvation. Without a clear sense of personal limit, a minister or helper easily succumbs to the need to respond to every hurt and problem in the community. Such a person can slip into a style of ministry described by my colleague, Dr. Evelyn Eaton Whitehead, as "promiscuous ministry"—ministering to every need that arises, in whatever form, and at the eventual expense of the minister's fidelity to and effectiveness in that specific ministry to which she is preeminently called.

One sign of a helper slipping into compulsive helping is an increasing seriousness about the needs in a community or the world. Overwhelmed by the troubles and endless demands of a hurting society, such a person becomes agitated, distracted, and eventually exhausted, not just by responding to but by worrying about all that "has to be done." Such a compulsiveness can be named a messianic complex: the person assumes responsibility for the salvation of the world, transferring this burden from God to his own shoulders. Calling this a messianic complex does not suggest the person is an egomaniac, but only that the minister has, probably unconsciously, assumed as his or her own responsibility the salvation of the world. The self-importance implied in assuming this responsibility is complemented by a practical loss of trust in God's guiding presence in the world.

An asceticism that seeks to exorcise this kind of compulsion will include an effort to turn the world and its salvation back to God. This can be both humiliating for the helper who is a compulsive responder and immensely relieving. With a less heroic sense of my own mission, I begin to have a better chance of helping others according to my gifts and limits. This specifying of the shape of a person's ministry can contribute to an increased focus and effectiveness, as well as recovering space in the person's day for less heroic, more "useless" activities such as recreational time with loved ones and quiet time with God. The fruit of this ascetical effort at making a person's time less compulsive is evidenced not simply in greater personal comfort, but also in the effectiveness and endurance of the person's ministry: with greater focus and less self-seriousness, our ministry can contribute to a community for decades instead of burning out after a short burst of enthusiastic service.

A second compulsion, theologically related to the first, arises from the profound temptation toward self-justification. Thus, some helpers and ministers not only need to be needed (a healthy trait but sometimes exaggerated in the professional helper), but are often inclined to believe that the good they do makes them more worthy in the sight of God. The preaching, counseling, and caring that I do give proof (I hope) of my own goodness, even perhaps earning my salvation. Few of us would consciously hold this theological position, but this deep-seated hope may lie at the root of some of our compulsiveness and busy-ness in ministry.

Again, if we participate in this kind of compulsiveness, it may be revealed in a reflection on our use of time. If we are compelled to "earn our way" with God, to repeatedly prove our worth by what we achieve in the vineyard of the Lord, then nonachievement time will appear a waste and be avoided. Time for prayer will lose its value because I am not *doing* any-thing, not helping anyone. Leisure time and vacation, which share the "uselessness" of time for prayer, will be avoided or at least apologized for. Periods of illness will be another time indicative of my compulsion for self-justification: Can I tolerate being ill, especially in its more docile forms (as the flu or a broken bone), or do I fight this different, more passive experience of time with its invitations to dependency and reflection? An uneasiness with the variety of empty spaces in my life time suggests that I need to be doing, achieving, earning my way. The grace of an illness or vacation is that it can reveal this compulsiveness, this unholy need to prove my worth to God and self, and can initiate the ascetical process of changing how I shape the time of my life.

These are but two compulsions commonly found in the lives of profes-sional helpers. The reader may well have hints of other forces more rele-vant to her or his own asceticism of time. Whatever the form of a person's compulsions, they are forces that make us unfree and unbalanced in our use of time. Each obsession distorts our time, focusing our attention and energy narrowly on unholy purposes—even when these unholy purposes have to do with helping others. Christian spirituality is concerned with the exorcism of these compulsions or demons and the liberating of our time.

If this assertive stage of our reflection is fruitful, it already begins to suggest the direction of a practical strategy or decision. With greater clar-ity about what influences the decisions that shape our life style and better awareness of the Christian Tradition's call to live in the presence of God, we can begin to design practical steps that will assist us in living in a ho-lier, more effective fashion.

The Decision-Making Stage

Practical Steps in Developing an Ascetical Life Style

The methods outlined in this section belong both to the third stage of de-cision and to the first stage of listening to our experience of time. That is, they are tools which allow a more careful listening to our experience of time, and are already part of an ascetical effort to manage time more ma-turely.

Invoking the imagination as an alternate source of information, a person might, after some quieting (already an asceticism), listen for an image or images that arise around the word *time.* In this exercise of a guided fantasy, a person listens not for a definition of time, but for feelings, biases, apprehensions that may be revealed in these images. When performed carefully and shared with others, this reflective imagining can offer some preliminary clues about our relationship to time in our life.

A useful reflective exercise on time management might be an analysis of how we concretely spend our time. A recent day might be charted according to our use of three different kinds of time—work, alone, and together time. Work time refers to those periods of the day when we were performing activities most directly relevant to our job or career (whether with others or not). Alone time refers to periods of quiet when we were neither working nor with others. This will include prayer, listening to music, or other quiet reflection. Together time describes periods of being with others in nonwork situations—conversation, meals, games, etc. Charting the percentage of a recent day spent in each of these times provides some of the information necessary for decisions about how to better use my time.

This exercise has several intents: to give a concrete portrait of my day, to invite me to define each of these kinds of time in my own life, and to gain an initial sense of their relative importance to me. This exercise is best performed with a small group of people, preferably those who know my life style and pace and so can confirm the accuracy of my chart. No magic formula exists for how a day is to be divided. Having delineated our own use of a specific day, it falls to each of us—with the help of those who support and challenge us—to judge our satisfaction with its balance. The Christian Tradition shapes this judgment in reminding us of the importance of time spent with God and time given to our loved ones. It does not, however, tell us how to spend our day; this is our own ascetical task, a task assisted by the specific information gained in this simple exercise.

A second exercise on our concrete use of time entails a prioritizing of our daily work involvements. Having kept a log of our activities over the past week, we are invited to divide them into three categories: "A" will include those activities most central to who we are and what we seemed called to do. These are the activities most definitive of our vocation. "B" includes other activities, which are important but do not enjoy the same central significance in our life. A third category, "C," comprises those support activities and chores that seem necessary—things that "have to get done," but are least definitive of our career or vocation.

The intent is, of course, to invite us to prioritize, to select out the more significant activities in our days. Having set out in some detail the many things we are involved in, the goal is not to lop off category "C" or "B." We may find we are comfortable with the distribution and quantity of activities in our life. (Though, if we are, we probably did not feel the need to do this exercise.) If we are not comfortable with our use of time, we are faced with concrete choices: Which of these "A" activities are most central to my vocation? What ones are important, but not necessarily to be done by me? What activities in "B" can be omitted not because they are unimportant, but because they less thoroughly match my gifts and limits? Again, without a concrete sense of what these gifts and limits are, we have no criteria by which to prioritize our work; everything is equally significant and makes an equal demand on us. Finally, how can I more efficiently accomplish my "C" tasks? What is the best time of the day for such activities?

In these and other exercises on our use of time the goal is greater clarity about our own actions. What forces lead me to spend my time in this fashion? What compulsions, religious ideals, and ambitions structure the time of my life? This clarification clears space for a recovery of our own agency; as we more clearly recognize the outside forces at work in our activities, we become freer to choose to align our energies with or resist these forces. We can also become more aware of ourselves as agents, as able to assertively structure the time of our life, and not simply respond to external demands. If such simple exercises seem beneath mature adults, it is useful to recall a common alternative to this ascetical effort at time management: indulging in such velleities as "If there were just more time," "I wish I weren't so busy," and "Where does the time go?"[13]

A crucial asceticism in a person's mature management of time is choosing what to do and what not to do. As the developmental psychologist Bernice Neugarten (1979) has indicated, a concern in the mid-years is for greater self-utilization—a better use of our talents in the context of our own limits. The challenge of psychological maturity is to choose, not just between good and evil, but among goods. Theologically, this means a specifying of my own ministry. Although the ideal of "being all things to all people" may excite me to new levels of generosity, it does not contribute to a specifying of my ministry, a specifying so crucial to a truly ascetical exercise of ministry.

Another practical challenge within this asceticism of time is learning to say no. If a person's vocation begins in the ability and courage to say yes to service and the needs of a community, this same vocation matures in the courage to say no. Enthusiasm and the sense that all things are possible are important and fitting elements of early adulthood. As an adult matures, an asceticism of denial attains new importance. The yes of each commitment entails a complementary no to other possibilities not to be pursued. Ministerial commitment to these few, limited modes of service includes the necessity of saying no to other important demands. The inability to say no appears most often not as a sign of holiness, but of an immaturity that can lead to exhaustion and ineffective ministry. For the compulsive responder, this asceticism of saying no must begin in small steps—refusing one demand this week, one demand next week— and in bearing the unpleasant taste of one's limitation, in the interests of a more focused and effective ministry.

Conclusion

Christian spirituality has always been concerned with time. Believers seek to become more aware of God's presence not only in their personal present, but also in their Tradition's past and in the future of humanity. Christians in liturgy and recollection recover God's presence in their past: in the Eucharist we re-call Christ's presence among his first followers and this historical presence penetrates and heals the present community. In hope Christians envision future time, foreseeing a more just and caring period of life. This vision beyond the present shapes their present actions of justice and care. In both temporal directions, then, Christians escape the restrictive immediacy of the present and its tendency to ignore the power of the past and be oblivious to the potential of the future.

The challenge of psychological maturity as well as religious growth is to become both alive to the past and future and still attentive to the present. Maturity and growth in the present fail when nostalgia or regret absorb our attention or future fantasies distract us from present needs. In both instances we become un-present, distracted from the loving and working in which we are invited to participate now. Christian spirituality and religious formation must provide believers with the opportunity to reflect on the practical influence of the past on their lives: To what extent does past time enliven and shape our present and to what extent does it determine and compel the present? ("We must do it this way because we have always done it this way.") This formation will also include training in the imagination—efforts in prayer and planning to envision a more just and Christian future, rather than using the imagination nonascetically to fantasize futures as a means of escaping the present.[14]

A major intent of the asceticism of time outlined in these pages is to recognize more clearly the religious quality of our life time. This may entail changing our view of time as a neutral medium—a given, non-negotiable aspect of life, thus irrelevant to Christian discipline. It may also necessitate a conversion from seeing time as enemy. Time is an enemy for the person who sees death only as annihilation and for the person whose religious belief locates the Holy outside of and beyond time. Believers who belong to a historical faith like Christianity are invited to resist these temptations, recognizing time as also a graceful medium, the place where we meet God and other loved ones, where our creativity finds expression. Time in this sense is neither neutral nor simply corruptive; it is the "culture" in which persons and communities develop. We mature in our ability to love and work *through* time. Time is not to be overcome, but to be befriended.[15] This asceticism intends the befriending of time. As we grow in awareness of God's presence in our life and as we more assertively structure our time in the direction of awareness and more effective service, we heal our relationship with time, befriending it. Responding to God's intervention into our life, we participate in making our life time more holy.

Finally, an ascetical use of time may be one of the ways Christian adults are called to witness to the secular society they live in. If a Christian is, indeed, gifted with different values and different perceptions about the quality and value of life, these should be evidenced in the way the person uses time. Rather than imitating the hectic, overly busy and distracted life style so common in American society today, ascetical Christians might be expected to give their work time a different quality. Someone who believes that our work and careers belong to a larger process of change and redemption, that we are not solely responsible for the future of the world, need be less frenetic and compulsive. Such a person can afford to be friendlier with time, and witness to a style of living both more relaxed and more aware. If Christians' work time might be expected to look different than that of unbelievers, so might their attitude toward "useless" time: such persons might allow more quality time for play and prayer. Less driven by a work ethic and/or a need to excel as proof of our worth, we Christians can be expected to live differently—but only if the religious beliefs we have inherited find practical expression in assertive and ascetical decisions about how we spend the time of our life.

Notes

1. This pattern is discussed by Michael D. Mitchell in "Consultant Burnout," in *The 1977 Annual Handbook For Group Facilitators* (LaJolla, CA: University Associates, 1977), pp. 143–46, and by Jerome Overbeck in "The Workaholic," in

Psychology Journal of Human Behavior 13 (August 1976):79–83. Of the five means of coping with this problem suggested by Mitchell, the first two concern a more careful management of time.

2. Both Plato and Aristotle were most interested in *chronos* as the measurement of duration. In the *Timaeus*, Plato defined *chronos* as "the moving image of eternity" (37d). The movement of this duration was cyclic (Aristotle's *Physics*, IV, 14), an interpretation challenged by the Christian conviction about time as linear, from an initiating creation to a concluding judgment.

3. In. A. E. Taylor's translation of Plato's *Laws* (in *The Collected Dialogues of Plato* [New York: Random House, 1963]), *kairos* is rendered as "circumstance" (709b), "momentous" (945c), and "critical point" (961c). In Book Two of *The Republic,* Plato argues the need for the members of the ideal state to contribute their own work and at the right time: "If one lets slip the right season, the favorable moment in any task, the work is spoiled" (370b).

4. Mircea Eliade reviews a variety of religious interpretations of sacred and profane time in his *Patterns in Comparative Religion* (New York: Sheed and Ward, 1958), Chapter 11. Eliade's fascination with a return to an original sacred time and the need to overcome time (see Chapter 5 of his *Myth and Reality*) make his approach to sacred time quite different than that of this article.

5. In the Book of Exodus, for instance, *kairos* translates as the time when Yahweh will send a plague on the pharaoh (9:14), the appointed time when the people are to celebrate the Passover (13:10), and other times when commemorative feasts are to be celebrated (see 23:14 and 34:18). In the prophets, *kairos* appears frequently in reference to a time of special tribulation (see Isa. 33:2 and Jer. 2:27, 30:7). In Chapter Three of Ecclesiastes, *kairos* translates as the notion of season, the right time for a certain kind of activity: "A time to be born and a time to die; a time to plant and a time to reap" (v. 2).

6. Barr emphasizes the inconsistency in the New Testament usage of these words, ignoring those frequent uses of *chronos* and *kairos* to translate duration and special opportunity. He does make an important critique of Oscar Cullman's (1964) narrow definition of *kairos* as "a definite point in time" (p. 39). *Kairos* refers not only to a moment, but often to an extended period during which a special opportunity or vulnerability is experienced.

7. In *Christian Life Patterns*, Evelyn Eaton Whitehead and I have sought to relate *kairos* to the experience of psychologial crisis in contemporary life. "Crises (such as may be experienced in a career change or divorce) are potentially kairotic moments in their vulnerability, their peculiar openness to learning and to the revisioning of life. For one who believes, a crisis is a place in which one might expect to encounter God" (p. 70).

8. Languorous swimming and a boiling sun in the first half of the book emphasize Meursault's directionless drift through life; during his imprisonment, in the second half, "the whole problem was, how to kill time."

9. Andreasen (1978) discusses this experience as that of "excess time" (p. 18) in which we feel bored or fatigued, and in terms of the weariness and distress of a pointless time (pp. 49–50). His remedy of rest complements the movement

suggested here toward a recovery of purpose and focus which energize our time.

10. This dichotomy begins with Plato's definition of time as "the moving image of eternity," and his distinction of the realm of eternal, unchanging ideas from the empirical world of shadow, change, and uncertainty. Plotinus' emphatic distinction between time and eternity influenced such early Christian thinkers as Origen and Augustine. (See C. A. Patrides' introduction to *Aspects of Time*.) Oscar Cullman, in *Christ and Time*, argues for a New Testament distinction between limited and unlimited time, instead of the more Platonic distinction of time and eternity (see p. 46). He argues against the notion of God as timeless, and for a Christian God who participates in time without being limited by it (pp. 62–3). For a contemporary (and struggling) effort to heal this dichotomy between time and eternity in Catholic piety, see Jean Mouroux's *The Mystery of Time*.

11. The intensity of awareness experienced in certain critical events (love, insight, danger) effects a distortion of time which has often been described in terms of nontime. Anthropologist Victor Turner, in an article, "Passages, Margins and Poverty" (*Worship*, 1972), judges that certain experiences of passage are "almost always thought of or portrayed by actors as a timeless condition, an eternal now, as 'a moment in and out of time,' or as a state to which the structural view of time is not applicable" (p. 399). Dualistic spiritualities which opposed soul and body, light and darkness, eternity and time, quite naturally led to a disparagement, even a hatred, of time. Thus Meister Eckhardt: "Nothing is more contrary to God than time, attachment to time, contact with time, and even the atmosphere of time" (quoted in Mouroux [1964], pp. 292–93). Powerful religious experiences, such as those described by Turner, can also be described in terms of the condensation or concentration of time: time continues but appears to slow as we become more alert to its content; the disruption of ordinary time (*chronos*) neither stops nor destroys time, but alters it, making us more present. This very different experience of time may merit the name of *kairos*.

12. I am indebted to Dr. G. V. Egan of the Institute of Pastoral Studies at Loyola University in Chicago for introducing me to this nexus of compulsions and asceticism. I borrow this, and no doubt many other of his ideas, with much affection.

13. Another method of an asceticism of time, perhaps overly intense and reflective for many, is the monitoring of our vocabulary about time: How often do we speak about time in compulsive vocabulary—"I have to do this. . . . I've got to run now"—assigning agency to forces outside ourselves? How can our vocabulary reflect our effort to be more of an agent in the use of time, *choosing* to be this busy or this free?

14. Subtle and crucial differences exist between our flight into fantasy to escape the challenges of the present (living out the Marxist critique of religion as an "opiate" which distracts people from present distress and the action necessary to relieve this distress), and our envisioning a future in ways that excite and empower us to change the present (the prophetic function of the imagination).

15. This befriending is aided by the recognition of the specific contribution of time to our growth in maturity and grace. Human growth occurs not despite

time, but (in part) because of it. The notion of becoming "seasoned" expresses this contribution to development: wine and humans do not simply change over time but can become better; proper aging effects the release of hitherto unavailable "virtues" in both wine and humans.

References

Andreasen, Niels-Erik. *The Christian Use of Time.* Nashville: Abingdon, 1978. An excellent reflection on time organized around the theme of the Sabbath as holy time and time for rest.

Barr, James. *Biblical Words for Time.* Naperville, IL: Alec R. Allenson, 1962. An analysis of *chronos* and *kairos,* as well as other words for time in the Old and New Testament. Barr warns against the simplistic selection of any of these words to construct a "biblical theology of time."

Cullman, Oscar. *Christ and Time.* Philadelphia: Westminster, 1964. A theology of Christian time, with a useful study of the New Testament terms *kairos* and *aion* (age).

Davidson, James. *Effective Time Management: A Practical Workbook.* New York: Human Sciences Press, 1978. A very simple but useful workbook designed for administrators or managers who wish to make better use of their work time.

Lakein, Alan. *How to Get Control of Your Time and Your Life.* New York: Wyden, 1973. Provides a variety of exercises which can clarify and help improve one's use of time.

Léon-Dufour, Xavier. *Dictionary of Biblical Theology.* New York: Seabury, 1967. See pages 600–6 for a clear discussion of the different understandings of time in the Old and New Testament.

Mouroux, Jean. *The Mystery of Time: A Theological Inquiry.* Translated by John Drury. New York: Desclee, 1964. A Catholic spirituality which describes human time as shaped by values which transcend time.

Neugarten, Bernice. "Time, Age, and the Life Cycle," in *American Journal of Psychiatry* 136 (July 1979):887–94. A valuable overview of current developmental research and theory concerning attitudes toward and experience of time at different points in the human life cycle.

Patrides, C. E. (Ed.). *Aspects of Time.* Toronto: University of Toronto Press, 1968. The chief virtue of this volume, many of whose essays are outdated, is its extensive bibliography on literary and religious interpretations of time.

Whitehead, Evelyn Eaton, and James D. Whitehead. *Christian Life Patterns.* New York: Doubleday, 1979. Chapter 2 includes a discussion of psychological crises in contemporary adult life and the relationship of these crises to *kairoi,* or times of special religious opportunity.

PART V

Implications for Ministerial Education

Education for ministry is centrally concerned with preparing Christians to reflect and act effectively in the Church and in the world. It is our conviction that this education must give Christian ministers greater access to the three sources of religiously relevant information.

Greater skill in attending to the Scripture must be complemented by an increased ability to listen to a community's religious concerns. Access to cultural information, especially the resources of the social sciences, must be part of ministerial education—as must training in skills of personal, interpersonal, and organizational awareness.

These skills are not merely techniques of management or manipulation. In the context of Christian leadership they are virtues—religious abilities requisite for effective ministry.

In Part V we discuss concrete ways in which the three sources of religious information can be incorporated in programs of education for ministry, concluding with an outline for a coordinated program of training in ministerial skills.

·11·

EDUCATION FOR MINISTRY— ACCESS TO THE SOURCES

The development of this model of reflection resulted in part from dissatisfaction with the current state of education for ministry—at both the seminary level and in programs of continuing education. In the experience of many, education for ministry today is vitiated by the disjunction between academic theological studies and experiential learning. Theological studies, relying largely on historical and philosophical methods, address only with great difficulty the theological learning latent in contemporary ministerial experience. As a result, the academic theology that ministry students learn, while judged to be very important, is rarely brought into contact with the experiences they are beginning to gain in the ministry.

Other factors contribute to this disjunction in seminary education. Ministry students, as we have noted earlier, are often intimidated by the complexity, stability, and sacredness of theological studies. At the same time, they may well recognize the marginal quality of the ministerial preparation provided in the seminary program. It is true that significant headway has been made in the incorporation of field education, clinical pastoral education and similar internship programs into the standard curriculum of seminaries and divinity schools. But in many, perhaps most, instances, there has been little success in integrating these learning experiences into the educational core of the theological degree program. Concluding their theological studies, many ministers begin their pastoral work with neither the skills nor the confidence to explore the theological import of their ongoing ministerial experience. Thus, intimidated by theology as a discipline and untrained in methods for experience-based learning, ministers enshrine this learning disjunction in their practice of ministry.

The theological method required in the practice of ministry differs from that to which many ministers are exposed during the course of formal studies. The philosophic tools of Tillich or Lonergan or Tracy may serve well as a guide for reflection in systematic theology; they are simply less useful in ministry. When these are the *only* methods presented to the minister, there can be a negative result. Ministers become convinced that theological reflection is important but that it is something in which, clearly, they are not qualified to participate. The minister's self-image becomes that of a functionary: ministers administer a religious Tradition that other persons (theologians or denominational authorities) shape. Thus, the crucial role of the minister in handing on—and thus handling—the Tradition is obscured.

Ministers, those persons involved in the daily work and pastoral activity of the Church, make the bulk of the practical decisions about the community of faith in its present and its future. It is through their action, not exclusively but significantly, that the Christian Tradition passes to the next generation of believers. To perform this role well—that is, faithfully and effectively—Christian ministers need both confidence and competence. Ministers must be confident in their role as "traditioners"—decisive stewards of a rich and often ambiguous heritage of faith. They must be competent in their ability to gain access to the sources of God's revelation that are available to them and to make theologically informed decisions in their ministry.

The model and method we present in this book are offered as tools of this ministerial competence. The goal of our discussion has not been theoretical understanding but working knowledge. We are interested in a process that can be used by persons in ministry. In the tripolar model we set out a framework of what such theological reflection includes; in the three-stage method we offer an image of how it works. In this chapter we will examine some of the implications for ministerial education that may be drawn from our discussion of theological reflection in ministry.

Access to Tradition

The challenge to education for ministry is to teach the Christian Tradition to future ministers in such a way that it becomes accessible to them as a resource in their ministry. The central role of Sacred Scripture in Christian Tradition makes the way that Scripture is taught a critical factor in giving ministers access to the Tradition. Thompson and Ulrich consider this challenge in detail in Chapter Two. Here, we will simply underscore what is obvious from their discussion. In a program of ministerial education Scripture will be taught with different goals and, therefore, different methods than those in effect in a doctoral program of academic theology.

The method of instruction will fall between that appropriate for developing Scripture scholars and that involved in merely providing for the student a set of interpretations of texts that may be handy in preaching. The model of theological reflection in ministry requires that students gain both an awareness of the pluriformity within Scripture and comfort with the richness and ambiguity that this pluriformity provides. Ulrich and Thompson have suggested several useful methods through which ministry students may gain access to the diverse scriptural sources of information and inspiration.

Another effective way in which the Tradition can be made more accessible to the ministerial student is through interdisciplinary teaching— where theology can be experienced in conversation with other disciplines and other perspectives. This may take many forms: team-taught courses, panel discussions, and selection of a particular ministerial issue as a common focus in several courses taught concurrently, or a day set aside in the curriculum for seminary-wide exploration of a single pastoral question. For any of these approaches to be educationally effective, the conversation must move beyond ritual politeness or defensive argumentation to a respectful dialogue of mutual exploration and challenge. Many factors in ministerial education today—indeed, in higher education—work against fruitful collaboration across disciplines. But when it is achieved, or even seriously attempted, students are provided a model of theology more adequate to the challenges that face the Church and the world—a theology that may serve as a practical resource to the minister.

We will look at two areas in which such interdisciplinary perspective can be especially valuable: ecclesiology and spirituality.

Ecclesiology courses are intended to provide ministry students with a theological and ministerial understanding of the Church. Traditionally, ecclesiology courses "begin at the beginning," combining a discussion of the Church in Scripture and the early history of our Tradition with philosophical reflection on the nature of the Church. In an interdisciplinary approach such a discussion can be complemented by reflection on two other sources of information: sociological discussion of the expectations and limitations of life together in American society[1] and the ministerial student's experience of Christian community in *this* parish, in this concrete and limited instance of Church. Such an approach displays that synthetic method of reflection on the Church that ministers are expected to exercise during their professional career. Ecclesiology courses have in the past too often consisted of analyses of disparate historical and philosophi-

cal notions of the Church. After such analyses ministers have been expected to apply these important but often abstract insights to a concrete
and sometimes confusing community of faith. Not having learned a synthetic method for reflecting on the Church, ministers most often find that
they cannot invent one in the midst of a busy ministry. Their ongoing theological reflection suffers and, we would argue, their effective ministry
suffers.

An interdisciplinary approach can serve the minister's understanding of
spirituality as well. Spirituality is a vital component of the minister's personal life. For many in ministry the role of spiritual guide is central in pastoral work as well. Development in spirituality is thus an integral if challenging part of professional education in ministry. Professional training in
Christian spirituality benefits from—even requires—an interdisciplinary
approach. To be effective as a spiritual guide, a minister must have some
awareness of the movement of spirituality in Christian history and also a
knowledge of the human person. In education for ministry the stress must
be on the *working* knowledge (knowledge that facilitates behavior) of the
person, a knowledge that the minister can not only appreciate but also put
to use. The developmental perspective in contemporary psychology can
provide a framework that Christian ministers can use as working knowledge to guide their efforts to invite adult believers to greater spiritual
awareness.[2] Thus, the developmental tasks of intimacy and generativity
that Erik Erikson notes as central in adult maturity can be illumined by
the wisdom of the Christian spiritual tradition concerning charity (*agape*)
and service (*diakonia*).[3]

In designing an educational program in spirituality it is useful to recall
that religious traditions always borrow and modify cultural understandings of the person, whether these be in the form of philosophical insights
or psychological perspectives. A religious tradition must, of course, be
aware of the nonreligious origins and limitations of these understandings
and so employ them in a nonidolatrous fashion.

Access to Experience

As we saw in Chapter Three, access to experience in a pastoral reflection
is not only a question of recalling what we know about a ministerial concern. Feelings, hopes, and apprehensions—all of which influence our reflection and decisions—need to be listened to, as well. Thus, extrarational
as well as rational means of access are required.

A new interest in the relation of theology and biography[4] attests to a
new awareness of personal history as a source of theological reflection.

This awareness has been a spur to the use of disciplined methods in journal keeping, many influenced by the work of Ira Progoff,[5] to assist in charting, at both a rational and extrarational level, the movement of God in one's life experience.

Appreciation for the extrarational aspects of experience has highlighted the imagination as an alternate source of information. The exploration of one's sense of personal ministry, outlined in Chapter Three, depends on the imagination to provide information about the images and feelings that accompany our exercise of ministry.

We tap the imagination most emphatically in exercises of guided fantasy.[6] An example of our use of guided fantasy in a theological reflection on the Christian Tradition may be useful here. A reflection on our sacred religious heritage seeks to better understand its historical and changing nature; here we turn to theological and philosophical notions of history and tradition as resources. But it also seems imperative for us to become more critically aware of some of our deeper feelings about the Christian Tradition and the authority and weight of our religious past. This latter exploration is probably not facilitated by asking for a definition of tradition (a strictly rational approach). We have found it useful, in an exercise of guided fantasy, to invite participants to listen for images that arise in their imagination around this general notion of tradition. The goal of such an exercise (and here, as in any educational endeavor, the manner in which this exercise is conducted is crucial to its effectiveness) is not a cognitive clarification of tradition, but an examination of deeper attitudes about it—attitudes that influence my study of the tradition even if I am not aware of them. Thus, one image may be of an immovable fortress, threatening and ominous; another might be of an ocean liner moving carefully but persistently through a dangerous sea; yet another image might be of a giant tree—strong, alive, protective.

A common error that can occur at the beginning of any collective reflection is to assume that, when we use an important word (e.g., *tradition*), we all mean the same thing. An initial exercise, such as the exercise of imagination outlined above, can assist the communal reflection in clarifying the various feelings and biases with which we come to a reflection. At this earliest stage of a reflection it is not important to evaluate these images to find which are "right." Rather, the goal is critical attending to experience at an extrarational level—to both clarify different starting points and to become more aware of our own feelings that will necessarily, but now more consciously, accompany the reflection.

The question of access to experience, especially at this extrarational level, recalls the broader question of education for ministry and for adult Christian living. Theological education, joined as it is with academic styles and goals, has traditionally addressed questions of history and philosophy much more effectively than questions of personal feeling and experience. Over the past decade of discussing these concerns with Christian ministers we have learned that ministers and, more generally, Christian adults are neither very aware of nor very comfortable with their feelings. Many Christians have been taught that their feelings reflect their more selfish needs. Feelings are judged to be volatile, unreliable, and at the very least "merely" subjective. Traditionally, the attention given to feelings was preeminently that of control rather than critical clarification. Evaluation of feelings frequently preceded this clarification, thus short-circuiting it. Lacking both the means and encouragement to listen carefully to feelings and imaginings, Christian adults not surprisingly lack a vocabulary for their feelings and other extrarational attitudes.[7] This lack of critical awareness blocks our ability consciously to bring these experiences—personal and communal—to theological reflection. The theology which supports the present model of reflection calls for critical and concrete access to our different feelings, so that these often powerful and always revealing aspects of our life experience may become conscious participants in reflection in ministry.

Access to Cultural Information

Theological reflection in ministry requires that ministers have access to information in the culture *both* in order that they may use the culture's resources *and* in order that they may be aware of its limiting assumptions and biases. This category of information includes many sources—contemporary philosophy, literature, the media, popular culture. In our discussion we have focused on the social sciences as vehicles through which the minister can have access to information about contemporary culture and to the values and mores through which our society interprets its life.

There is evidence that the Church is increasingly aware of the importance of the social sciences to its mission. More and more, as we noted in Chapter Four, Church leaders use the research methods of the social sciences to investigate questions of vital concern. They turn to the findings of the social sciences for information to guide their choices in planning and action. Programs of education for ministry can contribute to a more critical and effective use of the social sciences within the Church.

The minister is not a professional social scientist. Thus, for the minister, as for most nonspecialists, some translation is necessary if the social sciences are to be genuinely accessible. What is needed is not a translation "down," as though to a less intelligent or less alert audience. It is a translation "across," to an audience whose categories of thought and analysis are different but not inferior.

In regard to the psychological sciences, this translation is underway. There are sources to which the minister may turn for accurate and critical explanation of current psychological theory and practice. The Clinical Pastoral Education movement has raised the level of psychological sophistication among persons in ministry. Journals, such as *Pastoral Psychology, Religion and Health,* and the *Journal of Pastoral Care,* have made psychological concepts, theory, and technique available to the reflective minister. University-based religious authors have made important contributions—Don Browning at the University of Chicago, Howard Clinebell at Claremont, Eugene Kennedy at Loyola University in Chicago, James Lapsley at Princeton, Henri Nouwen at Yale, and others. As a result of these and other efforts, many religious people today are at home in psychology. They can draw upon and use appropriately its categories and approaches to illumine their pastoral understanding and to guide their pastoral practice. Increasingly, ministers are sufficiently critical to know the difference between psychology and religion and to bring the two perspectives into creative tension.

The same is not the case in regard to sociology. The work of Peter Berger, Joseph Fichter, and Andrew Greeley has brought sociology to the attention of some in ministry. But generally, there is much less familiarity with the concepts and approaches that guide sociological analysis, much less awareness of the connections between sociological findings and ministry, much less sense that there is anything of value here to be learned. The appearance of Gregory Baum's important work, *Religion and Alienation,* marks a significant step toward the remedy of this situation. Baum designated his effort "a theological reading of sociology." In it his goal is to "make use of sociological concepts and insights to understand more clearly what Christian practice should be in the present and how we can more adequately formulate the presence of the Holy Spirit in society."[8] The efforts of critical theology in Europe and liberation theology in Latin America offer additional examples of the dialogue between sociological analysis and theological interpretation, some of these influenced by Marxian analysis. In ministry today (and, therefore, in education for ministry), there is a need for increased sociological awareness.[9] Psychological insight often focuses on the individual. Sociology, on the other hand, tends to be interested in human corporateness; sociology is concerned with the social context in which the individual lives. When the psychological insight into the individual is not balanced by sociological awareness of the social context, there can be negative effects for ministry. One of these results is a reinforcement of a "privatized" mind-set, one which has its focus on the individual. The resulting problem is not so much narcissism, but a lack of appreciation of the ways in which individuals are influenced by social factors. Access to sociology can broaden the minister's awareness of structural evil, of the influence of social class on the individual's belief and behavior, of the subtle ways in which religious language and religious institutions can have effects that work against religious values.

The goal of our method—the goal of ministry education—is not to make ministers sociologists. The minister is invited to reflect upon the different levels of cultural experience not as a professional social scientist, but as a highly literate professional in ministry. And seminaries and continuing education programs can help ministers gain this level of literacy.

These programs can include among the faculty social scientists who can serve as translators, who can effectively "give away" to the nonspecialist not only the findings of the social sciences, but its orientation as well. By designing interdisciplinary learning events, programs of education for ministry can model the ways in which ministers can have access to the social sciences. These programs can show theologians, social scientists, and ministers who are aware of each other's vocabulary, who are respectful of each other's starting point, who can challenge each other's assumptions.

Seminaries and programs of continuing education can acquaint ministers with those journals that discuss the social sciences in ways open to the reflective nonspecialist. In sociology, for example, these would include *Sociological Analysis* and the *Review of Religious Research*. These educational programs can include a consideration of how to make appropriate use of the social science consultant and other resource persons in one's ministry. Ministers in studies can be assisted in developing a workable personal plan to keep themselves accountable to the professional discipline of ongoing reading in the social sciences. In each of these ways formal programs of education can help ministers gain the critical access to the social sciences that can support their theological reflection in ministry.

Notes

1. Among the resources in social science to be consulted are Jacqueline Scherer, *Contemporary Community: Sociological Illusion or Reality?* (London:

Tavistock, 1972); Rosabeth Moss Kanter, *Commitment and Community* (Cambridge: Harvard University Press, 1972); and Philip Slater, *The Pursuit of Loneliness: American Culture at the Breaking Point* (Boston: Beacon, 1970). In the specifically religious and Catholic area, one would want to include David O'Brien, *The Renewal of American Catholicism* (New York: Oxford University Press, 1972); Andrew Greeley, *The American Catholic: A Social Portrait* (New York: Basic Books, 1977); and Evelyn Eaton Whitehead, ed., *The Parish in Community and Ministry* (New York: Paulist Press, 1978).

2. Resources that can be useful to the minister seeking this working knowledge include Erik Erikson, ed., *Adulthood* (New York: Norton, 1978); Daniel Levinson et al., *The Seasons of a Man's Life* (New York: Knopf, 1978); Marjorie Fiske Lowenthal et al., *Four Stages of Life* (San Francisco: Jossey-Bass, 1976); and George Vaillant, *Adaptation to Life* (Boston: Little, Brown, 1977).

3. For an analysis of Erikson's perspective in relation to the Christian spiritual and moral tradition, see Don Browning, *Generative Man: Psychoanalytic Perspectives* (Philadelphia: Westminster, 1973) and Evelyn Eaton Whitehead and James D. Whitehead, *Christian Life Patterns* (New York: Doubleday, 1979).

4. An example of this trend can be found in James William McClendon, Jr., *Biography as Theology* (Nashville: Abingdon, 1974). The rescue of theology from being solely a philosophical coordination of doctrines and the clearer recognition of the Christian Tradition as essentially a story have helped this reorientation in theology. See John Dominic Crossan's *The Dark Interval: Toward a Theology of Story* (Chicago: Argus, 1975).

5. See his *At a Journal Workshop* (New York: Dialogue House, 1975). For a simpler and more explicitly Christian method, see George F. Simons, *Keeping Your Personal Journal* (New York: Paulist, 1978).

6. Our own mentor in this area of extrarational learning has been Dr. G. V. Egan of the Institute of Pastoral Studies at Loyola University in Chicago. Apprehension about the religious value of such exploration will diminish as we recover the central importance of the imagination in Judaeo-Christian history. The role of the imagination in the Israelite prophets and in Christian mystics such as John of the Cross and Juliana of Norwich will be better appreciated as theology continues to move from a discussion of dogma to critical reflection on the life stories that constitute the Christian story.

7. A contemporary asceticism for Christians can entail developing a vocabulary of feelings. As we are able to name our feelings, we bring them into greater consciousness and thus we can better appreciate their influence on and contribution to our actions. See John Wood, *How Do You Feel?* (Englewood Cliffs, NJ: Prentice-Hall, 1974) for useful exercises that may contribute to the ascetical effort to identify one's feelings.

8. *Religion and Alienation* (New York: Paulist Press, 1975), p. 4.

9. The absence of serious exposure to contemporary sociology that prevails in most programs of education for ministry is demonstrated in the survey of member institutions of the Association of Theological Schools conducted by Alvin J. Schmidt, Dean of Graduate Studies at Concordia Theological Seminary in Fort Wayne, Indiana, and reported in his paper to the Association for Professional

Education for Ministry in June 1978. See his "The Great Omission in Ministerial Education: Sociological Awareness," in *Report of the 15th Biennial Meeting of the Association for Professional Education for Ministry* (New Haven, CN: APEM, 1978), pp. 101–10.

·12·

SKILLS TRAINING IN EDUCATION FOR MINISTRY

We have discussed the method for theological reflection in ministry in terms of three sets of interrelated skills—attending, assertion, and decision making. In ministry these skills are relevant both to theological reflection and to the daily life of the believing community. The development of these skills—as elements of one's interpersonal style as well as of one's reflective stance—is part of the professional discipline of contemporary Christian ministry.

"Skills" have not enjoyed an especially favorable reputation in theological education. While an educator would expect exegetical training to include certain linguistic or methodological skills and philosophic reflection to involve definite intellectual skills, other behavior traditionally associated with ministry (administration and counseling, for example) has not been sufficiently translated as *ministeral* skills. Instead, these have often been interpreted merely as techniques borrowed from business administration or psychology and thus not genuinely theological or religious.

The past two decades have seen the elaboration of a range of life-management skills and skills for the professional helper. The pioneering work of Robert Carkhuff and Gerard Egan has moved the discipline of skills training beyond its early "how-to" stages into a mature period of theoretical refinement and practical technique. Models of helping skills (Egan, 1975), interpersonal skills (Egan, 1976, 1977), and life-development skills (Egan and Cowan, 1979) have been incorporated effectively in several ministry education settings.[1] Here the skills of effective ministry are treated not simply as techniques externally attached to ministerial behavior, but as essential ingredients of ministerial self-understanding. When skills are thus integrated into both training in spiritual leadership and methods of theological reflection, they make a major contribution to professional education for ministry. In this chapter we outline one design for the incorporation of skills training in education for ministry.

Let us begin with a restatement of our central conviction. The introduction of the ministerial skills of attending, assertion, and decision making into an educational program is related to a significant shift in the understanding of the role of the minister in the community. The minister or
priest is seen less exclusively as engaged in a one-directional ministry—
giving to others, preaching, forming the congregation. The minister is
called to attend to the faith of the community before preaching to it. The
initial attitude of the minister is that of listener—a behavior demanding
specific skills. Clearly, the minister must be attendant upon the Word of
Scripture. A theologically informed ministry requires that ministers incor-
porate the skills of listening that are appropriate to the data of pastoral
practice as well. In addition to skills which enable them to attend to the
texts of Scripture and to the history of the Church (a focus of the skills of
many professional theologians), ministers must also develop skills which
enable them to listen at the interpersonal level. Ministers must become
adept at discerning religious information as it arises in personal experience, in the community, and in the culture, as well as in the explicit formulations of Christian Tradition.

The skills of assertion are germane not only to the minister's decisive
role in the community but refer as well to the call of the community to be
assertive in witnessing to its religious conviction. As the minister moves
from a more authoritarian or dominant role in the community, he or she
must have and be able to provide to others the assertive skills which allow
for the appropriate—that is, respectful and nondestructive—sharing of
diverse convictions. Assertiveness is one of the religious skills that moves
the ideal of shared responsibility and collegiality beyond rhetoric and toward practical execution. Ministers and communities who possess skills of
assertion are more likely to be able to deal effectively with diversity. The
skills of assertion prepare us to sustain the ambiguity and tension that are a
necessary part of contemporary reflection in theology and ministry. Prepared to listen and to share conflicting convictions, we can more carefully
and confidently contribute to the larger theological reflection which describes the life of the Church in the world today.

Finally, the skills that facilitate practical decision making (goal setting
and action planning) take on religious purpose only in a theology that interprets each community as having an active contribution to make to the
larger Church. Such a theology understands the *sensus fidelium* not as a
uniform and passive reflection of the faith of the Church, but as a necessarily pluralistic and assertive witnessing of this faith by different commu-

nities. Such a theology expects and supports those decisions which, with all their limitations, exemplify the Church at work in the world. Specific skills give these decisions focus and practicality, as well as criteria of accountability.

Education for ministry will benefit from recognizing the analogous nature of these skills. Discernment in spiritual direction, the effective scrutiny of a scriptural text and its context, listening to "the signs of the times" in a culture—all these are learned behaviors of attending and each is an element of that virtue of attending required for effective ministry. Liturgical preaching, the management of a parish council, testing the Christian Tradition's view of homosexuality against the evidence of gay Christians today—all these are religious exercises of assertion and each is a part of that virtue of assertion demanded of the contemporary minister. Judging the import of a scriptural text; assisting a community to arrive at clear, practical decisions about its own commitment to justice; expressing theological insight in practical, ministerial action—all these are skilled actions of a decision maker and each is a facet of that virtue of orthopraxy: faith expressed in action.

The range of these skills moves from the more immediate and specific (attending to this question or person or community here and now) to the more general and historical (attending to a larger historical question about the Church's life and practice). As a people convinced that God has acted in special ways revealed in our Scripture and history and that God still acts today, we are called to develop this wide range of skills, or better, virtues, in order to better discern and witness to this continuing presence.

A Design for Ministry Skills Training

Our intention here is to outline a systematic program of skills training designed to build on ministers' attitudes of personal care and to enhance their style of pastoral leadership. The program, originally developed by our colleague, Rev. J. Gordon Myers, S.J., has been a basis of ministry skills-training components at the Jesuit School of Theology in Chicago and, earlier, at the University of Notre Dame. With some modification it has been incorporated in sequences of continuing education for ministry as well.

The program describes a sequence of learning events which focus upon personal enrichment and professional skill. The word *skill* is used here to

THE CONTINUUM OF THEOLOGICAL REFLECTION:
Analogous Skills are Required at Different Locations

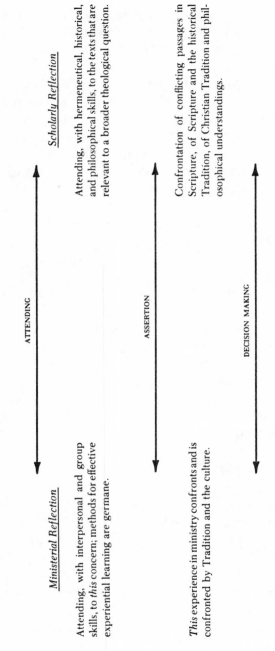

Scholarly Reflection

Attending, with hermeneutical, historical, and philosophical skills, to the texts that are relevant to a broader theological question.

Confrontation of conflicting passages in Scripture, of Scripture and the historical Tradition, of Christian Tradition and philosophical understandings.

The dialogue generates theological insight and conclusions, with implications for the life of the Church and, therefore, for ministry. Critical skills of analysis and synthesis are required.

ATTENDING

ASSERTION

DECISION MAKING

Ministerial Reflection

Attending, with interpersonal and group skills, to *this* concern; methods for effective experiential learning are germane.

This experience in ministry confronts and is confronted by Tradition and the culture.

The dialogue generates pastoral response to *this* concern; skills are needed both to reach and to implement this decision. Decisions reached have implications not only for *this* faith community, but also for the Church and for theology.

Figure 12

refer to more than a collection of techniques; it designates an ability to act, effectively, out of the richness of informed Christian consciousness.

The focus of the program includes self-awareness, professional mastery, and social interaction.

Self-awareness

The program intends to assist ministers to grow in an awareness of what they think, what they feel, and what they can do. Awareness here includes the development of a more nuanced vocabulary to accurately match personal experience. This growth in awareness and in one's vocabulary for expression leads to both personal growth and more effective ministry. More in touch with my own thoughts, feelings, and behavior, I am able, in turn, to be more empathetic with others as they seek to explore and understand their own identity and experience.

Professional Mastery

Mastery involves not only the development of skills, but an attendant increase in self-confidence. Mastery leads to the parallel development of a sense of my own worth and an awareness of my particular competence. Obviously enriching to the minister, this awareness carries over into the pastoral situation. The minister can function more competently; in addition, the person in need of assistance comes in contact with the minister's contagious and growing sense of hope and personal agency.

Social Interaction

Specialists in the helping professions (Carkhuff, 1973; Egan, 1975) point out that most persons who seek professional help are experiencing interpersonal difficulty with one or several other persons who are significant in their life. Similarly, issues of personal and social relationship are central in many questions that are brought to the minister. Ministers are assisted, in both their personal lives and their professional roles, by an increasing appreciation of the factors that are critical in social interaction—what works and does not work with people. Their professional responsibilities require that they become knowledgeable about the ways in which attention, acceptance, appreciation, affection, and alienation are likely to influence relationships. The ability to build and sustain relationships is important to ministers personally and vital for the effectiveness of their ministry.

The goal of this program of training is twofold: to introduce ministers to skills of awareness and interaction that are valuable in their personal life and to bring the minister-participants to a level of proficiency in these skills that will enable them to use them confidently and competently in their ministry.

Format

The *intensive workshop* format has proved successful in ministry skills training, especially where it is followed by opportunity for practice, feedback, and supervision in the use of these skills in one's ministry. The workshop format involves ten hours of concentrated work extending over an evening, the next day, and the following morning. Focusing upon the development of specific skills and their use in concrete situations, this time frame allows for theoretical presentation, definition, demonstration, and supervised practice. In this experience-based learning environment, the participants learn by observing, by acting, and by being coached in the immediate context of their practice of new behavior. A series of three intensive workshops is offered in each module, paced at intervals of three or four weeks apart. In the interim weeks, participants meet regularly for brief sessions of practice and review.

Description of the Training Modules
Ministry Skills for Pastoral Leadership I

This initial module introduces the basic skills necessary for effective interpersonal involvement. The skills include accurate understanding, empathic response, concreteness of expression, appropriate self-disclosure, immediacy in relationships, and responsible confrontation. The three intensive workshops focus on:

- the ministry of listening (attending and response)
- the ministry of sharing (self-disclosure and assertion)
- the ministry of reconciliation (confrontation and conflict-resolution).

Ministry Skills for Pastoral Leadership II

This module builds upon the skills developed in the earlier workshop experiences. These earlier skills, seen as critical in one-to-one pastoral situations, are now translated into the group context. Additional skills, specific to the group situation, are introduced. These latter include:

- responding and initiating in the group
- requesting and giving concrete feedback
- taking appropriate responsibility for the interaction of the group
- inviting the responsible participation of others in group
- collaborating in group planning and action.

The workshops of this module focus on:

- basic group leadership (translation of basic skills into group context)
- advanced group leadership (introduction of group specific skills)
- collaboration and problem solving in groups.

Ministry Skills for Pastoral Leadership III

The final module of the sequence presumes that participants have a knowledge of, and some proficiency with, those skills necessary for interpersonal and group involvement. With this foundation, the focus moves to issues of decision, value, and planning as these influence individuals and organizations.

The three workshops of this module are:

Values Clarification Laboratory

Strategies of value clarification have proved useful in religious education settings as well as in planning and counseling. This workshop enables participants to continue the supervised use of the individual and group skills learned earlier as they explore the value constellations that constitute their own and others' lives. In addition, there is opportunity to assess the situations and tools that are appropriate to a ministry of value clarification and commitment.

Laboratory in Life Planning

A key issue in the lives of individuals and families today concerns the reformulation of the meaning of time and how we spend our lives. Strategies of life planning are emerging as significant tools within this reformulation process. The goal of life planning is not to predict the future but rather to plan for it in such a way as to enable a person to move toward a future that is not only possible but that is preferable. Present experience does not flow automatically into a preferred future. We make creative and responsible choices for the future through reflection on and reconstruction of past and present experiences, followed by concrete planning and decision making.

This workshop involves the use of the interpersonal and group skills learned earlier as well as the continued exploration of one's effective values. It provides, in addition, concrete strategies designed to help the minister help others to evaluate present commitments, study alternatives, and make concrete decisions about possible changes in life direction.

Organization Development for Ministry

Just as individuals and groups can experience the need for clarification and change, so can organizations. This workshop focuses attention on the skills and strategies useful to effective change within organizations. The distinction between problem solving and planning is examined, along with criteria for judging when each is appropriate. Skills of problem analysis are practiced and participants engage in a variety of strategies for effective planning, action, accountability, and evaluation in the organizational context.

Note

1. The programs whose design we know best are located in Chicago. They include the several Master's level concentrations available through the Institute of Pastoral Studies at Loyola University, the M. Div. sequence at the Jesuit School of Theology, and the D.Min. program sponsored by the Center for Pastoral Ministry of the archdiocese of Chicago. For another discussion of the importance of the inclusion of skills in training for ministry, see Dennis C. Kinlaw, "Helping Skills for the Helping Community," in *Religious Education* 71 (November/December 1976):572–83.

Resources for the Skills-Training Sequence

Ministry Skills for Pastoral Leadership I

There are a number of well-developed approaches to comprehensive skills training that may be adopted. Our own preference is that developed by Gerard Egan and presented in his *Interpersonal Living: A Skills/Contract Approach to Human-Relations Training in Groups* (Monterey, CA: Brooks/Cole, 1976). Used in conjunction with the accompanying *Instructor's Manual* (by Michael Cowan, Gerard Egan, and Maureen Bacchi) and material in Egan's earlier *The Skilled Helper* (1975), this text provides a disciplined step-by-step approach to identifying and practicing the behavior useful in a wide range of ministerial situations.

The Rehabilitation Research and Training Center at the University of Arkansas offers another systematic program of skills training. See B. L. Means and R. T. Roesslar, *Personal Achievement Skills Training: Instructor's Manual* and also the *Participant's Manual* (Hot Springs, ARK: Arkansas Rehabilitation Research and Training Center, University of Arkansas, 1976).

The Human Resources Development Training Institute has also provided manuals for skills training. See G. L. Sydnor, R. Akridge, and N. L. Parkhill, *Human Relations Training: A Programmed Manual* (Minden, LA: HRDTI, 1972) and G. L. Sydnor and N. L. Parkhill, *Advanced Human Relations Training: A Programmed Manual* (Minden, LA: HRDTI, 1973).

Ministry Skills for Pastoral Leadership II

Here again Gerard Egan's work is a primary resource. His *Interpersonal Living* can serve as a text for the advanced work of this second workshop series. Thomas Gordon, another pioneer in the development of training in behavioral skills, deals with effective behavior in the leadership context in *Leadership Effectiveness Training* (New York: Wyden, 1977). The resources on decision making and problem solving, listed in Chapter Seven, include material that can be incorporated at this stage in the skills-training sequence.

There are two other resources that, while not dealing directly with skills training in group leadership, nonetheless may be useful to participants in this advanced workshop. In *Increasing Leadership Effectiveness* (New York: Wiley-Interscience, 1976), Chris Argyris discusses a model and theory of leadership. D. Barnes and F. Todd explore the dynamic of group interaction in *Communication and Learning in Small Groups* (London: Routledge and Kegan Paul, 1977).

Ministry Skills for Pastoral Leadership III

Values Clarification

A classic work in this area, still valuable, is Sidney B. Simon, Leland W. Howe, and Howard Kirschenbaum's *Values Clarification: A Handbook of Practical Strategies for Teachers and Students* (New York: Hart, 1972). Other useful resources are: Howard Kirschenbaum, *Advanced Value Clarification* (LaJolla, CA: University Associates, 1977); Sydney B. Simon, *Meeting Yourself Halfway: Thirty-One Value Clarification Strategies for Daily Living* (Niles, IL: Argus, 1974); Maury Smith, *A Practical Guide to Value Clarification* (La Jolla, CA: University Associates, 1977).

Those interested in an overview of the work that has been done in the area may consult R. K. Goodman, "Values Clarification: A Review of Major Books," in J. W. Pfeiffer and J. J. Jones, eds., *The 1976 Annual Handbook for Group Facilitators* (LaJolla, CA: University Associates, 1976), pp. 274–79.

Life Planning

Resources here are focused on both life management and on questions of career choice and change. R. L. Williams and J. D. Long deal with life management in their *Toward a Self-Managed Life Style* (Boston: Houghton Mifflin, 1975). In a somewhat more popular style, Tony Larsen treats a number of important questions in his *Trust Yourself: A Holistic Handbook for Self-Reliance* (San Luis Obispo, CA: Impact, 1979).

Career issues are dealt with effectively by John C. Crystal and Richard N. Bolles in *Where Do I Go From Here With My Life?* (Berkeley, CA: Ten Speed Press, 1974) and by Richard N. Bolles, *What Color Is Your Parachute?* (Berkeley, CA: Ten Speed Press, 1976).

Organization Development

The resources given in Chapter Seven in our discussion of decision making and problem solving are relevant here as well. In addition, Gerard Egan and Michael Cowan provide a developmental model for understanding and acting in the organizational setting in their *People in Systems: A Model for Development in the Human Service Professions and in Education* (Monterey, CA: Brooks/Cole, 1979) and in the accompanying workbook, *People in Systems: Personal and Professional Applications* (by Michael Cowan, Gerard Egan, and Norman Hetland).

Postscript

Our discussion of method, of skills, and of ordered reflection raises an important question: What place is there for mystery, for grace, and for the unexpected?

Method is, indeed, one of the ways we attempt to direct our actions. At times the commitment to method can seem to be an effort to control not only our lives, but God's influence in them. With this motive, method becomes a form of magic, a struggle to order and constrain God to fit our own plans.

But, as we have noted throughout this book, method can also be viewed as an expected part of Christian discipline—a systematic, enduring effort to attend to God's appearance in our lives. Method, in such an understanding, functions not to limit or control mystery and grace, but to allow these to be perceived.

Method in ministry—a way of reflecting together and coming to common effective action—carries us beyond vague instincts and deceptive rhetoric. An uncritical reliance on instinct can be cloaked in exhortations that we "trust the Spirit." And rhetorical injunctions, such as "let God guide us," may simply disguise a group's passivity or a designated leader's inability to elicit decision and commitment.

A method of communal reflection is required for those who envision the Church as groups of adult believers growing in their trust in the authority of their own lives with God. This growth takes place in the context of the authority of our religious heritage and the teachings of the Church. It is this context of several authorities that makes religious reflection both necessary and exciting.

There is great enthusiasm in the American Church today for shared responsibility and mutual ministry. To realize this vision we must be able to reflect together. Extraordinary trust and skill are required for such a potentially threatening enterprise. Our skills in sharing, concretely and respectfully, our own partial insights must be complemented by our faith that God is at work among us—even in our conflicts and disagreements. As Christian ministers and as communities of adult believers, we will succeed in mutual ministry not simply because we are exhorted to it, but because we have developed the discipline and skills of theological reflection. These skills, in helping us move responsibly toward Christian action, rescue Christian virtue from rhetoric.

Finally, a note on pluralism. A rich variety of styles of religious reflection is needed in the Church today. Some readers will be distressed to find not discussed in this model of reflection questions they see as significant to the theological enterprise. These persons will require a more sophisticated method of analysis. Others, to be sure, will find this model still too complex; they will require a simpler means for reflection together. This is as it should be. The model presented here is intentionally Janus-like: it faces both toward theology and toward practical ministry. As an effort in pastoral theology, it addresses the sometimes considerable gap between thought and action, between theology and ministry, that exists in today's Church. This is certainly too great a gap for a single method of reflection to heal. We invite others to join us in this open and somewhat exposed space.

This book has developed over several years of listening attentively to how effective ministers reflect and act. The book itself is an assertion. It awaits other assertions—confirmations and challenges, additions and alterations. The ensuing discussion, already begun among our often charitable critics and colleagues, will lead—we hope—not only to insight, but to the development of a range of practical styles of religious reflection. Such methods will assist our graceful attention to God's presence among us and our faithful response, in our own age, to this transforming presence.

Notes on Contributors

Peter J. Henriot, S.J. Political Science (Ph.D., University of Chicago) Director, Center of Concern, Washington D.C.-based center for analysis and education, focusing on international issues of social justice.

J. Gordon Myers, S.J. Educational Development (Ph.D. candidate, University of Wisconsin) Consultant in Ministry Education and Organization Development. 1974–1979: Coordinator of Ministry Faculty, Jesuit School of Theology in Chicago.

William G. Thompson, S.J. New Testament (S.S.D., Biblical Institute, Rome) Professor of New Testament, Jesuit School of Theology in Chicago. 1973–1975: Dean, Jesuit School of Theology in Chicago.

Eugene C. Ulrich Old Testament (Ph.D., Harvard University) Professor of Theology, University of Notre Dame. 1978–1979: Director of Ministry Program, University of Notre Dame.

Evelyn Eaton Whitehead Social Psychology (Ph.D., University of Chicago) Whitehead Associates, Consultants in Education and Ministry. 1973–1978: Graduate Theology Faculty and Co-Director of the Office of Field Education in Ministry, University of Notre Dame.

James D. Whitehead Pastoral Theology (Ph.D., Harvard University) Whitehead Associates, Consultants in Education and Ministry. 1973–1978: Graduate Theology Faculty and Co-Director of the Office of Field Education in Ministry, University of Notre Dame.

James J. Young, C.S.P. Theology (M.A., St. Paul's College) Rector, St. Paul's College, Washington, D.C. 1975–1978: Director of Ministerial Studies, Weston School of Theology, Cambridge, Massachusetts.

Bibliography

Abbott, Walter M., ed. *The Documents of Vatican II*. New York: America Press, 1966.

Alberti, Robert, ed. *Assertiveness: Innovations, Applications, Issues*. San Luis Obispo, CA: Impact, 1977.

———, and Michael Emmons. *Your Perfect Right: A Guide to Assertive Behavior*. San Luis Obispo, CA: Impact, 1974.

Andreasen, Niels-Erik. *The Christian Use of Time*. Nashville: Abingdon, 1978.

Argyris, Chris. *Increasing Leadership Effectiveness*. New York: Wiley-Interscience, 1976.

Barnes, D., and F. Todd. *Communication and Learning in Small Groups*. London: Routledge and Kegan Paul, 1977.

Barr, James. *Biblical Words for Time*. Naperville, IL: Alec R. Allenson, 1962.

Baum, Gregory. *Man Becoming: God in Secular Experience*. New York: Herder and Herder, 1971.

———. *Religion and Alienation*. New York: Paulist Press, 1975.

Berenson, B. G., and K. M. Mitchell. *Confrontation: For Better or Worse*. Amherst, MA: Human Resource Development Press, 1974.

Berger, Peter. "Some Second Thoughts on Substantive versus Functional Definitions of Religion." *Journal for the Scientific Study of Religion* 13 (1974): 125–33.

———. *The Heretical Imperative*. New York: Doubleday, 1979.

———, and Thomas Luckmann. *The Social Construction of Reality*. New York: Doubleday Anchor, 1967.

Bolles, Richard N. *What Color Is Your Parachute?* Berkeley, CA: Ten Speed Press, 1976.

Bower, S. A., and G. H. Bower. *Asserting Yourself: A Practical Guide for Positive Change*. Reading, MA: Addison-Wesley, 1976.

Bremmer, Lawrence M. *The Helping Relationship: Process and Skills*. Englewood-Cliffs, NJ: Prentice-Hall, 1979.

Bright, John. *A History of Israel*. Philadelphia: Westminster, 1959.

Brown, Raymond E. *Crises Facing the Church*. New York: Paulist Press, 1975.

———. " 'Other Sheep Not of this Fold': The Johannine Perspective on Christian Diversity in the Late First Century." *Journal of Biblical Literature* 97 (1978):5–22.

———. *The Community of the Beloved Disciple*. New York: Paulist Press, 1979.

———, J. A. Fitzmyer, and R. E. Murphy, eds. *Jerome Biblical Commentary*. Englewood-Cliffs, NJ: Prentice-Hall, 1968.

Browning, Don. *Generative Man: Psychoanalytic Perspectives.* Philadelphia: Westminster, 1973.

————. *The Moral Context of Pastoral Care.* Philadelphia: Westminster, 1976.

Bullmer, K. *The Art of Empathy.* New York: Human Sciences Press, 1975.

Camus, Albert. *The Stranger.* Translated by Stuart Gilbert. New York: Knopf, 1946.

Carkhuff, Robert R. *Helping and Human Relations: A Primer for Lay and Professional Helpers.* New York: Holt, Rinehart and Winston, 1969.

————. *How to Help Yourself: The Art of Program Development.* Amherst, MA: Human Resources Development Press, 1974.

————. *The Art of Problem-Solving.* Amherst, MA: Human Resources Development Press, 1973.

————, R. M. Pierce et al. *The Art of Helping III.* Amherst, MA: Human Resources Development Press, 1977.

Carr, Anne. "Theology and Experience in the Thought of Karl Rahner." *Journal of Religion* 53 (1973): 359–76.

"Case Study Method." *Theological Education* 10 (1974). Entire Issue.

Cobb, John B. *Theology and Pastoral Care.* Philadelphia: Fortress Press, 1977.

Coleman, John. "Vision and Praxis in American Theology: Orestes Bronson, John A. Ryan and John Courtney Murray." *Theological Studies* 37 (1976): 3–40.

Cotler, Sherwin B., and J. J. Guerra. *Assertion Training: A Humanistic and Behavioral Guide to Self-Dignity.* Champaign, IL: Research Press, 1975.

Cowan, Michael, Gerard Egan and Norman Hetland. *People in Systems: Personal and Professional Applications.* Monterey, CA: Brooks/Cole, 1979.

Cross, F. M. *Canaanite Myths and Hebrew Epic.* Cambridge, MA: Harvard University Press, 1973.

Crossan, John Dominic. *The Dark Interval: Toward a Theology of Story.* Chicago: Argus, 1973.

Crystal, John C., and Richard N. Bolles. *Where Do I Go From Here With My Life?* Berkeley: Ten Speed Press, 1974.

Cullman, Oscar. *Christ and Time.* Philadelphia: Westminster, 1964.

Davidson, James. *Effective Time Management: A Practical Workbook.* New York: Human Sciences Press, 1978.

Dulles, Avery. "The Apostolate of Theological Reflection." *The Way,* Supplement 20 (1973):114–23.

————. "The Meaning of Revelation." In Joseph Papin, ed., *The Dynamics of Christian Thought,* pp. 52–80. Villanova, PA: Villanova University Press, 1970.

————. "Review of David Tracy's *Blessed Rage for Order.*" *Theological Studies* 37 (1976): 307–9.

Egan, Gerard. *Change Agent Skills: Model and Methods for the Renewal of Systems.* Monterey, CA: Brooks/Cole, in press.

————. *Exercises in Helping Skills.* Monterey, CA: Brooks/Cole, 1975.

————. *Interpersonal Living.* Monterey, CA: Brooks/Cole, 1976.

————. *The Skilled Helper: A Model for Systematic Helping and Interpersonal Relating.* Monterey, CA: Brooks/Cole, 1975.

————. *You and Me: The Skills of Communicating and Relating to Others.* Monterey, CA: Brooks/Cole, 1977.

————, and Michael Cowan. *People In Systems.* Monterey, CA: Brooks/Cole, 1979.

Eliade, Mircea. *Patterns in Comparative Religion.* New York: Sheed and Ward, 1958.

————. *Myth and Reality.* New York: Harper and Row, 1963.

Erikson, Erik, ed. *Adulthood.* New York: Norton, 1978.

Fagan, Harry. *Empowerment: Skills for Parish Social Action.* New York: Paulist Press, 1979.

Finnegan, John. "Marriage Law." *Chicago Studies* 15 (1976): 281–304.

————. "The Pastoral Care of Marriage." *Origins* 5 (August 28, 1975).

Geertz, Clifford. *The Interpretation of Cultures.* New York: Basic Books, 1973.

Goldstein, A. P., R. P. Sprafkin, and N. J. Gershaw. *Skill Training for Community Living.* Fairview Park, NY: Pergamon Press, 1976.

Goodman, R. K. "Values Clarification: A Review of Major Books." In J. W. Pfeiffer and J. J. Jones, eds., *The 1976 Annual Handbook for Group Facilitators*, pp. 174–79. LaJolla, CA: University Associates, 1976.

Gordon, Thomas. *Leadership Effectiveness Training.* New York: Wyden, 1977.

Greeley, Andrew. *Priests of the United States: Reflections on a Survey.* New York: Doubleday, 1972.

————. *The American Catholic: A Social Portrait.* New York: Basic Books, 1977.

Greenleaf, Robert. *Servant Leadership.* New York: Paulist Press, 1978.

Gremillion, Joseph, ed. *The Gospel of Peace and Justice: Catholic Social Teaching Since Pope John.* Maryknoll, NY: Orbis, 1976.

Gustafson, James M. "The Relation of the Gospels to the Moral Life." In D. G. Miller and D. Y. Hadidian, eds., *Jesus and Man's Hope* 2:106–117. Pittsburgh: Pittsburgh Theological Seminary, 1971.

Gutierrez, Gustavo. *A Theology of Liberation.* Maryknoll, NY: Orbis, 1973.

————. "Theology of Liberation." *Theological Studies* 31 (1970): 245–58.

Hardy, James M. *Corporate Planning for Non-Profit Organizations.* New York: Association Press, 1972.

Häring, Bernard. *The Law of Christ.* Cork, Ireland: Mercier Press, 1963.

Haughton, Rosemary. *The Theology of Experience.* New York: Newman, 1972.

Hitchcock, James. "Thomas More and the Sensus Fidelium." *Theological Studies* 36 (1975): 145–54.

Ivey, A. *Microcounseling: Interviewing Skills Manual.* 2nd ed. Springfield, IL: Charles C. Thomas, 1977.

Kanter, Rosabeth Moss. *Commitment and Community.* Cambridge, MA: Harvard University Press, 1972.

Kaufman, Gordon. *An Essay on Theological Method.* Missoula, MT: Scholars Press, 1975.

Kaufman, R. *Identifying and Solving Problems: A System Approach.* LaJolla, CA: University Associates, 1976.

Kelleher, Stephen J. *Divorce and Remarriage for Catholics?* New York: Doubleday, 1973.

Kelly, C. "Assertion: The Literature Since 1970." In J. W. Pfeiffer and J. J. Jones, eds., *The 1977 Annual Handbook for Group Facilitators*, pp. 264–75. LaJolla, CA: University Associates, 1977.

Kennedy, Eugene, and Victor Heckler. *The Loyola Psychological Study of the Ministry and Life of the American Priest*. Washington, D.C.: National Conference of Catholic Bishops, 1971.

Kinlaw, Dennis C. "Helping Skills for the Helping Community." *Religious Education* 71 (1976): 572–83.

Kirschenbaum, Howard. *Advanced Value Clarification*. LaJolla, CA: University Associates, 1977.

Koester, Helmut. "*Gnomai Diaphoria:* The Origins and Nature of Diversification in the History of Early Christianity." *Harvard Theological Review* 58 (1965): 279–318.

Kuhn, Thomas. *The Structure of Scientific Revolutions*. Chicago: University of Chicago Press, 1970.

Lakein, Alan. *How to Get Control of Your Time and Your Life*. New York: Wyden, 1973.

Lange, A. J., and P. Jakubowski. *Responsible Assertive Behavior: Cognitive/Behavioral Procedures for Trainers*. Champaign, IL: Research Press, 1976.

Larsen, Tony. *Trust Yourself: A Holistic Handbook for Self-Reliance*. San Luis Obispo, CA: Impact, 1979.

Lasch, Christopher. *The Culture of Narcissism*. New York: Norton, 1978.

Léon-Dufour, X. et al., eds. *Dictionary of Biblical Theology*. 2nd rev. ed. Translated by P. J. Cahill *et al.* New York: Seabury, 1973.

Levinson, Daniel. *The Seasons of a Man's Life*. New York: Knopf, 1978.

Liberman, R. P., L. W. King, *et al. Personal Effectiveness: Guiding People To Assert Themselves and Improve Their Social Skills*. Champaign, IL: Research Press, 1975.

Lindgren, Alvin J., and Norman Shawchuck. *Management for Your Church*. Nashville: Abingdon, 1977.

Lonergan, Bernard. *Method in Theology*. New York: Herder and Herder, 1972.

Lowenthal, Marjorie Fiske, Majda Thurnher and David Chiriboga. *Four Stages of Life*. San Francisco: Jossey-Bass, 1976.

Mackey, J. P. *The Modern Theology of Tradition*. New York: Herder and Herder, 1963.

Means, B. L., and R. T. Roesslar. *Personal Achievement Skills Training: Instructors Manual and Participants Manual*. Hot Springs, AK: Arkansas Rehabilitation Research and Training Center, University of Arkansas, 1976.

Medellin Documents. *The Church in the Present-Day Transformation of Latin America in the Light of the Council*. Washington, D.C.: Latin American Bureau, United States Catholic Conference, 1970.

Meland, Bernard. *Fallible Forms and Symbols*. Philadelphia: Fortress Press, 1976.

Metz, Johannes. *Theology of the World*. New York: Herder and Herder, 1971.

McClendon, James William, Jr. *Biography as Theology*. Nashville: Abingdon, 1974.

McDonagh, Enda. *Gift and Call.* St. Meinrad, IN: Abbey Press, 1975.

McKenzie, John L. *Dictionary of the Bible.* Milwaukee: Bruce, 1965.

Mitchell, Michael D. "Consultant Burnout." In J. W. Pfeiffer and J. J. Jones, eds., *The 1977 Annual Handbook for Group Facilitators,* pp. 143–46. LaJolla, CA: University Associates, 1977.

Monden, Louis. *Sin, Liberty and Law.* New York: Sheed and Ward, 1965.

Mouroux, Jean. *The Mystery of Time: A Theological Inquiry.* Translated by John Drury. New York: Desclee, 1964.

Murray, John Courtney. "Introduction to 'The Declaration on Religious Freedom'." In Walter M. Abbott, ed., *The Documents of Vatican II,* pp. 172–74.

National Catechetical Directory. Washington, D.C.: United States Catholic Conference, 1978.

Neugarten, Bernice. "Time, Age, and the Life Cycle." *American Journal of Psychiatry* 137 (1979): 887–94.

Neibuhr, Reinhold. *Christ and Culture.* New York: Harper, 1951.

Neibuhr, Richard R. *Experiential Religion.* New York: Harper and Row, 1972.

Noth, Martin. *A History of Pentateuchal Traditions.* Translated by B. Anderson. Englewood Cliffs, NJ: Prentice-Hall, 1972.

———. *The History of Israel.* 2nd ed. Translated by P. Ackroyd. London: A. and C. Black, 1960.

O'Brien, David. *The Renewal of American Catholicism.* New York: Oxford University Press, 1972.

Ogden, Shubert. "What is Theology?" *Journal of Religion* 52 (1972): 22–40.

O'Meara, Thomas. "Toward a Subjective Theology of Revelation." *Theological Studies* 36 (1975): 410–27.

Our Mission Today. Document of the 32nd General Congregation of the Society of Jesus. Washington, D.C.: United States Jesuit Assistancy, 1975.

Overbeck, Jerome. "The Workaholic." *Psychology Journal of Human Behavior* 13 (1976): 79–83.

Patsavos, Lewis. "The Orthodox Position on Divorce." In James J. Young, ed., *Ministering to the Divorced Catholic,* pp. 51–64. New York: Paulist Press, 1979.

Pelikan, Jaroslav. "Theology and Change." *Crosscurrents,* 19 (1969):277–84.

Percell, Lawrence et al. "The Effects of Assertive Training on Self-Concept and Anxiety." *Archives of General Psychiatry* 31 (1974):502–4.

Phelps, Stanlee, and Nancy Austin. *The Assertive Woman.* San Luis Obispo, CA: Impact, 1975.

Pope John Paul II. *Redemptor Hominis.* Washington, D.C.: United States Catholic Conference, 1979.

Pritchard, J., ed. *Ancient Near Eastern Texts.* 3rd ed. Princeton: Princeton University Press, 1969.

Progoff, Ira. *At A Journal Workshop.* New York: Dialogue House, 1975.

Puebla Documents. *Proceedings of the Latin American Bishops Conference.* Unofficial Translation Coordinated and Distributed by Catholic Committee on Urban Ministry. Notre Dame, IN: CCUM, 1979.

Rahner, Karl. *Theological Investigations. I.* Baltimore: Helicon, 1961.

Ricoeur, Paul. *The Symbolism of Evil.* Boston: Beacon Press, 1967.

Scherer, Jacqueline. *Contemporary Community: Sociological Illusion or Reality?* London: Tavistock, 1972.

Schillebeeckx, Edward. *Marriage: Human Reality and Saving Mystery.* New York: Sheed and Ward, 1965.

————, and Bas Van Iersel, eds. *Revelation and Experience.* New York: Seabury, 1979.

Schmidt, Alvin J. "The Great Omission in Ministerial Education: Sociological Awareness." In *Report of the 15th Biennial Meeting of the Association for Professional Education for Ministers.* New Haven, CN: APEM, 1978.

Schoonenberg, Piet. *Man and Sin: A Theological View.* Notre Dame, IN: University of Notre Dame Press, 1965.

Segundo, Juan Luis. *The Liberation of Theology.* Maryknoll, NY: Orbis, 1976.

Shea, John. "Doing Ministerial Theology." In D. Tracy, ed., *Toward Vatican III,* pp. 188–95. New York: Seabury, 1978.

Simon, Sydney B. *Meeting Yourself Halfway: Thirty-One Value Clarification Strategies for Daily Living.* Niles, IL: Argus, 1974.

————, Leland W. Howe, and Howard Kirschenbaum. *Value Clarification: A Handbook of Practical Strategies for Teachers and Students.* New York: Hart, 1972.

Simons, George F. *Keeping Your Personal Journal.* New York: Paulist, 1978.

Slater, Philip. *The Pursuit of Loneliness: American Culture at the Breaking Point.* Boston: Beacon Press, 1970.

Speery, L., D. Mickelson, and P. Hunsaker. *You Can Make It Happen.* Reading, MA: Addison-Wesley, 1977.

Smith, John. *Experience and God.* New York: Oxford University Press, 1968.

Smith, Maury. *A Practical Guide to Value Clarification.* LaJolla, CA: University Associates, 1977.

Stendahl, Krister. "Biblical Theology, Contemporary." In *The Interpreter's Dictionary of the Bible* Vol. 1. New York: Abingdon, 1962.

Sydnor, G. L., R. Akridge, and N. L. Parkhill. *Human Relations Training: A Programmed Manual.* Minden, LA: Human Resources Development Training Institute, 1972.

————, and N. L. Parkhill. *Advanced Human Relations Training: A Programmed Manual.* Minden, LA: Human Resources Development Training Institute, 1973.

Taylor, A. E. *The Collected Dialogues of Plato.* New York: Random House, 1963.

Theodorson, G. A., and A. G. Theodorson. *Modern Dictionary of Sociology.* New York: Crowell-Apolla, 1970.

Tillich, Paul. *Systematic Theology.* Vol. 1. Chicago: University of Chicago Press, 1951.

————. *Theology of Culture.* New York: Oxford University Press, 1959.

Tracy, David. *Blessed Rage for Order.* New York: Seabury, 1975.

————, ed. *Toward Vatican III.* New York: Seabury, 1978.

Turner, Victor. "Passages, Margins, and Poverty: Religious Symbols of Communitas." *Worship* 46 (1972): 390–412, 482–94.

Vaillant, George. *Adaptation to Life*. Boston: Little, Brown, 1977.

Van Campenhoudt, Andre G. "The Local Churches." Mimeographed paper. Brussels, Belgium: Prospective, 1975.

Warren, D. J., and R. B. Warren. *The Neighborhood Organizer's Handbook*. Notre Dame, IN: Notre Dame Press, 1977.

Webster's New World Dictionary of the American Language. College Edition. New York: World Publishing Co., 1964.

Weiss, Robert. *Loneliness*. Cambridge, MA: M.I.T. Press, 1973.

————. *Marital Separation*. New York: Basic Books, 1975.

Whitehead, Evelyn Eaton. "Clarifying the Meaning of Community." *Living Light* 15 (1978): 376–92.

————, ed. *The Parish In Community and Ministry*. New York: Paulist Press, 1978.

————, and James D. Whitehead. *Christian Life Patterns: The Psychological Challenges and Religious Invitations of Adult Life*. New York: Doubleday, 1979.

Wilken, Robert. *The Myth of Christian Beginnings*. New York: Doubleday, 1972.

Williams, Oliver F., and John Houck. *Full Value: Cases in Christian Business Ethics*. San Francisco: Harper and Row, 1978.

Williams, R. L., and J. D. Long. *Toward a Self-Managed Life Style*. Boston: Houghton Mifflin, 1975.

Wood, John. *How Do You Feel?* Englewood Cliffs, NJ: Prentice-Hall, 1974.

World Development: The Challenge to the Church. Geneva: SODEPAX, 1968.

Young, James J. *Growing Through Divorce*. New York: Paulist Press, 1979.

————, ed. *Ministering to the Divorced Catholic*. New York: Paulist Press, 1979.

Name and Subject Index